Working
Method

The *Critical Social Thought* Series
edited by Michael W. Apple, University of Wisconsin, Madison

Tough Fronts: The Impact of Street Culture on Schooling
L. Janelle Dance

Political Spectacle and the Fate of American Schools
Mary Lee Smith with Walter Heinecke, Linda Miller-Kahn, and Patricia F. Jarvis

High Stakes Education: Inequality, Globalization, and Urban School Reform
Pauline Lipman

Rethinking Scientific Literacy
Wolff-Michael Roth and Angela Calabrese Barton

Learning to Labor in New Times
Nadine Dolby and Greg Dimitriadis, editors

Working Method: Research and Social Justice
Lois Weis and Michelle Fine

Working
Method

Research and Social Justice

Lois Weis
Michelle Fine

Routledge
Taylor & Francis Group

NEW YORK AND LONDON

Published in 2004 by
Routledge
270 Madison Avenue
New York, New York 10016
www.routledge-ny.com

Published in Great Britain by
Routledge
2 Park Square
Milton Park, Abingdon
Oxon OX14 4RN
www.routledge.co.uk

Routledge is an imprint of the Taylor & Francis Group.
Printed in the United States of America on acid-free paper.

Chapter 1: "Dear Zora: A Letter to Zora Neale Hurston Fifty Years After *Brown*" previously appeared in *Teachers College Record*. Reprinted with permission.

Chapter 2: "Race, Gender, and Critique" previously appeared in *Signs*, vol. 27 no. 1, Autumn 2001. Copyright © 2001 by The University of Chicago. All rights reserved. Reprinted with permission.

Chapter 3: "Civics Lessons" previously appeared in *Teachers College Record*. Reprinted with permission.

Chapter 4: "Gender, Masculinity, and the New Economy" previously appeared in the *Australian Educational Researcher*, vol. 30 no. 3, 2003. Reprinted with permission.

Chapter 5: "Participatory Action Research" previously appeared in *Qualitative Research in Psychology: Expanding Perspectives in Methodology and Design*, pp 173–198. Copyright © 2003 by the American Psychological Association. Reprinted with permission.

Chapter 6: "Extraordinary Conversations in Public Schools" previously appeared in the *International Journal of Qualitative Research*, vol. 14 no. 4, 2001, pp 497–523. Reprinted with permission. www.tandf.co.uk/journals.

10 9 8 7 6 5 4 3 2 1

Library of Congress Cataloging-in-Publication Data

Weis, Lois.
    Working method : research and social justice / Lois Weis and Michelle Fine.
        p. cm. — (Critical social thought)
    Includes bibliographical references and index.
    ISBN 0-415-94825-8 (hardback : alk. paper)—ISBN 0-415-94826-6 (pbk. : alk. paper)
    1. Social problems—Research. 2. Social justice. 3. Equity. 4. Social sciences—Research—Methodology. I. Title: Research and social justice. II. Fine, Michelle. III. Title. IV. Series.
    HN29.W3983 2004
    361.1'072—dc22

                                                    2004004886

Table of Contents

Series Editor's Introduction

We are witnessing an attack on critical understanding of the relationship between education and power and on the critical research that underpins it. The Bush administration has installed a definition of what counts as "legitimate" inquiry that returns us to the days of unreflective positivism, at the same time that its own agenda is based on either very poor research or at times almost no serious research at all (Smith et al., 2004). Not only is this definition of research based on an eviscerated understanding of science—one that bears little resemblance to the ways in which the best of scientific inquiry actually goes on—but it ignores the truly major gains that have been made through the use of a wide range of tools and perspectives. These include qualitative and ethnographic models, discourse analysis, critical policy studies, historical work that captures both the richness of daily life and the effects of official policies, conceptual and philosophical analysis, and so much more. The attempted evacuation of these traditions from the definition of "officially sponsored" research is bad enough. But even more worrisome are the effects on new approaches that are both empirically detailed and socially and culturally critical at one and the same time. Indeed, with the current Rightist attacks on the progressive gains that have been made in programs in education, the economy, health care, housing, and so many other areas (Apple, 2001; Katz, 2001), this makes these new approaches more necessary now than ever before.

All of this cannot be understood unless we realize that, with the worsening fiscal crisis being experienced in higher education and research institutes throughout the country, the search for sources of revenue to support research activities has intensified beyond the already intense pressure that existed before. Unfortunately, in educational research as in so many other communities, in times such as these there is a tendency for rationality to follow funding. That is, even when the researcher may not totally agree with the perspectives embodied in particular official definitions of important questions or the increasingly pre-specified ways of answering them, the pressure is on to abide by conservative educational and methodological priorities, and ultimately the social interests that underpin them, so that the intense financial problems are dealt with.

We need to be honest about the economic realities that universities now face since many of our institutions of higher education have had their budgets drastically cut and are increasingly "public" in name only, with most of their funding now coming not from public funding but from tuition and private sources. But we also need to be just as honest about the ideological effects and the effects on people's lives and careers. It's a risky time and real people face these risks.

Even in the face of these problems, however, the growth of critical research models and agendas has gone forward with increasing vigor. For example, we have a number of models of empirically and conceptually nuanced research that document the effects of current policies and provide spaces for alternative policies to evolve. The recent works of McNeil (2000), Gillborn and Youdell (2000), Lipman (2004), and others have "born witness to the negativity" of what is currently happening as neoliberal and neoconservative policies litter the landscape of education with the inequalities their policies have generated.

While it is crucial, "bearing witness" is not enough, however. We also need research that points to the complexities of real people's understanding of what they are facing and of what they can do about it. We need models and examples of how this socially committed research might be done by individuals and groups made up of people like you and me. This is where *Working Method: Research and Social Justice* enters.

As I have said elsewhere, while there may be gains to thinking of the world as a social construction, as a product of "discourse," such a position needs to come to grips with the gritty materiality of class dynamics, of political economy, of "worlds of pain" (Apple et al., 2003). In some ways, it is too reminiscent of the unattached intelligentsia of Karl Mannheim (1936), that group that has no class position itself but can stand above society and deconstruct its relations without having to commit itself to anything in particular. The universalism of the intellectual who stands above it all, observes and deconstructs the positions of others, has of course a long tradition in education and elsewhere. Adorno's vigorous attack on such "innocuous skepticism" is telling here. As he put it, such a standpoint "calls everything into question and criticizes nothing" (Osborne, 1996, p. xii).

Lois Weis and Michelle Fine will have none of this. They understand that the society in which we all live is characterized by social antagonisms and structurally generated relations of dominance—and by social movements and people who refuse to accept these relations and antagonisms. Weis and Fine are committed as well to doing something about these things. The kind of research that they argue for and *demonstrate* through rich examples points to ways in which our inquiries can contribute to giving voice to counter-hegemonic possibilities. Because of this, *Working Method* is a significant contribution to our understanding of the ways research can function as part of a larger set of movements for social justice.

MICHAEL W. APPLE
*John Bascom Professor of
Curriculum and Instruction and
Educational Policy Studies
University of Wisconsin, Madison*

References

Apple, M. W. (2001). *Educating the "right" way: Markets, standards, god, and inequality.* New York: RoutledgeFalmer.

Apple, M. W., et al. (2003). *The state and the politics of knowledge.* New York: RoutledgeFalmer.

Gillborn, D., & Youdell, D. (2000). *Rationing education.* Philadelphia: Open University Press.

Katz, M. B. (2001). *The price of citizenship.* New York: Metropolitan Books.

Lipman, P. (2004). *High stakes education.* New York: RoutledgeFalmer.

Mannheim, K. (1936). *Ideology and utopia.* New York: Harcourt, Brace, and World.

McNeil, L. (2000). *The contradictions of school reform.* New York: Routledge.

Osborne, P. (1996). Introduction: Philosophy and the role of intellectuals. In P. Osborne (Ed.), *A critical sense* (pp. vii–xxviii). New York: Routledge.

Smith, M. L., et al. (2004). *Political spectacle and the fate of American schools.* New York: RoutledgeFalmer.

Acknowledgments

Numerous people have aided in the preparation of this manuscript. We thank, in particular, Michael Apple for seizing upon our idea and encouraging us to place the volume in his series, Ilene Kalish who signed us with Routledge, and Catherine Bernard who happily inherited us when Ilene Kalish left. Catie LaLonde, a graduate student at the University at Buffalo, State University of New York, was indispensable as we put the volume together. Craig Centrie continues to push us as we work through the relationship between the visual arts and what we do as ethnographers, and we are forever in his debt. Amy Ferry, once again, saw to the preparation of the final manuscript and we thank her most sincerely for staying with us through numerous edits. Thanks, once again, to Tereffe Asrat, Sara Asrat, Jessica Asrat, David Surrey, Sam Finesurrey, and Caleb Finesurrey for loving us as we will always love you. This volume is dedicated to all those—past, present, and future—who struggle toward a better world.

Introduction
Compositional Studies in Four Parts: Critical Theorizing and Analysis on Social (In)Justice

Lois Weis and Michelle Fine

This book sits at the intersection of theory and method; it offers, perhaps, a *theory of method* for conducting critical theoretical and analytic work on social (in)justice (Daiute, 2003). We write the book for both veteran social scientists and graduate students eager to move among history, political economy, and the lives of ordinary people, for that is what we think we do best. For more than 20 years we have, individually and together, tried to write with communities under siege and to document the costs of oppression and the strengths of endurance that circulate among poor and working-class youth and young adults in America. Producing this work in schools, communities, and prisons, we seek in this volume to reveal the story behind the method that allows us to theorize and interrogate (in)justice in times when neoliberal ideology saturates and the Right prevails.

This volume is our attempt to theorize and explicate how scholars and activists can situate analyses of inequity, power, privilege, and deprivation within and beneath structural circumstance. We offer a detailed introductory essay on what we are putting forward as "compositional studies," in which analyses of public and private institutions, groups, and lives are lodged in relation to key social and economic structures. The remainder of the book wanders through a series of projects we have undertaken over the past two decades so as to reveal the intellectual infrastructure of work that dances as compositional study.

To capture our process, we borrow from what some have described as oscillation (Alford, 1998; Deleuze, 1990; Farmer, 2001; Hitchcock, 1999), a deliberate movement between theory "in the clouds" and empirical materials "on the ground." In this introduction, we articulate compositional studies as frame and elaborate on how we oscillate from local to structural, how we analyze in ways that reveal what photographers call the "varied depths of field," and how we try to position the work to "have legs," that is, to be useful to struggles for social justice. Writing to name the assumptions of our "compositional studies," we reflect here upon its possibilities for theory and activism and consider the limits of this work.

We write well-educated and influenced by ethnographers who have written powerful "oscillating" works (see Anzaldua, 1999; Crenshaw, 1991; Fanon, 1967; hooks, 1984; Ladson-Billings, 2000; Matsuda, 1995). Paul Willis (1977) and Valerie Walkerdine et al. (2001), for instance, have crafted analyses of White working-class youth situated explicitly in historical and class politics, with a keen eye toward development and identity. Patricia Hill Collins (1991), like Mari Matsuda (1995), Gloria Ladson-Billings (2002), and Patricia Williams (1992) have crafted the Critical Race Theory to speak explicitly back to the webbed relations of history, the political economy, and everyday lives of women and men of color. Barrie Thorne (1993) has boldly broadened our understandings of gender, arguing fervently against "sex difference" research, insisting instead that gender be analyzed as relational performance. Paul Farmer (2001) moves from biography of individuals living in Haiti who suffer tuberculosis to the international politics of epidemiology, illness, and health care, while Angela Valenzuela (1999) skillfully helps us come to know Mexican American youth across contexts in school, home, and community. These scholars produce writings centered on the rich complexity within group, offering complex, detailed, and sophisticated analyses of a slice of the social matrix, theorizing its relation to the whole (see also Bourgois, 1995; Connell, 1995; Duneier, 1994; Foley, 1990; Rubin, 1976; Scheper-Hughes & Sargent, 1998; Stack, 1997; Stepick, Stepick, Eugene, & Teed, 2001; Twine, 2000; and Waters, 1999).

In compositional studies, we take up a companion project, writing through multiple groups of this social puzzle we call America, fractured by jagged lines of power, so as to theorize carefully this relationality and, at the same time, recompose the institution, community, and nation as a series of fissures and connections. While there is always a risk that the in-group depth may be compromised at the expense of cross-group analysis, we try, in this essay, to articulate how this method responds to questions of social critique, social justice theory, and advocacy.

To be more specific, in *The Unknown City* (Fine & Weis, 1998) and in *Working Class Without Work* (Weis, 1990) analytically speaking, we have argued that White working-class men (at least in the urban northeast of the United States) can be understood only in relation to a constructed African American "other," with the most powerful refraction occurring in relation to African American men. These men must be theorized and their words analyzed, then, in relation to "bordering" groups—White women, African American men and women, gay men across racial/ethnic groups, and so forth. While their narrations rarely reference history or the global economy explicitly, we have had to situate these men, as they move through their daily lives and narrate their social relations, in the shifting historic sands of social, economic, and political conditions.

The key point here is that social theory and analyses can no longer afford to isolate a group, or to represent their stories as transparent, as though that group were coherent and bounded; instead, we must theorize explicitly, that is, connect the dots, to render visible relations to other groups and to larger sociopolitical formations. The emergent montage of groups must simultaneously be positioned within historically shifting social and economic relations in the United States and globally. While the specific bordering groups are uncovered ethnographically and may vary by site, deep theorizing and analysis are required to join these seemingly separate and isolated groups and link them institutionally and ideologically. More broadly speaking, our notion and practice of qualitative work suggests that *no* one group can be understood as if outside of the relational and structural aspects of identity formation.

At the heart of compositional studies lie three analytic moves we seek to make explicit. The first is the deliberate placement of ethnographic and narrative material into a contextual and historic understanding of economic and racial formations (see Sartre, 1968). Without presuming a simple determinism of economics to identity, we nevertheless take as foundational that individuals navigate lives in what Martín-Baró (1994) and Freire (1982) would call "limit situations," within historic moments, unequal power relations, and the everyday activities of life. As Jean-Paul Sartre articulated in 1968, weaving a method between Marxism and existentialism, "If one wants to grant to Marxist thought its full complexity, one would have to say that man [*sic*] in a period of exploitation is at once both the product of his own product and a historical agent who can under no circumstances be taken as a product. This contradiction is not fixed; it must be grasped in the very movement of *praxis*" (p. 87).

And yet, when we engage ethnographically, speak to people, collect survey data, or conduct a focus group, it is most unusual for individuals to articulate the relations between and among their own "personal lives" and the historic, economic, and racial relations within which they exist (Mills, 1959). History appears as a "foreign force"; people do not recognize the "meaning of their enterprise . . . in the total, objective result" (Sartre, 1968, p. 89). That is indeed the insidious victory of neoliberal ideology (Apple, 2001); people speak as if they are self-consciously immune and independent, disconnected, and insulated from history, the state, the economic context, and "others." As social theorists, we know well that the webs that connect structures, relations, and lives are essential to understanding the rhythm of daily life, possibilities for social change, as well as the ways in which individuals take form in, and transform, social relations. Thus we work hard to situate our analyses of communities, schools, and lives historically, economically, and socially so that the material context within which individuals are "making sense" can be linked to their very efforts to reflect upon and transform these conditions.

Second, in our work we rely more on categories of social identity than many of our post-structural scholar-friends do. That is, while we refuse essentialism, resisting the mantra-like categories of social life—race, ethnicity, class, gender—as coherent, in the body, "real," consistent, or homogeneous, we also take very seriously that these categories become real inside institutional life, yielding dire political and economic consequences. Even if resisted, they become foundational to social identities. Even as performed, multiple, shifting, and fluid, the technologies of surveillance ensure partial penetration of the politics of social identities (Butler, 1999; Foucault, 1977; Scott, 1990). You just can't hang out in poor and working-class communities, a suburban mall, a prison, or an elite suburban golf course and believe that race, ethnicity, and social class are simply inventions. Thus, with theoretical ambivalence and political commitment, we analytically embrace these categories of identity as social, porous, flexible, and yet profoundly political ways of organizing the world. By so doing we seek to understand how individuals make sense of, resist, embrace, and embody social categories, and, as dramatically, how they situate "others," at times even essentializing and reifying "other" categories, in relation to themselves. This is, we argue, what demands a relational method.

Third, as a corollary principle to our interest in categories as fluid sites for meaning-making, we seek to elaborate the textured variations of identities that can be found within any single category. Thus, as you will hear, our method enables us to search explicitly for variety, dissent within, and outliers who stand (by "choice" or coercion or both) at the dejected or radical margins, those who deny category membership or who challenge the existence of categories at all. Analytically, it is crucial to resist searching for in-group coherence or consensus as anything other than a hegemonic construction, although, as we argue, the search for modal forms is exceedingly useful. Nevertheless, it is critical to theorize how variation and outliers in relation to such modality re-present the larger group (Bhavnani, 1994).

These three moves—contextual, relational, and a focus potentially on and through individual variation while seeking modal forms—are crucial to what we are calling our "theory of method." Indeed, we would argue that this theory of method is conceptually akin to what an artist does, and this leads us to call our articulated method "compositional studies." A visual artist has no composition without paying explicit attention to both the positive and negative spaces of a composition. Positive space (the main object) must have a negative referent, and the negative referent, visually speaking, is as important to the whole composition as the positive. It is these "blank" or "Black" spaces in relation to "color" or "White" that we pay attention to in our work. Like the artist, then, we explicitly explore the negative bridging spaces within the composition; we intentionally explore the relationship between "negative" and "positive" spaces and understand that no positive exists except in relation to the negative. Again, this is an artistic metaphor, but one that offers great power as we reflect upon and name our ethnographic practice.[1] Under our theory and practice of method then, relevant bordering groups (those groups that border the primary subject of interest in the ethnography) are as essential to the ethnographic composition as any primary group under consideration. Thus, our specific genre of ethnographic practice historically implies a *particular* analytic method, one that considers the in-between, the gauze that glues groups together, even as it is narrated to distinguish "them."

Extending our notion of compositional studies, we also argue that no group, even as in relation to other bordering groups, can be understood without reference to the larger economic and racial formations within which the interactions take place. The in-between, like DuBois's color line, grows to be as theoretically and politically critical as that group that initially captures our ethnographic attention. Like the Black arts movement in the 1960s and 1970s then, we intentionally and self-consciously politicize our artistic/compositional metaphor, arguing that our ethnographic compositions sit at the nexus of structural forces and individual lives and agency.[2]

In so doing, we locate *dynamism* as a core element of our method, self-consciously embracing movement rather than the freezing so characteristic of a wealth of prior ethnographic practice—movement in relation to larger economic and social formations as well as bordering "others." Given the shifting nature of all parts of what we call the "composition," our method enables and encourages us to capture this shifting over time and space.[3]

We offer, in this book, a series of compositional designs—ethnographic inquiries designed to understand how global and national formations, and relational interactions, seep through the lives, identities, relations, and communities of youth and adults, ultimately refracting back on the larger formations that give rise to them.

Sculpting the Work: On Design in Composition

In a desire toward clarity, but at the risk of being didactic, we sketch below various forms of compositional design, offering images of each in subsequent chapters. We elaborate this list not because we believe it is exhaustive, nor prescriptive, but because we have learned that frame matters, images help, and a bit of methodological advice goes a long way. Thus, we sketch below a series of possible design frameworks that may prove useful in research on social (in)justice (see Bhabha, 1990; Farmer, 1999; Twine, 2000; Winant, 1994). These broad frameworks, we suggest, can be employed with qualitative and/or quantitative methods and data. They share, at base, a commitment to framing and/or reframing questions of theory, policy, and politics from within sites of contestation.

Full Compositional Analyses

These studies aim to map the full community (see Fine & Weis, 1998) or institution (as in the schools) and to document the aggregate view and the ideological representation of the whole. Full compositional analyses allow us to view the site through a lens of coherence and integrity. Often reproducing dominant representations, these full analyses nevertheless allow readers to grasp the familiar frame before the research ventures into more fractured analyses. Within the full composition, however, it is important to tease open any apparent (or not so apparent) fractures.

First Fracturing Analyses

The first fracturing analysis produces an interior analysis of the institution/community through lines of difference and power. These analyses destabilize the representation of institutional coherence, integrity, and stability, typically activating the first challenge to "well-established facts" (Law & Mol, 2003).

Counteranalyses

While the first fracturing analysis interrupts representations of coherence, this call for counteranalyses presses the move to destabilize further. That is, in these analyses, we juxtapose the principle fracture lines with other lines of challenging analysis. By placing these varied analyses adjacent to one another, they reveal the many competing stories that can be told about and within institutional life and power (see Bowen & Bok, 1998 for an excellent example; Lather, 1991). Ironically, such comparative analyses reveal existing fault lines, suggesting where mobilization can begin and radical change is possible.

Historic Trajectory

These studies are designed to trace, over time, the continuities and discontinuities of identity, relations, and material lives. Relying upon longitudinal and/or archival materials, designs for historic trajectory enable us to see the "field of forces" through which development, change, structural advantages, and structural assaults shape how individuals and groups live and narrate their everyday social practices.

Revealing Sites for Possibility

As part of our theoretical and ethical commitment, we construct, at once, designs that fracture ideological coherence and designs that document those spaces, relations, and/or practices in which possibility flourishes or critique gets heard. Our commitment to revealing sites for possibility derives not only from a theoretical desire to re-view "what is" and "what could be," but also from an ethical belief that critical researchers have an obligation not simply to dislodge the dominant discourse, but to help readers and audiences imagine where the spaces for resistance, agency, and possibility lie. We craft research that aims toward Lather's "catalytic validity": research to provoke action.

The above design strategies seek to trace how obviously related, and yet seemingly remote, structural conditions shape local contexts, group identities, and individual lives. It is relatively easy to write up institutional stories as thick, local qualitative descriptions without revealing the webs of power that connect institutional and individual lives to larger social formations. Yet, if we do not draw these lines for readers, we render them invisible, colluding in the obfuscation of the structural conditions that undergird social inequities. It seems clear that researchers, as public intellectuals, have a responsibility to make visible the strings that attach political and moral conditions with individual lives. If we don't, few will. Rendering visible is precisely the task of theory, and as such, must be taken up by method.

Importantly, our notion of compositional studies invites a rotating position for the writer/researcher; that is, compositional studies afford researchers the opportunity and obligation to be at once grounded and analytically oscillating between engagement and distance, explicitly committed to deep situatedness and yet shifting perspectives as to the full composition. Our theory of method, then, extends an invitation to the researcher as multiply positioned: grounded, engaged, reflective, well-versed in scholarly discourse, knowledgeable as to external circumstances, and able to move between theory and life "on the ground." Whether in a school, prison, neighborhood, cultural arts center, community center, or religious institution, we invite researchers and writers to travel between theory "in the clouds" and the everyday practices of individuals living in communities as they (and we) negotiate, make sense of, and change positionalities and circumstances. This method suggests then, an articulate, intellectually and personally flexible, and engaged individual who really does respect what others have to say. The responsibility of placing these interactions, narrations, and all that we have come to refer to as "data" largely, as we suggest here, lies with us.

Organization of the Book

In this volume we offer examples of our work as emblematic of each design. In so doing, we encourage other researchers to work with the design category, envisioning how future studies add to our knowledge in the targeted area.

Section 1: Full Composition and Initial Fracturing

We begin with an essay entitled "Dear Zora," written as a letter to Zora Neale Hurston who, in 1955, authored a scathing critique of the *Brown v. Board of Education* decision in the *Orlando Sentinel*. We write this piece off of a participatory research project with youth from across communities, zip codes, races, ethnicities, class, sexualities, and (dis)abilities to speak back to *Brown* and to Hurston and to speak forward to the ongoing struggles for racial and class justice in American schools. The research represents at once a full compositional design and a fracturing analysis. That is, Michelle and colleagues, with youth researchers, surveyed, interviewed, and conducted focus groups and participant observations in some of the wealthiest and poorest schools in America. We write a full compositional story of the state of public education in urban and suburban America, but can only craft that argument with a searing recognition of the inequities that shatter the presumption of (educational) "justice for all."

Section 2: Deep Work Within a Fracture

As a complement, the second chapter, "Race, Gender, and Critique," provides a fracturing analysis within feminist studies of women's experiences of community and domestic violence. In this piece Lois reveals at once the common experience of violence in the lives of African American and White low-income women, and then the turns that race, ethnicity, class, and position enforce with respect to how the women respond to abuse in the home and in public. The power of this piece lies in the recognition of class- and gender-based shared experiences of violence, and then the racially disparate responses to the abuse. Like Patricia Hill Collins, who elegantly distinguishes experience and consciousness, this piece allows us to "see" the oppressively democratic distribution of fists on women's bodies and to think through the racialized options "available" to women living simultaneously in very different worlds.

The third chapter, "Civics Lessons," intentionally enters a specific class fracture—poor and working-class youth in California—who attend schools in substantial disrepair, with undercredentialed faculty, insufficient instructional materials, and exceedingly high teacher turnover. In this piece, written for a class action lawsuit on behalf of children in underresourced schools throughout California (*Williams v. California*), after speaking with more than 100 children and teens, we hear incisively about the social policies that have situated these youth inside extremely oppressive educational "limit situations." Here, youth critically detail the inadequacies of their schooling, painfully revealing their belief that the state views them, fundamentally, as worthless. This chapter exposes the texture, complexity, and variability within a particular class fraction by documenting meticulously how social policies and state priorities shape contexts within which youth *witness* public betrayal and thereby *learn* alienation, even as they embody and narrate hope and desire.

Section 3: Designs for Historic Analysis

Chapter 4 draws from Lois's most recent work, *Class Reunion* (2004b). Given kaleidoscopic changes in the world economy in the past several decades, Lois's follow-up study of individuals who initially are the subjects in *Working Class Without Work* (Weis, 1990) drives home the point that identities are constructed over time and in relation to the constructed identities of others, as well as dialectically in relation to the broader economy and culture. Long-term ethnographic investigations enable us to track this set of interactions and relationships over time. Here is the unique contribution of Lois's *Class Reunion*: She uses data gathered in 1985 in a working-class high school and then re-interviews these students 15 years later. This form of *ethnographic longitudinality* enables us to shift our eyes from pieces drawn at one point in time to those drawn at another, opening ever further the specter of compositional ethnography.

Section 4: Designs to Document Sites of Possibility

The two chapters in this section represent our desire to write, at once, toward both critique and possibility. "Participatory Action Research" (chapter 5) documents a participatory action research project conducted with prisoners as co-researchers, within a women's maximum security facility, in which we interrogated the impact of college in prison on the women prisoners, their children, the prison environment, and post-release outcomes. With participatory commitments to design, analysis, and writing, Michelle and colleagues set out to understand the extent to which college in prison—once widely available in 350 prisons nationally and today available in less than a dozen—can enable intellectual, social, and political possibility in a space that does violence to the spirit and is bereft of hope. In this piece we articulate the relation of national security and prosperity to the swelling prison industrial complex, the racialized darkening of the prison population, the ruptures in community life for poor and working-class youth of color, and the implications of the 1995 decision to withhold Pell Grants for prisoners. We take delight in the vibrant stories of transformation, radicalization, and liberation narrated by prisoners who attend college, are released from prison, and return at significantly lower rates than their less educated peers. In this piece we aim to reveal the delicate dynamics of participatory work under surveillance, the power of educational access even (or especially) in prison, the long arm of federal realignment of dollars and priorities away from public education and toward prison containment, and the vibrancy of a small program that can, we argue, turn the world upside down.

"Extraordinary Conversations in Public Schools" (chapter 6) continues this same rhythm: the scholarly obligation to document sites of hope even, or especially, in institutions of deep despair. In this chapter, we reflect upon the power of small safe spaces, fractures in the hegemonic armor, in which youth come to reimagine the world and their subsequent shaping of it. We write at the nexus of reproduction theory and resistance analyses, eager to imagine research in which possibility flourishes without occluding the marks of oppression. Thus, in this final piece Lois and Michelle jointly theorize the delicate relation of injustice and persistence, despite the odds. And we suggest, perhaps somewhat arrogantly, that to document sites of possibility is indeed to keep them alive and nurture their survival. In the epilogue we revisit these themes as we reflect upon our designs and emblematic chapters.

Full Composition and Initial Fracturing

CHAPTER 1

Dear Zora:
A Letter to Zora Neale Hurston
Fifty Years After *Brown*

Michelle Fine, Janice Bloom, April Burns,
Lori Chajet, Monique Guishard,
Tiffany Perkins-Munn, and María Elena Torre

Dear Zora:

Sorry that it has taken so long to respond. Actually, it's been 48 years. For the benefit of readers, we'll reprint your prophetic letter to the editor of the *Orlando Sentinel* and offer a rather lengthy response:

> Editor: I promised God and some other responsible characters, including a bench of bishops, that I was not going to part my lips concerning the U.S. Supreme Court decision on ending segregation in the public schools of the South. But since a lot of time has passed and no one seems to touch on what to me appears to be the most important point in the hassle, I break my silence just this once. Consider me as just thinking out loud. . . .
>
> I regard the ruling of the U.S. Supreme Court as insulting rather than honoring my race. Since the days of the never-to-be-sufficiently-deplored Reconstruction, there has been current the belief that there is no greater delight to Negroes than physical association with whites. The doctrine of the white mare. Those familiar with the habits of mules are aware that any mule, if not restrained, will automatically follow a white mare. Dishonest mule traders made money out of this knowledge in the old days.
>
> Lead a white mare along a country road and slyly open the gate and the mules in the lot would run out and follow this mare. This ruling being conceived and brought forth in a sly political medium with eyes on '56, and brought forth in the

same spirit and for the same purpose, it is clear that they have taken the old notion to heart and acted upon it. It is a cunning opening of the barnyard gate with the white mare ambling past. We are expected to hasten pell-mell after her.

It is most astonishing that this should be tried just when the nation is exerting itself to shake off the evils of Communist penetration. It is to be recalled that Moscow, being made aware of this folk belief, made it the main plank in their campaign to win the American Negro from the 1900s on. It was the come-on stuff. . . .

It is well known that I have no sympathy nor respect for the "tragedy of color" school of thought among us, whose fountain-head is the pressure group concerned with this court ruling. I see no tragedy in being too dark to be invited to a white school social affair. The Supreme Court would have pleased me more if they had concerned themselves about enforcing the compulsory education provisions for Negroes in the South as is done for white children. . . . Thems my sentiments and I am sticking by them. Growth from within. Ethical and cultural desegregation. It is a contradiction in terms to scream race pride and equality while at the same time spurning Negro teachers and self association. That old white mare business can go racking on down the road for all I care.

Zora Neale Hurston, Eau Gallie
(August 11, 1955, Orlando Sentinel)

In 1955 you understood what few were willing to acknowledge. More than that, you dared to speak aloud, in unpopular dialect, about the white mare that seduces with promises of equality, freedom, and choice as it guarantees continued oppression and betrayal. As you suggest, promises of racial equality in public education in the United States have been covert operations that reproduce privilege. Nevertheless, with the wisdom of hindsight, we view *Brown* with a DuBoisian dual consciousness: as a radical interruption of law and educational practice, subverted almost immediately by the white mare of persistent racism.

The dual legacy of *Brown* reveals itself in the project of desegregation, which has indeed led African Americans, Asian Americans, African Caribbeans, Latinos, low-income White youth, undocumented immigrant students, youth with disabilities, girls, gays, and lesbians into institutions, clubs, and communities from which their great grandparents, grandparents, and parents may have been barred. In many cases, however, these students—youth of color and those who live in poverty, in particular—participate within such desegregated settings, from the margins. Academically, they witness excellence, but most sit just a classroom away. More African American and Latino students attend segregated schools than was true just a decade ago (Orfield & Easton, 1996).

And yet at the same time, in the spirit of *Brown*, a number of desegregated districts are interrogating questions of the "gap." Maybe not as deeply as we would wish or as radically as we would hope—but they are interrogating. And, even more compelling, in urban areas throughout the

United States there is a proliferation of intellectually exciting, inquiry-based, vibrant, bold small schools dedicated to overcoming the odds for youth in poverty, immigrant students, and adolescents of color. And community-based organizations, youth activists, and parent groups throughout the country are organizing with and for public education as a site of democratic, liberatory possibility (see Sisters and Brothers United, personal communication; Anand, 2003; Guishard et al., 2003). These schools, districts, and neighborhood organizations toil in the legacy of *Brown*. Refusing the white mare of persistent racism, they understand that with struggle comes resistance. They have dipped in the puddles of rich educational possibilities, slipped in the muddy waters of relentless in-equality, and currently wade through the waters of despair. We write with a dual purpose: to recognize the power of *Brown*'s progeny and to reveal where the persistent inequities continue to undermine. We write to honor what has been rich and powerful, to canvass the topography of *Brown* then and now, to "out" the duplicitous white mares of today, and to excavate the puddles of radical possibility that carry a genetic trace to the spirit of the *Brown* decision. You will be flattered to know that 23 years after you wrote this letter to the editor, the amazing writer Alice Walker spent much time theorizing your stance in literary and political history. In 1979 Walker wrote: "Is Hurston the messenger who brings the bad news, or is she the bad news herself? Is Hurston a reflection of ourselves? And if so, is that not, perhaps, part of our 'problem' with her?" (Walker, 1979, p. 2) And 25 years later, Zora, you are still on our minds.

We Begin With Echoes:
Hearing Voices Across Fifty Years Since *Brown*

> I am no fool; and I know that race prejudice in the United States today is such that most Negroes cannot receive proper education in white institutions . . . a separate Negro school, where children are treated like human beings, trained by teachers of their own race, who know what it means to be black in the year of salvation 1935, is infinitely better than making our boys, and girls doormats to be spit and trampled upon and lied to by ignorant social climbers, whose sole claim to superiority is ability to kick "niggers" when they are down. (DuBois, 1935, pp. 328–329).

> Most people, for some reason unknown to me, accept injustice. Why is that? When God created us, did he make us in the image of a welcome mat? No. So why are so many people getting stepped on? Speak Up! Let your voice be heard with the intent to inspire others. (Travis Marquis, 2002)

We write through an echo chamber of historic struggle and resistance, satu-rated by the words of DuBois in 1935 and Travis Marquis, age 21, of the South Bronx in 2002. Surrounded by the vibrant and electric words of civil rights struggles of the past and the yearning, despair, and resistance of youth today, we deepen our critical understandings of the legacies of *Brown*. Zora, we work with your analysis acutely in our consciousness because we believe that the spirit of *Brown*, in its fullest sense, sits at the core of our national democracy. But *Brown*, of course, has been "hijacked," as Asa Hilliard III (2002) would tell us—for it was always intended as a strategy toward justice, equity, and intellectual freedom, not a mechanistic formula of body counts and color codings. We review here the racialized life of public education today in a northeastern corner of the United States, to understand the victories and the ongoing struggles from the perspective of youth who live in the shadows of *Brown*, and who will determine its future.

The evidence we present reveals that the struggle for academic racial justice has, indeed, been "hijacked" by the better-funded movement for White and elite privilege that founded, and currently governs, America. The public sector of public education has been fiscally hollowed, with the demand for equal resources trivialized into a (denied) quest to sit beside a White child. The fire of *Brown* for equity, power, and justice has been blanketed, watered down. Youth of color today learn about a victory 50 years old as they daily confront largely segregated, underfunded schools, high-stakes tests that terrify and punish, with only some educators credentialed to teach. They are constantly witnessing locks being secured on the doors of Higher Education. A publicly financed welcome mat for African American and Latino youth sits at the barbed-wire rim of America's prisons and, with college tuition rates rising and financial aid drying up, the promises of military life seduce those most vulnerable (Fine, Anand, Jordan, & Sherman, 2000). Somewhere in their souls, though the numbers may be unknown, young people in New York know that in 1994, for the first time in history, their state expended more of its budget on prisons than on public universities (Gangi, Schiraldi, & Ziedenberg, 1998).

The radical realignment of the public sphere requires serious reflection on *Brown* and its progeny.

But before we're through, Zora, we'll also tell you about those spaces in schools and communities throughout the United States where youth are learning and teaching, organizing and demanding, laughing and embodying *the other legacy of Brown*—the legacy of fighting back, never giving up, struggling for racial equality in a sea of greed and neoliberal individualism. We listen as youth yearn for and demand equity in public education in the United States, at the beginning of the 21st century.

Echoes: The Faultlines of Racial Justice and Public Education

Fifty years after *Brown v. Board of Education*, we continue to confront what is called an "achievement gap" across racial and ethnic groups, and across social class fractions (Anyon, 1997; Bowles & Gintis, 1976; Ferguson, 1998; Fine, 1991; Fordham, 1996; Hochschild, 2003; New York ACORN, 2000; Orfield & Easton, 1996; Wilson, 1987).[1] In 2001, a series of school districts within the New York metropolitan area, in suburban New York and New Jersey, joined to form a consortium to address this question of the "gap" and invited us to collaborate on research. Drawing on the writings of Ron Hayduk (1999) and Myron Orfield (1997), we conceptualized an ethnographic regional analysis of the political economy of schooling as lived by youth in and around the New York City metropolitan area.

By crossing the lines separating suburban and urban areas, integrated and segregated schools, deeply tracked and detracked schools, we designed the work to reveal joints across county lines and to identify important contrasts (Orfield, 1997). We sought to document the codependent growth of the suburbs and the defunding of urban America and to reveal the fractures of inequity and the pools of possibility that fill the topography of "desegregated" suburban and urban communities and schools. We hoped, finally, to capture some of the magic of those schools in which rich, engaging education flourishes for youth across lines of race, ethnicity, class, geography, and "track."

We undertook this project committed to a textured, multimethod critical ethnographic analysis of urban and suburban schooling. Youth and adults designed the project to speak back to questions of racial, ethnic, and class justice in American education. To reach deep into the varied standpoints that constitute these schools, we created a participatory action research design with youth representing the full ensemble of standpoints within these urban and suburban desegregated settings (Anand et al., 2002; Fals Borda, 1979; Fine et al., 2001; Freire, 1982).

The Design

We have, since January 2002, been collaborating with youth from eleven racially integrated suburban school districts, one New Jersey urban district, and three New York City high schools, crossing racial, ethnic, class, gender, academic, geographic, and sexuality lines. We designed a series of research camps in schools, on college campuses, and in communities ranging from wealthy Westchester suburbs to the South Bronx of New York City.

At the first research camp, a 2-day overnight at St. Peter's College in Jersey City, New Jersey, youth participated in "methods training": learning about quantitative and qualitative design, critical race theory, and a series of methods including interview, focus group, observation, and survey research (e.g., we read with them Harding, 1987; Collins, 1991). Urban and suburban students and those of us from the Graduate Center crafted a survey of questions on the "gap," incorporating some of Tony Bryk's items on school climate and trust, as well as some of Constance Flanagan's items on civic engagement. The survey was intended to be distributed across districts, focusing on youth views of distributive (in) justice in the nation and their schools.

The youth insisted that the survey *not* look like a test, and so creatively subverted the representations of "science" by including photos, cartoons for respondents to interpret, a chart of the achievement gap, and open-ended questions such as "What is the most powerful thing a teacher has ever said to you?" Available in English, French Creole, Spanish, Braille, and on tape—because the inner ring suburbs are far more diverse than most believe (Orfield, 1997)—the survey was administered to close to 7,000 9th and 12th graders across districts. Within 6 weeks, we received more than 4,000 completed surveys—brimming with rich qualitative and quantitative data that could be disaggregated by race, ethnicity, gender, and "track." Beyond the surveys, over the past year we have engaged in participant observations within four suburban and two urban schools, arranged four cross-school visitations, and conducted over 20 focus group interviews. In addition, five school "teams" pursued their own questions crafted under the larger "opportunity gap" umbrella.

The Children of *Brown*: Civic Engagement and Equity

Although the history of today's desegregation is a complex montage of victories and disappointments, we have gathered a glistening layer of evidence about how youth in desegregated settings think about education and racial justice. In these data you can find the proud progeny of *Brown* and the white mare of betrayal. Consistently and across racial and ethnic lines, young people who attend desegregated schools hold high aspirations for college and strong values for multiracial justice and education. They embody a sense of the power and the unfulfilled promise of a multiracial/multiethnic democracy. They appreciate attending desegregated schools, but worry that the nation has walked away from the struggle for racial justice; they worry that their classrooms remain largely segregated. These young women and men are, indeed, ambassadors for a campaign for racial justice but are at a loss for how to make it real. Many feel betrayed by a nation that has abandoned multiracial democracy. And then, within the broad-based cohort support for desegregation, on every measure, we see a marbleized race/ethnicity effect: African American, Caribbean American, and Latino youth are significantly more troubled by the ripples of injustice that flow through their schools than are White American and Asian American youth.

On Academic Aspirations

As a group, the young women and men we surveyed are dedicated to attending college, with more than 90% of the respondents from each racial/ ethnic group indicating that "college" is important to their future. However, African American and Latino students, particularly those who are not in AP or honors level courses, worry significantly more that high-stakes testing and finances could obstruct their academic pursuits.

On Civic Engagement

We created a Civic Engagement Index, which measures students' desires to help those less fortunate, to work against racial injustice and to work for change in community and nation. The results indicated that students from desegregated high schools, overall, endorse high levels of civic commitments. Across all groups, more than 40% of the youth indicated that civic engagement was important to their future. Additionally, significant race/ ethnicity and gender differences emerge. On individual items and the Civic Engagement Index, African American and Latina girls scored significantly higher than all other groups ($\chi^2 = 122.71$, $df = 9$, $p < .001$). When asked how important "ending racism" is for future well-being, more than half of African American, Caribbean American, and Latino students, compared to only one third of White American students, selected "very important."

In parallel, more than 60% of all students indicated strong agreement with "It is very important to help my country," with little cross-race variation. Yet, in response to the item "We need to create change in the nation," White Americans were significantly less likely to agree (32%) than Asian Americans (43%), Latinos (52%), African Caribbeans (60%), and African Americans (61%). Again we see overall endorsement of strong civic commitments, but also a strong belief among students of color (African American, Asian American, Caribbean American, and Latino) that the nation has to change to be true to its democratic principles.

On Racial Equity in Schools

Turning to our Attitudes Toward School Desegregation measure, these students, as a cohort, are strong advocates for desegregation. A full 76% of the entire sample "agrees/strongly agrees" that "attending a school that is 'mixed' or integrated is very important to me." (This high level of support has been replicated in a sample of youth in Delaware attending desegregated middle and high schools, $N = 2,075$.) While they appreciate attending desegregated schools, however, students across the board recognize that access to *rigor and academic success* is unevenly distributed throughout their schools. Many register concern—even those who presumably benefit from the skewed distribution of educational resources (see Table 1.1).

TABLE 1.1 Views of Racial Justice in Schools (% Agree/Strongly Agree)

Statement	Asian American	White American	African American	Caribbean American	Latino
Classes are not as mixed as my school.	50	47	70	73	49
Everyone in my school has an equal chance of getting into the hardest classes.	67.5	63.6	39.2	45.6	58.1
My school is not good at equal opportunity.	18.9	17.7	40.9	41.4	35.6
There is an achievement gap in my school.	60.9	60.4	70.4	71.6	59.1
If I mess up, educators in my school give me a second chance.	53.4	50.9	37.6	38.8	47.8
N	210	1,491	286	138	274

Classes not as mixed as they should be: $\chi^2 = 78.11$, $df = 4$, $p < .001$.
Equal chance of getting in: $\chi^2 = 74.09$, $df = 4$, $p < .001$.
School not good at providing equal opportunities: $\chi^2 = 119.02$, $df = 4$, $p < .001$.
Achievement gap: $\chi^2 = 15.93$, $df = 4$, $p < .001$.
Second chance: $\chi^2 = 23.459$, $df = 4$, $p = .000$.

On every item of Views of Racial Justice in Schools, students expressed substantial concern about academic inequities: almost 60% agree that there is an achievement gap, more than 50% agree that "classes are not as mixed as my school," and more than 40% believe that "students do not have an equal chance of getting into the hardest classes." While equity concerns are cross-sectional, African American, Caribbean American, and Latino students are significantly more likely to rate their schools critically than White and Asian American students.

Confirming the writings of Braddock, Dawkins, and Wilson (1995), Crain and Wells (1997), Oakes, Wells, Yonezawa, and Ray (1997), and others, there are significant civic as well as academic consequences to attending desegregated schools. Yet the struggle for racial justice and equity within public education remains far from over, and different bodies worry differently about the inequities.

We offer here a few slices of our results on how youth theorize and embody racial/ethnic and class injustices that continue to define public education—how they conceptualize the betrayal by the white mare. In so doing, we document how youth positioned within varied and multiple social categories spin identities as students, researchers, and activists when they "discover" how deeply historic inequities are woven into the fabric of U.S. public education. We search to understand how young people who are engaged, aspiring, and committed experience "separate and unequal" across and within schools, today, even though many youth feel just like James (9th-grade African American youth researcher from the suburbs) when he stated, "*Brown v. Board* got my back."

Through the Windows of Betrayal: Reading/Riding the White Mare

The empirical materials presented have been carved out of the larger project, at twinned fracture points where youth confront structures, policies, practices, and relations that organize, naturalize, and ensure persistent inequity. We enter through these cracks—the enduring blood of *Brown*—because we find them to be compelling windows into how privileged and marginalized youth negotiate political and intellectual identities, dreams, and imaginations in an educational system in which privilege translates into merit and being poor and/or of color translates into worthlessness. We watch and monitor as youth in urban and suburban schools develop selves of resistance, capitulation, and outrage—as youth of color and poverty act on their academic desires through the gauze of alienation.

Interrogating Educational Finance Inequities

At the first research camp, "differences" of class, geography, race, and ethnicity were displayed boldly and interrogated subtly. Just after the camp, "shocked to hear what school sounds like when the kids from suburbs talk," the students from East Side Community High School decided to document the causes, justifications, and consequences of finance inequities in New York State. Working in an intensive high school elective on Youth Research with Lori Chajet and Janice Bloom, they met weekly to study original documents and to collect original information about the Campaign for Fiscal Equity lawsuit in New York City. Knowing much about the *Brown* decision, they could not quite believe that "separate and unequal" was the standard, accepted financing practice in New York State (so successfully challenged in New Jersey).

They gathered legal documents and interviewed activists, scholars, students, organizers, lawyers, and educators about the case. They read Justice Leland DeGrasse's 2001 decision in the *Campaign for Fiscal Equity* case:

> This court holds that the education provided New York City students is so deficient that it falls below the constitutional floor set by the Education Article of the New York State Constitution. The court also finds that the state's actions are a substantial cause of this constitutional violation. (*Campaign for Fiscal Equity (CFE) v. State of New York,* 2001)

And then they learned that just 17 months later, based on an appeal filed by Governor George Pataki, Justice Lerner of the Appellate Division overturned the DeGrasse decision:

> A "sound basic education" should consist of the skills necessary to obtain employment, and to competently discharge one's civil responsibility. The state submitted evidence that jury charges are generally at a grade level of 8.3, and newspaper articles on campaign and ballot issues range from grade level 6.5 to 11.7 . . . the evidence at the trial established that the skills required to enable a person to obtain employment, vote, and serve on a jury, are imparted between grades 8 and 9. (Supreme Court Appellate Division, June 2002)

Dismayed by this reversal, the youth researchers set out to document the consequences of finance inequity on students and graduates of high- and low-resource schools. They decided to visit one anothers' schools—in New York City and wealthy Westchester suburbs (districts that receive approximately $7,000 per child and more than $15,000 per child, respectively).[2]

Well rehearsed in their "researcher identities," they planned to visit schools just 20 miles north that receive almost double their per capita State revenues. As juniors, they traveled to several wealthy Westchester communities and documented differential access to computers, books, libraries, AP classes, and so on, although they were disturbed that "there's like no minorities in those top classes." Seeing privilege up close, however, was not merely an academic exercise. All too familiar with racist representations of "them," they confronted on the visits what they could not know—the striking material and intellectual capital accumulated through privilege.

Sitting on green grass waiting for their train back to the city, students expressed amazement at the differences between their own school and the large suburban complex they had spent the day visiting. "Did you see the auditorium? Okay, our auditorium looks like . . . [crap] compared to that one." "Because they have money, they could actually have a darkroom that they can do photography in," another exclaimed. Others focused on the library: "They have a lot of books!" "It's like a regular library." "The computers!" One student highlighted the difference in access to technology within the classroom and its effect on student learning: "I went to [a science class where] a girl gave a presentation about abortion. She had slides to show everyone [on a slide projector and a computer] . . . when we had that in our school we just did a poster." Several, having also visited science classes, followed up with remarks on the "real" science laboratories: the lab equipment, the sinks in the rooms, the materials for experiments.

As seniors, this same group visited another Westchester high school. Now adrenalin filled with the terror and excitement of their own college application processes, these young people toured the building with a sense of awe, depression, and disgust. Nikaury mumbled, "This school *is* college." José continued the conversation, "They already take psychology and advanced math and English." Emily, perfectly assessing the gravity and reality of the situation, stated, "*We're* going to compete with *these* students when we get to college?" A confrontation with profoundly unjust social arrangements provoked a psychological glide between outrage and shame; a rainbow of emotions spilled onto the sidewalks and consumed the air on the train ride back home.

These students know the contours of racism and global capitalism intimately. In the name of neighborhood gentrification of the Lower East Side, the pair corrode and devour the schools, neighborhoods, and dreams. They also know well the strength, resilience, and endurance of culture, community, and family. But with these visits, their fantasy of education as the relatively uncontaminated space for mobility was shattered. They were shocked by what privilege looked like up close. Traveling across county lines, they walked into a mirror that marked them as worthless. About to confront a series of high-stakes exit exams at the outer rim of their senior year, they bumped into the recognition that they were being failed by a state and set up by a school system, both of which have slipped surreptitiously off the hook of "accountability." In their work as critical youth researchers, they came to appreciate the courage of *Brown* and the *CFE* lawsuits. At the same time, they came to recognize the depth of our national refusal to grant them deep, full citizenship in the moral community called America.

On the Other Side of the Tracks Within Desegregated Schools

> African Americans wanted . . . their fair share of the resources for education in order to have a curriculum that was legitimate and culturally salient. . . . The evil system of segregation had to be destroyed. . . . [but] The demands of the American community were hijacked in the court system. (Hilliard, 2002, p. x)

Beyond the rim of the city, we visited and worked with eleven desegregated suburban schools. We could not help but notice that although diverse bodies pass through the integrated school doors, most funnel into classes largely segregated by race, ethnicity, and social class. Within these buildings, race, ethnicity, and class graft starkly onto academic tracks, overdetermining who has access to academic rigor and who does not.

Drawing from our survey data, we were able to document the sharp edges of stratified life on the other side of the schoolhouse door: the extent to which students from distinct race/ethnic groups participate in AP and honors courses. As Table 1.2 reveals, the patterns replicate racial stratification in the nation at large.

TABLE 1.2 Participation in AP/Honors by Race/Ethnicity and Parental Education

	Asian American	White American	African American	Caribbean American	Latino
Total sample: % in AP/honors	58	56	33	35	27
Students with college-educated parents: % in AP/honors	69	65	42	42	43

$\chi^2 = 387.43$, $df = 4$, $p < .001$ for total sample; $\chi^2 = 87.85$, $df = 4$, $p < .001$ for students with college-educated parents.

For the full sample of suburban youth, race and ethnicity overdetermine who participates in AP and honors courses while in high school.

We pulled out those suburban students with college-educated parents; however, the patterns were distressingly parallel. We constructed "segregation indices" for each participating suburban school: On average, 60–70% of Whites and Asians were enrolled in AP and honors classes, in stark contrast to the 20–40% of African American, Caribbean American, and Latino students.

This racialized bifurcation of "desegregated" schools was disturbing for the full school sample and ever more so for the middle-class subset, particularly because of the significantly more positive academic outcomes accrued by students in AP and honors courses. Students in AP and honors courses are significantly more likely than their peers to report feeling challenged academically ($F = 28.72$, $df = 1$, 2690, $p < .001$), they experience educators as being more responsive ($F = 29.340$, $df = 1$, 2827, $p < .001$), they are more likely to feel that they are known and understood by educators ($F = 81.775$, $df = 3$, 3052, $p < .001$), and they are more confident that they are being academically well prepared for college ($F = 35.538$, $df = 3$, 3020, $p < .001$). Based on students' responses about educators, the Positive Influence of Educators scale was created. This scale assesses how students perceive their teachers in terms of being understanding and caring, believing in the students, and exhibiting fair and impartial treatment regardless of race/ethnicity or socioeconomics. Fifty percent of White and Asian students in AP and honors classes, 47% of White and Asian students in regular and remedial classes, 37% of African American, Caribbean American, and Latino students in regular and remedial classes, and then 31% of AP and honors African American, Caribbean American, and Latino students offer strong positive ratings of their educators.

Given the differential access to rigor, it came as no surprise that students of color and students in lower tracks were extremely worried about high-stakes testing. Across schools and communities, African American, Caribbean American, and Latino youth—especially those in low tracks—expressed the most consistent fear that standardized tests could prevent them from graduation, a poll tax of sorts for the 21st century. When asked to assess the statement, "Standardized tests can prevent me from graduation," almost half of the Caribbean American, Latino, and African American students, one third of the Asian Americans, and just over one quarter of White Americans indicated that they agreed or strongly agreed with the statement ($F = 100.677$, $df = 3, 3022$, $p < .001$); students in AP and honors are significantly less anxious that standardized tests could prevent their graduation.

When we started this work, we had little idea how profoundly and consistently, across communities, academic tracks organize and racialize suburban schooling. And yet in each quantitative analysis, and with every focus group and interview we conducted, we learned of the significant impact of track on student engagement, motivation, confidence, identity, peer relations, and achievement. Indeed, a CHAID (chi-square automatic interaction detection) analysis of race/ethnicity, gender, parents' education, and track as predictors of various items of academic engagement, motivation, confidence, and achievement demonstrates that on many outcomes track is a stronger predictor than race/ethnicity—for example, on Importance of education to me: $F = 30.09$, $df = 3, 3966$, $p < .001$; Importance of civic engagement to me: $F = 11.73$, $df = 1, 2199$, $p < .001$; School has prepared me as well as any other student for college: $F = 38.32$, $df = 3, 3867$, $p < .001$, and Cantril's ladder measure of satisfaction with where you stand, now, compared to other students: $F = 26.21$, $df = 3, 3531$, $p < .001$.

Being placed in high-track classes bears obvious positive consequences for academic and civic well-being. It is thus doubly troubling that most students of color (African American, Caribbean American, and Latino) are placed in regular or remedial classes, and further, that those in the highest tracks who benefit in significant ways also consistently report the highest level of critique of their schooling. High-track African American, African Caribbean, and Latino students report intense alienation from and experience of racialized bias in their school experiences compared to White and Asian students in top classes.

To understand these dynamics more fully—the alienation of the middle-class, top-tier student of color—we turn to a focus group among varied youth who have come together to discuss academic tracking within their schools. These students attend desegregated schools in which almost 70% of Whites and Asians are in AP and/or honors classes, while approximately 35% of African American and Latino students are. We listen now as, 49 years post-*Brown*, students justify and challenge the schools in which they are being educated.

Charles: My thoughts? When we just had [one group in a class] . . . you really don't get the full perspective of everything. You know what I mean? If they were in tracked classes, they wouldn't get to interact. And like . . . when you're in class with like all White people, because I know the same thing happens at [my school] like sometimes I'm the only Black male in class, and you do feel sort of inferior, or you do like sort of draw back a little bit because you have nobody else to relate with, you know. If it's more integrated, like, you know, you feel more comfortable and the learning environment is better . . . you just get more sides of it because, I don't know, it's hard to even with math, everybody learns the same thing in math, but if it's all White people, you know what I mean? They're going to learn it somewhat different. It's not that they don't get the same education, but they're going to miss that one little thing that a Latino person or a Black person could add to the class. . . .

Jack: [I don't think we should detrack entirely], maybe not in like all classes, but that really like what they, like maybe if they just had all freshman classes like that, you know, it would help out a lot . . . [to change it all] . . . you know the kids that might not have achieved so much in the past could see like, you know, like "I do have a chance." And you know, "I don't . . . I just don't have to stop. I can keep going and keep learning more stuff." So I don't know, maybe not like every class should be tracked, but they should definitely be exposed.

Tarik: It starts from when you graduate eighth grade. In eighth grade they ask you, "would you want to be in [TOP TRACK]?" It depends on your grades. If your grades are good enough to be in TOP, then you can, but if not, you have to choose the [regular] level.

Jane: Because, like you know, some people even say that, you know, the smart kids should be in a class by themselves because it's more conductive to their learning. But then the other people would say like well the special education kids . . . they need to be with their kind so they'll learn better.

Charles (an African American in high- and medium-track classes) volunteered to speak in the focus group first. He chose to open the conversation by revealing his discomfort with racial stratifications in his school. He critically challenged the racial layering of the school (showing anger and a bit of shame), and he proudly smuggled in the possibility that African American or Latino students may have "one little thing" to contribute. Jack (a White, high-achieving student) followed, diverting the group's focus onto the [low track? Black?] students' (lack of) motivation. Tarik, who sits at the top of an under-resourced school comprised entirely of students of color, lengthened Jack's line of analysis, foregrounding individual motivation and choice. Jane, a White girl in top tracks, returned the conversation to school structure, but now—given that low motivation and bad grades are "in the room"—she justified tracks as responsive to, or "needed" by students at the top and the bottom.

In less than 2 minutes, race was evacuated from the conversation, replaced by the tropes of "smart" and "special education." Black and Latino students were demoted from potential contributors to needy. Tracks were resuscitated from racist to responsive. Sounding like contemporary embodiments of what Morris, Hilliard, and Morris describe as the "unusual Negro" of the early 1900s, Melanie and Emily (both biracial, high-achieving students) then entered the conversation, challenging how they have been turned into the "unusual Negroes" in their schools (Morris, Hilliard, & Morris, 2002; Deleuze, 1992):

> **Melanie:** Like tracking has been in the whole school system that I've been going to like from the beginning, and if you grow up in a tracking system, that's all you can know. So if you grow up and the whole time I've been in honors classes, and a lot of the time, and I'm mixed so a lot of the time when, if you want to hang out with different people and you're forced, and the other students in your classes and you're kind of forced to hang out with some people that you don't normally, wouldn't normally like hang around with. And at the same time, it's like a lot of emphasis put on by the parents and teacher, I remember a lot of the time, like "You're a good" . . . like teachers would tell me, "You're a good student but you need to watch out who you hang out with, because they're going to have a bad influence on you." They didn't see me doing anything. I was just walking down the hallway talking to somebody. It wasn't like, you know, we were out doing whatever. But a lot of times it is the teachers and the parents' first impressions of their ideas that come off. . . .

> **Emily:** But I want to say like . . . Melanie and I are a lot alike because we're both interracial and we were both in like honors classes. But with her, a lot of her friends are Black and with me a lot of my friends are White. And I get really tired of being the only . . . one of the very few people in my class to actually speak up if I see something that's like . . . or if I hear something that's not . . . that bothers me. And then I feel like I'm all of a sudden the Black voice, you know. Like I'm all Black people. And it's not true at all. I . . . lots of people have different kinds of opinions and I want to hear them. It's just that I think a lot of the time, like Charles was saying, when you're the only person in the class, you do get intimidated. And voices aren't heard any more then because of everyone else overpowering.

Across this focus group, as in their academic lives, youth carve identities individually and privately in relation to state and school practices that stratify "race" (see Cross, 1991). Today, at the moment of contact—the visits or the perched view from the top track in a desegregated school—African American, Caribbean American, and Latino youth voice a bold and cutting critique of a system of racialized segregation. They sculpt themselves in a nation, community, and in localized buildings in which racialized signifiers have come to be the organizational mortar with which intellectual hierarchies are built and sustained. A few challenge the seeming meritocracy, even as they trespass with ambivalence across the rungs of a color-coded ladder of opportunity. All witness the unchallenged hierarchy, many through the gauze of alienation.

African American, biracial, and Latino students—like Charles, Emily, and Melanie—traverse and negotiate social policies and practices of symbolic and material violence as they survive a torrent of everyday representations within their desegregated schools. Some do beautifully; others—not represented in this group—fall. To this task they import DuBois's "double consciousness," watching through a veil:

> The Negro is a sort of seventh son, born with a veil and gifted with second sight in this American world—a world which yields him no true self consciousness but only lets him see himself through the revelation of the other world. It is a peculiar sensation, this double-consciousness, this sense of always looking at one's self through the eyes of others, of measuring one's soul by the tape of a world that looks on in amused contempt and pity. One ever feels his twoness—an American, a Negro; two souls, two thoughts, two unreconciled strivings; two warring ideals in one dark body, whose dogged strength alone keeps it from being torn asunder. (DuBois, 1990, p. 9)

The veil connects and separates. The veil doubles as a shield of protection that "keeps [the self] from being torn asunder" and as a mote of alienation. Through the veil, youth of color see, hear, and witness. As Charles admits, he may "draw back a little." Some narrate pain, some pleasure, and a significant group claims that they do not allow the words to penetrate. In response to the question, "What is the most powerful thing a teacher has ever said to you?" African American students were the only group in the survey who answered in significant numbers with "NO EFFECT," "Can't remember a thing," "Nothing they say has affected me," "Not one thing."

While we do not believe that youth fully internalize the blaring messages, neither do we believe that they are fully inoculated by the wisdom of their critical analysis. The living structures, relations, and practices of power—inequitable State financing, school organization, school size, classed and racialized access to rigor, as well as deep-pocket private supports that privileged students enjoy—undoubtedly penetrate. These structures, relations, and practices enter the "bodies" accumulating consistently differential outcomes within and across schools mistakenly viewed as race-derived rather than institutionally and historically produced (Gramsci, 1971).

All lives are formed in unequal power arrangements, historic and contemporary, global and local. Our evidence suggests that most youth read this through the vantage of their daily life positionings. Youth of privilege typically represent themselves, discursively, as if untouched by and immune from these structural forces. They explain, largely, that they succeed on the basis of merit, hard work, good luck, and committed parenting. In contrast, most youth of color and/or poverty more finely season their explanations with critique, outrage, and the twinned attributions of structural and personal responsibility. They know that history, politics, the contours of oppression, and the power of culture shape their opportunities and their desires. And they, like you, Zora, dare to narrate it for us all. These youth feel seduced and betrayed, bewildered and a bit silenced, by the white mare that promised integration and delivered segregation within. They bear witness to the race/ethnicity gap that swells through the most penetrating fissures that form America. They recognize that urban/suburban finance inequities live and assure the gap, and that in suburban schools, academic tracks vivify and produce an embodiment of it.

And yet, just as *Brown* interrupted a century of fortified racism, we have discovered again that the gap is neither inevitable nor natural. Schools do not have to reproduce social formations. Many of the small, detracked urban schools in our study, as you will see next, were designed, like the *Brown* decision, to resist.

Small, Detracked Urban Schools: A Funny Thing Happened to *Brown* on the Way to the 21st Century

Zora, you must be feeling vindicated at this point. It would be easy to conclude from these data, the surveys, interviews, observations, and graduate follow-ups, that race and ethnicity differences in achievement are, indeed, embodied in the youth and enduring across contexts. Has *Brown* failed? We hear often, in whispers, "Is it true that *even* in suburban schools there's an achievement gap?"

The story is complex: *Brown v. Board of Education* sparked a revolution in social consciousness; important shifts in educational legislation, social policy, and school-based practice followed (Kluger, 1977). And yet as a nation we forgot, or we refused, to dismantle the structures and guarantees of race and class privilege. Therein lies the dialectical swagger of the white mare—the seduction and the betrayal. The persistence of a gap—which the youth call an opportunity gap, not an achievement gap—is sewn into the seams of our national fabric.

And yet tucked away in the recesses of a massive database lie a set of schools that reveal "what could be" *if* public schools were dedicated to the rigorous education of all, including poor and working-class youth, African American, Caribbean American, Latino, White, and Asian American. Surviving on inadequate fiscal resources but enlivened by the spirits and dedication of educators committed to changing the odds, the small schools movement in New York City and nationally flourishes—despite finance inequities, the assault of high-stakes standardized testing, and a bureaucracy that refuses to grant intellectual and political space to schools organized for "what must be." Living the visions of *Brown*,[3] these small schools are designed to educate America's poor and immigrant youth to be scholars, critics, and activists, to see critically what is and to imagine and enact the possibilities of what must be.

These schools breathe the spirit of *Brown*, the spirit that demanded a radical possibility for the education of African American and (since then) Latino youth, poor youth, and youth not privileged by birth to wealth. Some are desegregated, meaning that White students attend. Most are not. These schools receive just over half of what their sister institutions receive in the suburbs, with students whose parents are significantly less well educated. And they deliver. These schools educate each child as if she or he is going to college; the educators take it as their responsibility to help young people reach heights they never thought they could.

We included four such schools in our survey. It was stunning to notice that on every measure of student engagement, comfort, dropping out, graduation, aspirations for college, sense of being known, engaged by curriculum, and connected to educators, students in the small schools surpassed their peers in the suburbs, looking more like the White and Asian students in the suburban-tracked schools than the African American and Latino students.

On Civic Engagement

On every item of civic engagement we find that students in small schools are significantly more likely to "strongly agree" than students in large schools. On the overall Civic Engagement-Social Consciousness Scale, 51% of students in large schools compared to 62% of students in small schools consider acts of civic responsibility to be very important. More specifically, students in small schools are more likely to strongly agree that they should work to end racism (56% small vs. 43% large), protect the environment (30% small vs. 24% large), help those less fortunate (33% small vs. 26% large), change how the country is run (29% small vs. 14% large), and work to improve the local community (38% small vs. 25% large).

As other studies have demonstrated (Wasley et al., 1999), small schools develop in students the social capital by which they come to see themselves as critical and responsible agents in school and in their communities. We can see from these data that the sense of personal agency extends so that students in small schools also take up a responsibility to work for change in the nation.

On Perceived Responsiveness of Educators

Students in small schools were significantly more likely to report that teachers are academically responsive ($\chi^2 = 33.46$, $df = 1$, $p < .001$), that the curriculum is challenging ($\chi^2 = 5.58$, $df = 1$, $p < .01$), and that educators treat students fairly across lines of race and poverty (89% strongly agree, compared to 78% in large schools). Students in small schools are significantly more likely to strongly agree that "In my school, all students can achieve if they try" (52% of small-school students vs. 35% of large-school students) and significantly less likely to indicate that "There is an achievement gap in my school" (3% of small-school students strongly agree vs. 17% of large-school students).

Students in small urban schools rated educators as significantly more responsive than did any of their suburban peers (89% of small-school students agree or strongly agree, compared with 72% of high-track White/Asian Americans, 67% of low-track White/Asian Americans, 63% of high-track African Americans/Caribbeans Americans/Latinos, 59% of low-track African Americans/ Caribbean Americans/Latinos, and 55% of students in large urban high schools). On the item "Teachers know and understand me," 6.3% of suburban students strongly agreed, compared to 30.3% of small-school students; on "Teachers care about students like me," 11.5% of suburban students compared to 45.7% of small-school urban students strongly agreed; and for the item "Teachers give me a second chance," 6.2% of suburban students vs. 23.3% of small-school urban students strongly agreed. For "strongly agree/agree," these numbers swell to 76% small-school, urban students, 54% high-track White/Asian Americans, and 40% low-track African Americans, Caribbean Americans, and Latinos. To the more critical item, "Teachers treat students differently based on race/ethnicity of students," 81% of suburban students agreed compared to 44% of small-school urban students; for "Teachers believe all students can achieve at high levels" these percentages flip, with 36% of the suburban students agreeing, compared to 70% of the small-school urban students.

Turning from sense of belonging to sense of academic press (Bryk & Driscoll, 1988; Lee et al., 1999) and preparedness for college, we find similar patterns in the data. Students from the small detracked urban schools were significantly more likely to say "I feel challenged" by my coursework than all students in the suburban sample (76% of small detracked students, 66% of high-track White/Asian Americans, 58% of high-track African Americans/Caribbean Americans/Latinos; 63% of low-track White/Asian Americans, 54% of low-track African American/Caribbean Americans/Latinos). They reported feeling significantly more prepared for college (17% of suburban students strongly agree compared to 25% of small-school urban students) than low-track African American, Caribbean American, and Latino students, as well prepared as low-track White/Asian Americans and high-track African Americans/Caribbean

Americans/Latinos in the suburbs, and significantly less prepared than high-track White/Asian Americans in the suburbs. Finally, students in the small detracked urban schools hold academic aspirations as ambitious as the aggregated students in the suburbs, but significantly more ambitious than low-track African American and Latino students in the suburbs (90% expect to earn a Bachelor's degree compared to 85% of low-track African American/Caribbean American/Latino students in the suburbs).

While these rigorous, detracked small schools clearly help poor and working-class youth beat the odds, the question remains: To what extent are aspirations, engagement, motivation, and achievement primarily functions of cultural capital in the home? To this question we found very intriguing responses. As predicted, when we ran correlations between levels of parental education and youth engagement with educators, curriculum, and aspirations for college, we found maternal education and paternal education to be correlated with student engagement, motivation, and aspirations in the large suburban schools ($r = .087$, $p < .001$ in suburbs; in urban areas, not significant). Students whose parents were better educated were more engaged with faculty and curriculum, held higher aspirations for college, and felt better prepared for college than youth with relatively undereducated parents. In significant contrast, however, in the small urban schools, parental education was not correlated with student level of engagement or aspirations for college.

These small detracked schools recognize and resist the extent to which parental education overpredicts academic performance in the United States, interrupting the well-established but conceptually (and methodologically) problematic correlation of family educational status and student aspirations, engagement, motivation, and achievement. Typically poor children get under-resourced schools—and, as our data suggest, even in quality schools they do not enjoy the same educational opportunities. Thus the relation of family background is always empirically mediated by quality of education. Educators in these small detracked schools, in contrast and by design, have created contexts in which all students are exposed to academic rigor and respect. Educators assume it is their responsibility to provide the scaffolding required to master such materials. By so doing, these schools have fundamentally decoupled the long-standing and stubborn correlation of parental education and student achievement.

The challenge posed, then, to the rest of our schools is: How do we design the intellectual and emotional souls of our schools as they touch and are contaminated by the perverse stratifications that constitute America? Should school walls be simply porous to the winds of social inequity that so define our nation? Or should schools be designed to interrogate, challenge, and help youth resist what is and imagine and work toward what could be? Is that not the legacy of *Brown* for the 21st century?

"I'm Sick and Tired of Being Sick and Tired" (Ella Baker)

Across data sets, coasts, and zip codes, we witness youth across race/ethnic groups, rich and poor, pleased to be educated in desegregated settings, and yet yearning to be educated with adequate resources, rigor, and respect— that is, in schools and societies "not yet" (Greene, 1995). We hear discomfort with finance inequities and tracking from all, including privileged youth who benefit from the stratification (Burns, 2004). We hear the dire price paid most dearly by urban youth of color, but also by suburban youth, due to inequitable state policies, tracking systems, and racialized (mis)representations. And we see the power of youth standing together—across lines of race, ethnicity, class, geography, and academic level—to speak back to educators and to America. The struggle for racial justice is far from over; the spirit of *Brown* lives on in the "not yet" outrage and wisdom of youth and the everyday erosion of their belief in their America. The white mare now dresses in vouchers and high-stakes testing. The promise of privatization serves as the Trojan horse for continued racialized oppression. Youth are watching for how adults challenge, or collude, with the white mare.

We leave you with a scene from a recent "speak back." Youth researchers in a suburban school were presenting their findings to the faculty. Quite critical of racial and ethnic stratification in his school's academics and disciplinary policies, Nozier explained to the almost all-White teacher group that he, as an African American male, spends "lots of time in the suspension room . . . and you notice it's mostly Black, right?" Hesitant nods were rapidly erased by awkward discursive gymnastics: "Well, no, actually in June it gets Whiter when the kids who haven't shown up for detention have to come in," followed by "Sometimes there are White students, maybe when you're not there." But Nozier persists, with the courage of speaking his mind to educators who may or may not listen, standing with peers across racial and ethnic groups and a few adults willing to bear witness as he speaks truth to power.

Nozier is no more optimistic than we that in his school, at this moment, his critique will be heard and will transform local policy. In our research camps, we rehearse the school presentations expecting engagement and resistance. In the folded arms of faculty disbelief, the institution declares, "We are integrated, we are fair, it's not about race." But now, skillfully able to slice the school by analyses of race, ethnicity, and track, and able to read the tables and the discursive analyses, Nozier knows he stands not alone. He insists, "I don't speak just for me. I'm speaking for 1,179 other Black and Latino students who completed the survey and report high rates of suspensions." Suddenly his once dismissible, personal "anecdote" transforms into fact. He stands tall and represents the concerns of hundreds of African American and Latino students in his school, and from more than a dozen other schools, who report that suspensions, and access to rigor, are unevenly distributed and that opportunities are denied or discouraged. Flanked by White, African American, and biracial students, allies, together they have a job to do. They are the legacy of *Brown*. Nozier writes that he will not "walk away, to swagger to the policies of life." He will, instead, continue to deepen his analysis and outrage, surrounded by allies and representing hundreds, with the critical skills of participatory research toward social justice.

When asked, "Do you think it's fair to teach students of color about racism and critical consciousness and involve them in this work? Doesn't it depress you?" Jeneusse, a youth researcher from the South Bronx, assured an audience at Columbia University, "We've long known about racism; that's not news. What I know now, though, is that I can study it, speak about, and we need to do something to change it." Nikaury, a youth researcher from the Lower East Side of Manhattan, stunned an audience with her astute reflection on participatory action research and its benefits: "I used to see flat. No more . . . now I know things are much deeper than they appear. And it's my job to find out what's behind the so-called facts. I can't see flat anymore." These young women and men have, indeed, come to appreciate the complexity of the composition, the shape of the fractures, and their own capacities to repaint the canvas of the future. Youth who speak through "critical analysis of the 'gap'" speak back to our nation and ask us to re-view the very fractures of power upon which the country, the economy, our schools, and our fragile sense of selves are premised and to imagine, alternatively, what they could be. They, like their great-great-grandparents who longed for the *Brown* decision, know that social justice is always just around the corner. And even more than their great-grandparents, they can imagine allies of privilege eager to create multiracial schools of and for social justice.

These young women and men are asking for help from adults and from those who look like we have benefited—those of us who own the white mares or have enjoyed their company.

Zora, we need now, desperately, a movement of youth, parents, community, and educators to make good on the radical vision embodied in *Brown*. As they flourish in the puddles of educational possibility throughout the nation, they are drowning in severe public sector betrayal. But because of you, they know to beware the white mare.

We'll write again,

Michelle Fine, Janice Bloom, April Burns, Lori Chajet, Monique Guishard, Tiffany Perkins-Munn, and María Elena Torre

SECTION 2

Deep Work Within a Fracture

CHAPTER 2

Race, Gender, and Critique: African American Women, White Women, and Domestic Violence in the 1980s and 1990s

Lois Weis

In this chapter, I focus on young adult working-class and poor African American women and White women. Both groups currently lead lives of pain, frustration, and passion, lives that are directly linked to historically rooted racism, patriarchy, the privileging of white skin, and the new economy, as well as to the current dismantling of the urban public sector. Given historically distinct racial trajectories, I ask here, where do these women lodge social critique? Where do they locate the cause of and imagine the remedy for the troubles they endure? My analysis of "critique," or expressed site of problems, does not stem from data gathered in response to direct questions about critique per se. Rather, it is critique as woven throughout in-depth narrative responses that constitutes the site for analysis. As I will suggest, it is easy to hear pain, alienation, and blame. While these broad parameters are common across all races, women of different races place blame differently. As sociologists and social psychologists have long contended, *where* people locate critique—that is, where they place blame and responsibility for tough times—bears serious consequence for how they conceptualize remedy, if they can imagine alternative possibilities for themselves and their children, and whether they can see themselves as potential activists engaged for social change (Crosby, 1976; Fine, 1991; Janoff-Bulman, 1979; Weis, 1990).[1]

Elsewhere, Michelle Fine and I have explored where African American and White men center critique and have focused on race-based differences among poor and working-class men (Weis & Fine, 1996). Here I argue that gender-based differences are equally as strong and divisive, in the sense that gender "produces" different social analyses in the same way that race does. To be specific, when I code for critique I analyze narrative data as they relate to an articulated understanding of the current position (in the economy, family, and/or community) of the individual and/or group under consideration. While all those interviewed are poor and/or working class, men and women of varying ethnic and racial groups do not frame critique in exactly the same way. As I will argue here, in the case of White and African American men and women, their race and gender prefigure the ways in which they fashion social critique around issues of family, community, and the economy. Thus, although all are poor and/or working class, their demographic characteristics mean both that they have different experiences and that they offer differing interpretations of experiences that may, in fact, be similar.

The rapid recent deindustrialization of the urban northeast has meant a precipitous drop in blue-collar jobs from 1960 to 1990. In Buffalo, the city where interview data reported here were collected, blue-collar jobs dropped 21% during this time period. Although loss of jobs has hit all racial groups, it has had particularly devastating consequences for White men, who were the major beneficiaries of jobs under the industrial labor market. As this market constricts, White men have, therefore, the most to lose. This partially explains the sharpest rise in poverty of White males relative to other groups during this time period, although women's labor has simultaneously enabled families to increase the gap in mean family income relative to that of African Americans and Latinos (Fine & Weis, 1998). Because of industry closings, almost one quarter of blue-collar jobs have disappeared. While many of these men have, over time, landed employment elsewhere, they have most often taken jobs in the rapidly grow-ing and lower-paying service sector, rendering family income considerably less than before.

Buffalo, with a total population of 328,000 (not including the well-populated surrounding suburbs), is a predominantly Black–White town, with only 4.5% being foreign born. It sits in the Rust Belt and, as noted above, experienced deindustrialization in the latter 1970s. With the loss of jobs has come a steady decline in population—more than 35,000 since the 1980s.

The loss of heavy industry has meant a rising proportion of people living in poverty and a depressed income generally across demographic groups.

In 1990, 18% of Whites lived in poverty, compared with 38% of African Americans and 52% of Latinos. In 1980, only 14% of Whites lived in poverty, compared with 36% of Blacks. Data for Latinos are not available prior to 1990. Poverty rates are climbing for all groups, but are climbing relatively more for Whites than for African Americans, because of the disproportionate effects of deindustrialization on the poverty rates for this group (Fine & Weis, 1998).

In this context it is noteworthy that White men critique their situation largely in terms of marking the boundaries of what constitutes acceptable and unacceptable behavior (Weis & Fine, 1996; Weis et al., 1997). Rather than draw a critique of White elites who have directed the recent restructuring of the American economy, rendering the White working class superfluous, the White male version of social critique is, by and large, a clear, targeted, and critical litany of judgment on the focused actions and behaviors of others, particularly African Americans and particularly men. This critique includes charges of African American men not working and, more importantly, not wanting to work; welfare abuse; and the horrors of affirmative action, which, they allege, excises many White males. Although many of the White men interviewed have themselves been out of work and received government benefits including food stamps, they draw themselves as deserving of such benefits in contrast to African Americans, whom they see as freeloaders. Race affords them the opportunity to project and deny, authoring themselves as men who know how to take care of the family and "not live off the government," even though, at times, they know they must.

Unlike White men, African American men, as a group, offer a broad-based critique (Weis & Fine, 1996). Rather than locate blame in an individual or group, their critique is of racism and society, powerfully woven around notions of job availability. Astonishingly consistent in their narrations, the African American men Michelle Fine and I interviewed have an expansive systemic critique that wraps itself around the interrelated issues of lack of jobs, police harassment, the social scripting of the Black man by the media, and the social production of the drug economy.

At root, community problems derive from the lack of jobs for men. Due to the lack of good jobs, many men turn to trafficking in drugs, selling at the street level. The men we interviewed are critical of this "turn," even as much as they might understand it. It is here that the analysis of racism and the racial order begins to weave through the narratives. The police harass residents, particularly men, who live in poor central city areas. This is linked to the discursive construction of the Black male as criminal, thief, and drug dealer. Thus the availability of jobs (in both the broader legitimate economy and the drug economy) and police harassment, are, in the minds of those interviewed, inextricably linked.[2]

Both sociologists and psychologists have examined attributions or explanations for poverty and racial inequality (Hochschild, 1995; Jones, 1997a). Jennifer Hochschild's work on the American dream suggests widely divergent perspectives by race. As Hochschild argues:

> Whites believe it [the American dream] works for everyone; blacks believe it works only for those not of their race. Whites are angry that blacks refuse to see the fairness and openness of the system/blacks are angry that whites refuse to see the biases and blockages of the system. If that disparity persists or worsens, as it has every appearance of doing, the American dream cannot maintain its role as a central organizing belief of all Americans. (1995, p. 68)

Indeed, Blacks and Whites increasingly diverge in their descriptions of and explanations for America's racial situation:

> The two races share an overwhelming support for the American dream as a prescription for their own and other American's lives. The races disagree only slightly when people consider the American dream as a description of their own lives but they disagree considerably when people consider the dream as a description of others' lives. African Americans increasingly believe that racial discrimination is worsening and that it inhibits their race's ability to participate in the American dream; whites increasingly believe that discrimination is lessening and that blacks have the same chance to participate in the dream as whites. I call that finding the paradox of "what's all the fuss about?" (Hochschild, 1995, p. 55)

This finding, that there are race and gender attributional differences in explanations for poverty, points to the importance of situating social critique. Here I focus specifically on race-based differences among women and the ways in which race and gender are related to a fashioning of critique. The comparison between African American and White women, all poor and working class, speaks to recent criticisms within feminist scholarship, where Elizabeth Spelman (1988), bell hooks (1984, 1989), Barbara Christian (1985), and others point to a distinctly White middle-class bias. Work within recent years by White women and women of color has attempted to open up feminist thought to the perspectives and practices of those who are not middle class and not White (Crenshaw, 1991; Kennedy & Davis, 1993; Mullings, 1997; Stacey, 1990). While this intellectual project is ongoing, much work remains to be done. As Spelman argued a number of years ago:

> Feminists have rightly insisted that to talk simply about relations between whites and blacks, between rich and poor, between colonizer and colonized, masks gender distinctions within each group; for example, the problem with an explanation of inequality based simply on class ignores inequalities based on gender, but for similar reasons, talking simply about relations between men and women masks race and class distinctions among men and among women. (1988, p. 186)

Here I contrast data drawn from White poor and working-class women with those drawn from African American women of similar class background with an eye toward unpacking the varying perspectives and practices of women from non-middle-class White and African American ancestry.

The Sample

The quasi-life history approach relies on a series of in-depth interviews I conducted with men and women of varying ethnic and racial groups between the ages of 23 and 35 (what economists would classify as young adult). Seventy-five to 80 adults were interviewed in Buffalo and, in the larger study, the same number in Jersey City, although I do not draw on the Jersey City data here. In Buffalo, the sample relevant to this chapter included 15 African American women, 15 White women, 18 African American men, and 13 White men. We collected data between 1993 and 1996. We generally conducted interviews in two segments, each segment lasting from 1 to 2 1/2 hours. Thus we have between 2 and 5 hours of taped interviews with 154 individuals. We conducted many of the interviews ourselves, but talented graduate students of varying race and ethnicity assisted us; their names appear in the interview segments reported below. Interviewees were split more or less evenly among White, Latino/Latina, and African American men and women in each city and were drawn from "meaningful urban communities," to use William Julius Wilson's phrase (1987), which includes schools, early childhood programs such as Head Start, literacy centers, churches, workplaces, job-training centers, and social agencies such as Hispanics United and the Urban League. We had, in each city, unbelievably helpful advisory groups of activists and community leaders; they shaped questions, identified sites for recruitment, reviewed drafts, and invited our testimony at public hearings.

We also held extensive focus group interviews among targeted groups, a technique that enabled us to probe further issues raised in individual interviews. While focus groups tend to produce somewhat more optimistic statements (in the sense that interviewees share how to improve upon negative situations), as we employ them, they serve to offer elaboration on ideas expressed earlier. We held focus groups with African American women who currently send their children to an early childhood center and White women who send their children to a diocesan elementary school. Focus groups ranged in duration from one long meeting to groups that carried on for more than 2 months, and one still meets a year later. I highlight these selection principles to indicate that interviewees are currently connected to meaningful social networks and do not represent the most alienated members of any community under consideration. Many poor and working-class

White women, though, described themselves as being left in the city while their more affluent relatives fled up and out.

We asked all individuals to respond to an identical set of probe questions. Representative questions include: Can you describe your family when growing up? Can you tell me about the neighborhood you live in now? How is it the same as/different from the neighborhood you grew up in? The open-ended questions encourage people to talk about their lives—their experiences, hopes, problems, defeats, and dreams. And talk they did; but different ethnic/racial groups sang a different song, one rooted in their own experiences in the United States. Thus, men and women sound different across racial and ethnic group. Whites chant a song of despair, yet it is different in tone and cadence to that of Blacks. This chapter probes these sounds of critique among White and African American women, stressing *difference* in spite of broader sites of shared despair and hopelessness.

I have been intentionally "data heavy" in this chapter. This is partly a stylistic matter, as our broader project appreciates voices of those who are generally not heard from. In this case, too, the data are so compelling that we urge readers to take the time to work through the interviewees' points. Rarely are the voices of the poor and working-class heard, as more and more policies are made *in their name*, presumably for their own good. Thus the decision to have rather lengthy segments surface is intentional.

White Women's Critique of Neighborhood and Community

Poor and working-class White men across a number of studies (Fine, Weis, & Addelston, 1997; Weis & Hall, 2001) exhibit a searing critique of African Americans, particularly males. This critique stretches across the sites of the economy, neighborhood/community, and the family. In each space, African American men are implicated in the lowering of the White male position. White males spend much time envisioning themselves as superior to men of color and, as such, offer virtually no critique of White elites whose economic moves are diametrically opposed to working-class economic interests across race. The positioning of the African American male as a viral "other" is part of the terrain of White male identity, and White poor and working-class women in this study, while they may be racist to be sure, held more positive attitudes toward African Americans than their male counterparts (Fine & Weis, 1998; Hall, 2001; Weis, 1990; Weis & Fine, 1996).

Although studies do exist that explore the issue of racism among White females, few sociological analyses focus on the distinct ways in which racism emerges within the identities of White women (Frankenburg, 1993).[3] Over the past 20 years, some authors have examined racism among

White women in the women's movement (Amadiume, 1987; Spelman, 1988), and others have looked at racism among White females as related to the workplace (Hine, 1990; McIntyre, 1997). Other investigations consider racism among White women historically (Gilmore, 1996; Golden & Shreve, 1995; Ware, 1992). It is striking, though, that few scholars take as central *how* White females elaborate upon these tendencies as they construct identity.[4] Given that expressed racism does not emerge among women in the same ways as it does among men (Weis & Fine, 1996), the question arises: Where in White poor and working-class female identity does such racism emerge?

White poor and working-class men (like their high school counterparts, as uncovered in earlier studies such as Weis, 1990) spend a great deal of time engaged in the "self–other" co-construction that requires Black men. The White working-class male self in the northeast is highly dependent upon the construction of a Black "other," one who holds an unpleasant set of social characteristics against which the White male self can be drawn. No similar process has been uncovered for girls or women, either in past studies or here. White women's identities are not forged *fundamentally* in relation to the co-construction of an "other" of color, against whom they judge themselves to be virtuous in all areas. In fact, like Sue below, White poor and working-class women, at times, specifically argue against the construction of Black males so evident among their menfolk:

Sue: I'd say, a lot of men, in discussion about Blacks, they would be [more] opposed to Blacks, I would say, than women. Like the L.A. riot [Rodney King]. A lot of guys would say, I think, the cops really did their job. Where the women would say that was violent and they shouldn't have done it that way. A lot of the time it would be split up [by gender]. The men against the women in conversation. Mostly with that case. It's always the guys think that the cops did their job and they should have done that. [The guys say] they [police] had to do everything they could, and the women are, like, well, there were six people standing around, they [police] could have done it differently.

Lois: Can you give me any other examples where the men would take one side and the women might take another?

Sue: In general about the Blacks . . . I'd say anything you talk about. Things, like, to the men, Blacks are on welfare. They don't do nothing. They don't try. They're all standing on the corner. . . . They're just more willing to, like, put the Blacks down, where I think the women aren't. I'm sure some women say all Blacks are on welfare, but then there's some that say, "oh, no." They're not against Blacks as much as the men are. . . . The other day, my youngest daughter just asked me, "How come Daddy thinks all Black people are bad?" I tell her "I don't know why." But I try telling her that they're not all bad. Because I don't want her to be afraid of every Black person, because not every Black person is mean or nasty. Just like every White person is not mean or nasty. I try to get them [children] to like people of different races and not to judge them.

Women, like Sue, recount attempts to rewrite wholly negative race scripts perpetrated by the men in their lives. At times, they actively attempt to interrupt such racist ideology through direct intervention with children or, in the case below, try to undermine messages handed down by fathers:

Kathy: I had a lot of Black friends growing up that my father didn't know about.

Lois: In high school?

Kathy: No. Actually there were only two by the time I left; there were only two girls in that White school who were African-American descent. And I knew them both. But this was back in grammar school, and outside of school. They weren't in my school. And I had this one little Black girl that I got along [with] great, and I brought her home for dinner, and my father wouldn't let her eat dinner. Well, and she had to go home. Made me feel like I did something wrong. And that's the first time I was ever actually, for the lack of a better word, turned on to the fact that she was different than I was.

Kathy later recounted the following incident:

My father had a very big problem with prejudice. I think the only thing in my life that I did against my father, or to intentionally piss him off, was when my brother had given me a Michael Jackson poster when I was just thirteen years old. And I was infatuated with Michael; I loved the way he danced, the way he sang, everything about the man, I loved. So I put it up on my wall. And my father said, "you better take that nigger off my wall." And that floored me. I had never heard that word before. I knew what it was, but I never heard it used in context. I went through every magazine that I had. Cut out every picture of Michael Jackson that I had, and I had two sliding wooden closet doors. You couldn't see my doors when I was done with them. I plastered them with Michael Jackson. That totally pissed my father off. He just flew off the handle, ranting and raving. I thought he was going to, like, break out and tear up my room or something. And I didn't care. Because I don't know why I did it. You know, I had never done anything to intentionally piss my father off, but for some reason, I just felt that, to me, that I didn't feel the same way [about Blacks as he did].

White women do, to some extent, challenge their menfolk on issues of race. Many are unwilling to accept blanket assertions about racial groupings, and racially rooted discourse does not lie at the heart of their identity. Women's racial discourse, however, does emerge in relation to neighborhood concerns, safety, and particularly around issues of children. It is here that White women express their strongest social critique and where they begin to sound like White working-class men. For White women, racism seeps into their language routinely at the point of discussing safety in the neighborhood and particularly as it affects children, although they may or may not tie neighborhood demise to the behavior of one particular racial group (Fine & Weis, 1998). Women's primary social critique centers on what they see as demise of neighborhoods within which they must raise their children. Carol, Cindy, and Judy exemplify these points:

Carol: But now, you have a lot of absentee landlords [speaking about the neighborhood]. So you've got a couple of houses on the street that should be torn apart, but they aren't. And you've got more of your Puerto Ricans and Blacks starting to come in. And, like I said, not to be prejudicial or anything about it; it's just, it just doesn't suit me being there anymore. And it, you got to start thinking about going now. You know, leaving now. And there were two people on my block that got their purses robbed. And, you see, there was a day, not too long ago, I'm walking out to work and this guy walks by, so I slow myself down. I mean, I'm an easy target; you knock me down, I'm gone, you know. [Carol is small in stature.] I'd say, "Here take my purse, you know, just don't hurt me." And, I wasn't going to walk in front of him or behind him, and I just slowed myself down. And he just asked me, "Have you seen my bank card?" And it alarmed me.

* * *

Cindy: I only had one problem with one neighbor and we got rid of them.

Amira (interviewer): What do you mean you got rid of them?

Cindy: Well, because they were, not that, well, I wasn't prejudiced when I was growing up, but I sort of am now because we had so many problems. These Black people used to live next door in the back, and when they first moved in they were nice, and we got along. And then through the years, oh, my God, they were so bad.

Amira: What did they do?

Cindy: They used to play the music till four or five in the morning. I mean it was blasting, like they were right in my room. And they had drug dealing going on and stuff, and we got rid of them.

* * *

Lois: What's making you leave the city? [She and her husband bought land in a surrounding suburb.]

Judy: Well, his brothers are out there now. Although my brothers are out north, like Kenmore, we always were out there, and we always loved the land, the grass, the trees. More country type of setting. Number one, we want to leave the city because we just feel like we don't belong here anymore. We're being kind of pushed out now. I drive by in my car and they might say, "Who's this White girl. I'm going to pick her up." I don't even want to look at them in the eye. It's a terrible fright like that. . . . The neighborhood used to be Italian; now it's more minority people. More Spanish, Black. It's just more like that.

White poor and working-class women, in many cases, feel under siege in their neighborhoods, as their men do (Fine & Weis, 1998; Weis, Proweller, &

Centrie, 1997). They fear crime and are worried about their own personal safety and that of their children. In spite of the fact that they often paint their reality with a racist brush, being overeager to portray Blacks and Latinos as the "cause" of problems, they are, nevertheless, far more willing to judge individuals as individuals than are White men. Shirley, in a focus group discussion with other White women, states, "If a Black couple came to look on our street, I would tell my friends, you know, don't panic, give them a chance, you know . . . I mean, I live right on the city line. The [border town] school bus stops, and all these little Black kids are getting off. And I mean, these houses are gorgeous. It's like, their houses are nicer than mine, you know. If you can afford it, live wherever you want. I think that's what has to be drummed into people."

White poor and working-class women express concern about people of color when they face community safety concerns, particularly those revolving around children. Evonne, also a member of the focus group, states that her primary concern is "protecting my kids. I mean before [during her parents' generation], you could go out, and the kids could go around the block, you weren't worried about them. And now they go around the block, and you want to know what time they're going to be back, and where they're going. I mean, it's just a different situation from when I was smaller. Because my parents used to sleep with the front door open at night." Suzanne concurs, stressing that her neighborhood is mixed racially and that the issue is lack of respect for other people:

> I think the only thing that would make me want to move is, like I said, the parents aren't teaching their kids respect for other people. They're not even teaching them respect for adults. Some of those kids walk up and spit in your face because they felt like it. But I've got no real problems with our neighborhood. It's not a bad neighborhood. It's a Black/White neighborhood. We all live together. You have your thefts. You have your little break-ins. That happens no matter where the heck you are.

I have suggested here that the primary site of social critique among poor and working-class White women interviewed for this study is the neighborhood. Although more nuanced in its racism than what is expressed by White men, White women, by and large, tie their critique of what is happening in the neighborhood to those "others" (Blacks and Hispanics) who are moving in and dragging the neighborhood down. They, like White men, do not target White elites who are responsible for an inhospitable economy. They, like White men, do not target an economy that encourages an alternative drug economy to spring up within poor communities. Indeed, they do not target the drug economy at all. They fully and freely center critique on neighborhood, that space within which they must raise their children, and hold "others" of color largely responsible for its demise.

African American Women's Critique of Neighborhood and Community

Like White women, African American women interviewed here center much of their critique around neighborhood concerns. Both White and Black women have primary responsibility for raising children and are concerned about raising their young charges in increasingly inhospitable spaces. But, given the trajectories of gender, social class, and race in the United States, Black women offer a different fall guy as they attempt to explain neighborhood demise. Most of the African American women interviewed talk in great detail about how violence has swelled around them, overtaken their community. With fears for their own safety and that of their children, they are vigilant about keeping the kids "locked in the house after school."

The caring for children and shouldering of burden is not new to African American women; bell hooks (1990) has fully explored the creation of "home-place" as a dual site of love and resistance. What is relatively new, however, at least in the urban north, is the narration of the constant search for "safe spaces" in which to live and raise the next generation. And it is, without question, the drug economy of the 1980s and 1990s that Black women finger as cause for the demise of community, family, and self. Carolyn and Ayisha talk about their neighborhood now as compared with when they were younger:

> **Tracey (interviewer):** Can you tell me about the neighborhood that you live in now? How is it the same or different from the neighborhood that you grew up in?
>
> **Carolyn:** It's a lot different.
>
> **Tracey:** You made a face. . . .
>
> **Carolyn:** I live in an environment with a lot of drugs. It's hard to keep your kids in the yard when there's a lot of activity going out in front. And they want to go out and watch it. It's a lot different. Where I grew up, it was peaceful. And now it's, like, rough. Real rough.
>
> * * *
>
> **Lois:** Talk to me a little more about your neighborhood. You say that it's so different from when you grew up.
>
> **Ayisha:** Fourteen, fifteen, sixteen. In this particular neighborhood [where we are talking], they're selling drugs. They [young people] think that that's the only way they can get the things they want, and what really upsets me about it, is that their parents know and they're not trying to do anything

about it. I know when we were growing up, if we came in the house with something, we better have an explanation as to how we got it, where we got it. And they'll tell their parents anything and they'll believe it. I mean a hundred and fifty dollar sneakers and things like that. And the parents don't say anything. It's like they don't even care. Everybody is so wrapped up into doing their own thing, and that bothers me. There's a lot of young kids in the neighborhood, and what if these guys [who] think that they know everything about selling drugs ever run in with somebody somewhere else, and they come over and start shooting; there's so many young kids around here. Maybe the oldest one out of a group of the young kids is maybe seven or eight. It's not fair that they can't live and enjoy their life the way that we were given a chance. There's been many times where we would be sitting out on the porch and somebody may pull up in a car and jump out with a gun. You know that this is what they have in their hand is a gun. Now what they're getting ready to do with it, you don't know. The bullets don't have no name on them. And you're just scared.

Ayisha and Carolyn narrate being "under siege." For Ayisha, movements are further and further restricted. She and her son can go only certain places. She cannot go safely to the store. Her son cannot play safely on the streets. She cannot sit safely on her own porch or her mother's. Young people are taking over her space, many of whom are involved with drugs and have "no respect" for themselves or others. That guns accompany the drug trade makes space in the inner city perilous. Kathy concurs:

As some say, it's definitely not a good neighborhood to bring your kids up in, especially if you're a person like I am with any morals. I protect my kids. I *like* to protect them. Sometimes I may be a little too overprotective, but there is a lot of shooting over here, possibly drive-by shooting. There's a lot of drugs, you know, being sold over here. I'm pretty sure that somewhere there is a much quieter neighborhood for our children to grow up in. Parents not having to worry about keeping their kids either in your house or in the backyard, being able to let them go out on the sidewalks and ride their bikes or play with other children, you know, but in this neighborhood, I can't do it. I have to keep them, in the summertime and wintertime when they want to go outside and play, I have to keep them in the backyard, you know. I don't feel comfortable letting them out in the front to play.

Phillippe Bourgois (1995) points out that it is hard to guess the number of people who use or sell drugs in poor neighborhoods. Most residents in the neighborhoods where we interviewed stated they had nothing to do with drugs. The majority are law-abiding people who are not involved in the drug economy at all. The problem, however, as Bourgois points out, is that the law-abiding majority has lost control of public space. In his work in El Barrio in East Harlem, regardless of their absolute numbers or relative proportions, hard-working, drug-free Harlemites have been pushed onto the defensive. Most of them live in fear, or even have contempt, for their neighborhood. Worried mothers and fathers maintain their children locked inside their apartments in determined attempts to keep street culture out. They hope someday to be able to move out of the neighborhood.

The drug dealers that residents in Buffalo describe are, likewise, only a small proportion of the neighborhood population. But, like those in East Harlem, they set the tone of public life. Residents fear getting caught in the crossfire as anger swells over bad drug deals, as the well-known "craziness" associated with lethal crack overtakes their streets, and as young people turn increasingly disrespectful with dreams of big money made by participating in the crack economy. Again, these are the few, but they control public space; they set the tone for lives that law-abiding residents have to live. Mothers have to protect their children—from drug deals gone bad, from the lure of making large amounts of money that can be made on the streets. For, as women tell us, dealers want young runners—they are only prosecuted as youthful offenders—and mothers want to save their kids from possible death. The constant struggle between the inside of the house and the outside of the streets is played out across the community as children grow older.

There is a tremendous sense of hopelessness among African American women surrounding the narrations of neighborhood, community, and drugs. There seems to be no way out because neighbors, men, police, and government are all implicated in the abandonment of the inner city and its residents. It has become a space where there is almost no place to hide from drug deals gone bad. The most painful aspect of this, according to the interviewees, is the effect on children. Virginia talks passionately about what has changed since she was a child. The daughter of artists, one African American and one White, she grew up associated with a neighborhood art center, where she now works. She is an artist, works 40 hours a week, earns little money, and receives food stamps. She lives with her husband and two young children. Her infant sits on her lap as we talk, and she reminisces about the past:

> **Virginia:** I grew up on Dodge and Rollers . . . in that neighborhood. There was always a gang around, but the difference that I noticed, in that same neighborhood today, is the gangs—when we were growing up—had a tendency to take care of their turf, or their neighborhood, and now the gangs don't. They have a tendency to just milk it for what it's worth.

> **Lois:** Can you say more about that? What do you mean that the gangs took care of their neighborhood?

> **Virginia:** Well, I know it will sound strange to somebody, but they don't—as opposed to robbing the people who live in your own neighborhood—they robbed the outside people [laughter]. You know what I mean. They don't, they didn't let another gang come in and bother nobody.

Lois: They sort of protected the place?

Virginia: Yeah, they didn't—you know, how little kids will pester the old people sometimes and get on their nerves; they [gang members] pick them up and tell them not to do that, take them home to their mother. Or, if their mother wasn't home they'd say, "You shouldn't be doing that." You know, "Leave that old guy alone."

Lois: And that's not the case now?

Virginia: No. They just milk it for all it's worth.

Lois: Why do you think that's changed?

Virginia: I think the drugs are a lot harder. That's a part of it. It makes people a lot crazier than they used to be. The drugs used to sort of mellow people out. Now it makes them crazy. And they'll do anything, and they don't know who you are. It's like somebody could look at you now and they might be fine when they're straight. But if they're high they'll do anything to anybody because they don't, you know, they care less and less. Probably because, at least when I was little, there wasn't much in the neighborhood, but there was, like, there was a Boys Club where you could go do stuff. There's nothing else for them to do, you know. The system's taken everything away from them. Nothing for them to do. It's like when we were little, we could go to the Science Museum, cuz it was free. Now the Science Museum isn't free anymore, so it's not available to anyone in the neighborhood.

Virginia has an expansive critique of what is happening in the neighborhood—her community, the community in which she works and where her parents still live. For her, the plight of the inner city is due to a structural dismantling of services available to the urban poor (the science museum now charges; there is nothing for these kids to do) as well as a pillaging on the part of gangs of the very neighborhood they used to protect. Contrast this with the nature of social critique among White women we heard earlier. Virginia's, though, is not a romantic understanding of the past. Her brother was in a gang for many years, and she recognizes the problems associated with her youth. However, the gangs of her past were an integral part of the community in which gang members lived. They did not prey on friends. They did not try to get young children addicted to drugs in order to make more money. They had some respect for the community to which they were tied. This is no longer the case. Crack has "made people crazy." Gang members plunder their communities. They no longer feel any need to give back. In fact, the community is just a marketplace—a place to find young children to be drug runners, a place to sell from, and to sell to, irrespective of the consequences for the space where they live.

Women are trying to set up safe spaces in their homes as ways of protecting against the outside streets. Leith Mullings (1997) has written poignantly on this same point, based on her brilliant work in Central Harlem:

> People are adamant about trying to keep children safe. Women spend an extraordinary amount of time escorting children, limiting their movement, and trying by any means to keep them away from the violence of the streets. There are building-by-building and block-by-block struggles (often unsuccessful) to expel drug dealers. At the same time, proceeds from the sale of illegal drugs may be the only source of income for some families. As I interviewed residents of Central Harlem, people repeatedly expressed acute concern about losing the children—to the drug culture, to early death as a result of substance abuse, to the often random violence associated with illegal drugs in poor neighborhoods. Today, the leap of faith to envision continuity through children must be as great as it was during the days of slavery. (p. 93)

I have suggested here that the nature of social critique regarding community differs by race and gender. While we see vibrant social critique of the economy, the social representation of Black people, and the social institutions that "serve" the urban poor among African American men, African American women center critique on more immediate concerns related to the rearing of their children. In this, though, they differ from White poor and working-class women in that they focus on both the effect of the drug economy and, at times, the structural dismantling of the social institutions of the city. White women, in contrast, focus only on the Black and Latino "other" who, they argue, is moving in and destroying their neighborhood. At this point they sound very much like their menfolk, although White men have a far more intense and broad-based critique involving men of color. White women target people of color at the point where they see them as intersecting with neighborhood and children concerns.

White and African American Women on Violence in the Home

The Black and White women considered here share a further reality, that of domestic violence. Again, although violence touches both groups, Black and White women narrate this issue differently. Here it is striking that White women are reluctant to name domestic violence as a problem in the community, although it obviously is, whereas Black women speak openly and directly about the violence in their homes. White women are willing to name "others" as a problem in their neighborhood, but they are unwilling to name the White male "self" in any consistent way as a perpetrator of violence in their own homes. Black women, in contrast, hold Black men responsible for the violence in their homes and hold a more abstract drug economy responsible for the demise of their communities.

While many argue that violence in the home appears across social classes, it is now generally understood that there is more such abuse among the poor and working class, and that abuse can run across the life cycle for many girls and women (Kurz, 1995). In our database, White working-class women appear to experience more abuse than women from other cultural backgrounds, but White women are far more apt to deal silently with their "secret." As we will see, African American women share stories of abuse as well, but their stories are less frequent and, at the same time, more public.

We did not, when we began, intend to do a study on domestic violence. Indeed, this was, in some sense, far from our minds. However, 92% of the White working-class women whom we interviewed across Buffalo and Jersey City described histories or contemporary experiences of abuse. These women have been severely beaten, and many have been repeatedly abused by the men in their lives, and/or their sisters are or have been beaten. While the proportion of women being abused is incredibly high—higher than estimates in the literature, which hover around 70% (Kurz, 1995)—even more striking is that this is a well-guarded secret in White working-class communities. "Settled living" women, to use Joseph Howell's (1973) term—or, in other words, those who are married and whose husbands earn an adequate living—are at great pains to keep this information secret as they go about raising their children and protecting the ideology of the "good" White family life. Only when White working-class women become "hard living," that is, they exit from the nuclear family arrangement, are they willing to speak aloud about abuse in their homes. "Settled" White women would speak to us softly in the confines of our individual interviews, telling us their terrifying histories about individual men, but, once we pulled them together in focus groups, these same women were no longer willing to speak about their histories of abuse.

Looking into the private worlds of two of our White narrators—Suzanne and Kathy—opens up the whole cloth of women's pain, passion, and violence that fester beneath the surface of White working-class women's lives. Suzanne, a 31-year-old White married mother of four, is unemployed and currently volunteers in a local school. She and her husband have applied for public assistance but were denied funds because they earned over the designated income line for qualification. In her story of growing up, alcohol abuse saturates her family and all who were associated with this family:

> I grew up in an alcoholic family. . . . Both parents were alcoholics, so we basically were left alone a lot. . . . We were raised, basically, in the back room of a bar. . . . We didn't have a good home life as far as that goes. There was always degrading things said to us. . . . There was none of the self-esteem stuff [no attempt to build the children's self-esteem], or anything else like that. We were always called dumb and stupid and told we weren't going to amount to anything.

Suzanne draws attention to the ways in which alcohol and violence were, for her, linked. According to Suzanne, many of her siblings were unaware of the family's dysfunctions while growing up and, today, are living lives filled with the same forms of abuse:

> [Talking about her nonalcoholic sister] She lived in la-la land. I always tell her, I don't know where she lived, because she didn't live in our house. . . . You know, she's so condemning of my [alcoholic] sister. And I told her, but look at what we were raised in. And that's the first thing my other sister [the alcoholic] will say is, "Well, mom and dad did it and we're all here." But we're not all here. You know, my brother killed himself because of it. And, she actually lost her life because of it, because she's so busy drinking. She's not raising her kids either. So her kids are going through the same thing, basically, all over again. And she also, my mother was abused by my father all the time. And my sister let men beat her up too. She used to get beat up terrible all the time. So, her kids have seen that already too. And they say that's another trend. . . . The abuse. . . . You try to find somebody like your father and you end up in that type of situation. And just like my brother, my brother hated to see my father beat up my mother. But at the same time, he beat the hell out of his girlfriends. So . . . it's a thing; after you see it, you think it's normal even though it's not.

She comments further on how she used to defend herself from the outbreaks at home and the ways those experiences affect her today:

> And with me with my father, he tried once. He used to try to, used to fondle me. And that was about it. So, and then one time he grabbed me and smacked me and I smacked him. It was the only time I ever hit my father because I don't believe that you should ever hit your parents, but I swore that he was not going to do to me what he did to the rest of that family. And since that time, he never touched me because I'm bigger than him. . . . And my mother . . . [is the same size] . . . I used to tell my mother, why didn't you sit on him? He was so thin and so little; you could have just sat on him instead of getting beat up all the time. But my mother wouldn't. She was afraid of him. Yeah, I used to get to the point where I stood in between the two of them, praying that neither one of them would hurt each other, and I'd end up getting punched in the middle because I couldn't stop them and get them departed.

Contrary to the Norman Rockwell images of the nuclear family sitting down to eat dinner, Suzanne, as a child, is entangled in a set of family relations that drown in alcoholism and, according to her, the violence associated with that drinking. As she states, "the scariest thing is never knowing if you were going to wake up and have a mother and a father" or facing what would be going on when she awoke. She recounts sleeping in her clothes every night in the event that she had to flee her house in the middle of the night. She sees and feels the fact that she now sleeps without clothes as an act of immense liberation. Among the White women interviewed, however, Suzanne's stories are not the only examples of such abuse and are not even necessarily the most extreme. As evidenced in the data, these White working-class women's lives are marked by concentrations of fear and violence that seem to mount from the moment they are born. Although not every White poor and working-class household looks this way, the violence that does exist is rough and hard and has a lingering presence.

Kathy is a 24-year-old White female. Currently unemployed, she worked previously at Our Lady of Victory Infant Home as an aide to physically and mentally handicapped adolescents. Kathy is not married but is in a relationship. She has an infant son and a 5-year-old daughter, neither of whom is the child of the man who she sees currently. Kathy received WIC (Women and Infant Care) benefits but has not applied for welfare. Her savings, which she lives off at the moment, amount to $1,500. Kathy's life has been filled with violence from every direction. A prototype of the "hard-living" woman, she was raised by an abusive father, raped when she was 12, and brutally assaulted by the father of her first child when she was 18. Kathy remembers the things that frightened her while growing up:

> My father terrified me. . . . He had a very bad temper . . . and my mother's drink-ing. My father would never physically hurt my mother because she would have packed us up in a heartbeat. But he mentally abused her. Nothing was ever good enough; nothing was ever right. She wanted to go back to work. He kept telling her, "no, no, no. Your place is here. . . ." Like . . . like, no matter which way she turned, he was there with a blockade, trying to stop her from being her own person, developing her own will. . . . She started drinking . . . I don't remember when she started, but I do remember one instance very vividly. My brothers don't remember this. I was ten. We were down in Georgia, visiting my father's sister and her husband. . . . My mother was, had a glass and it was half full of wine, and what she kept doing was drinking it and filling it back up to half when my father was home. And I saw this, like, well, my father caught on to her. And my father was a big man. He was probably about 6'1" or 6'2". . . . He grabbed all three of us, picked us up and threw us in the Winnebago and took off. And he was going to leave her there. And I remember screaming. We must have gone about four or five miles out and may be even more than that. We were screaming, screaming, "We don't want to leave mama, we don't want to leave mama." He was just going to leave her down there and take us with him. . . . At that point, I didn't care if he hit me or not. I just kept screaming and screaming and screaming. And if he hit me I was going to scream even louder. I wanted to go back, and I didn't care what he did. You know, if he slapped me for screaming, I was going to scream louder. I screamed myself hoarse and he finally turned around.

In Kathy's case, her mother was the alcoholic. The scenario of vio-lence, however, is similar to that of Suzanne. Both Kathy and Suzanne narrate lives filled with shock and shame, with hitting, crying, verbal abuse, and insecurity. The young Kathy did not know whether her mother would be abandoned by her father in Georgia, and Suzanne slept in clothes each night of her childhood in case she had to escape for help or safety.

Growing up in poor and working-class White homes, these women have been subject to various forms of violence throughout their lives. Their bodies carry scars and memories of abuse. Suzanne and Kathy describe sexual, verbal, and physical abuse. As Kathy approached her teens, she used to run by the railroad tracks to get away from home. There, one day, she met another 6th grader—a boy—who raped her in her secret hiding place, that private space to which she would run to escape her abusive father. Left pregnant at the age of 12, her friend's mother arranged for her to have an abortion. Kathy has been lurched from one violent encounter to another, as have many of the women we have interviewed. If they have not been beaten, as a child or now, it is their sisters who face abuse by current husbands or lovers.

The hand of the male is not soft and supportive for Suzanne, Kathy, and many of the other White working-class women we interviewed, but instead is violent and brutal—a force to be feared. Given this, one would expect that poor and working-class White women would voice some critique of men and family. Yet they do so only rarely; and the intimacies shared in an interview about individual men do not translate into collective sharing, nor do they spur a critical analysis of the role of family, heterosexuality, and/or men in ways that begin to break the patterns of violence that regulate gender relations inside some poor and working-class White families. While White women were willing to tell us a great deal in the secret space of our individual interviews, they refused to share in focus groups, and they wrapped their narratives of the loving family in tones of reconciled contentment. What little critique they have is tied to the actions of individual men rather than domestic relations in general and the violence that may be linked to these relations.

Black women, on the other hand, are, in this study, much more outspoken in their critique of domestic relations overall and the violence accompanying these relations. While the instance of reported domestic abuse is lower for African American women in our sample than for White women (67% as opposed to 92% in the two cities), their stories are more public. Unlike White women, African American women spoke in focus groups as well as in individual interviews, where they shared experiences of pain and suffering as well as strength and hope. They tell and retell stories of abuse to one another, with sympathetic nods all around the group. They call police (who are generally unresponsive), seek orders of protection (with little avail), flee to shelters. Listen to the focus group discussion held with a group of African American women in an early childhood center:

Lois: Has anyone experienced domestic abuse?

Ayisha: If there is anybody in a relationship, somewhere down the line there is some type of violence or domestic violence.

Gloria: It's not a pretty picture. I went through it twice. One time I was lucky. Two [the second time], it was to the point where the violence was so strong, at the point where you had to wait for this person to go to work to escape from your home. So I was like, my safety for my kids had to come first. He would want to be the controller. He wanted me to listen to him. He wanted me to bow down by his rules. Next thing you know, my son walked into the room and he seen me get abused real bad, to the point where I went to the hospital and I was abused from the thigh down, from the back down, and he [the son] was like, "Well, are you still going to let that man abuse you, Mommy?"

There is a great deal of domestic violence in the lives of both African American and White poor and working-class women. Either they were abused as children, their mothers were abused by their fathers/stepfathers, they were abused by former boyfriends/spouses, and/or their sisters are currently being abused. What is striking in the White women's stories, however, is the extent to which the violence is a well-kept secret that only leaks out through cracks in our interviews.

This is not the case for the poor and working-class African American women with whom we worked. Whereas White women are deeply involved in protecting the images and wage worlds of their spouses, fathers, brothers, and so forth and, more importantly, protecting the image of the domestic unit as a whole, there is little comparable cover among poor African American women. This is not to say that these women do not deeply respect and desire the domestic unit, nor to say that they do not worry about protecting African American men from police and public scrutiny (Mullings, 1997), but rather to suggest that there is open and honest discussion of these issues among poor and working-class African American women in a way that is taboo within the working-class White community. White women spend a good deal of time propping up the image of the nuclear family and hiding the abuse, while poor and working-class African American women are openly suspect of the institution and spend more time in self-healing through participation in group discussion.

Among African Americans interviewed here, women reach out to other women to discuss aspects of their lives, breaking the silence surrounding abuse. We might speculate as to why this is the case, in distinct contrast to White women. To begin with, there may be less to be gained historically or today by hanging on to the ideology of the nuclear family among African American women, given that Black men have not had access to a "family wage" in the same way that White men have (Mullings, 1997; Steady, 1981). White women have, therefore, more reason for preserving the image of the nuclear family since it has worked for them in economic terms better than it has for Black women. Also, it is arguably the case that the ghetto is the "new tenement" of old, and that the interdependence of people within these sites encourages more sharing of information regarding all aspects of life than the more individuated living situations characteristic of the current White working-class (Howell, 1973; Rubin, 1976). Linda Gordon's (1993) historical work on battered immigrant women suggests that the information regarding battering was shared historically, much as is the case today among African American women. White working-class communities have become far more filled with presumably autonomous families than were former White immigrant communities, in which new immigrants packed together in tighter spaces. Turning inward as a result of the "freedom" that less crowded housing affords, becoming less interdependent, White working-class women buy into the secret of domestic violence in a way that poor Black women in the 1990s have not and cannot.

Both Gloria and Ayisha in Buffalo discuss what happened when domestic violence arose in their respective homes and, in so doing, reveal the very public nature of domestic violence events among poor African American women. (This discussion with Gloria and Ayisha continues the previous discussion.)

> **Gloria:** I don't think God put me on this earth to take abuse from any man. So I figured, well, hey, I love myself, I can't live without myself, I can do bad by myself and I can do good by myself. I don't have to live by man, or be with man. So it took a lot for me to make that step. He went to work one day, and I had the, it was like a prayer, I swear I was so broke, down to my last nickel, and I said I don't got no money to try to get this stuff out of this house, and it was like, oh, God, please help me. I went, put my numbers in [played the numbers], next thing I knew my number was in, and they said okay [she won some money from playing the numbers]. Then I went in and called U Haul and got everything out of my house. When he got off work he came home to an empty house. What I hated was that *I* had to run, and I had called the cops, and they told me they could not do anything, because for the simple fact that he was with me in my household. So what I had to do was take everything that I had in my house and my kids, and I left.

> **Ayisha:** If you do something to protect your own self, you get in more trouble with the law. It's easier for you to take actions into your own hand [than trust the cops and/or courts], but then you're in trouble with the law. It takes longer to settle it through the law. And to me it causes too many problems for the law to be able to take care of it. You have to go through so much. You have to get a restraining order. You have to go through being put on the calendar in the court system. You have to go through trials, where this person might show up and this person might not show up. So that [the abuse] keeps happening. Then they just throw it out of court. [All the women are shaking their heads in strong agreement.]

The police and court systems are highly unresponsive for this group. Central to poor African American women's collective wisdom is a deep suspicion of these systems (Collins, 1991; Jones, 1997a). Police do not come. Restraining orders expire. Court appointments are not kept. So women, their families, and friends take matters into their own hands. They leave; they fight back. The whole affair becomes highly public. Ayisha describes the highly public nature of a beating she suffered at the hands of her boyfriend:

> The police were called. I didn't call the police. What happened was, my son was there and he was so upset and crying, and he went to sleep. I was bleeding. I think [my boyfriend] was trying to stop me from calling anybody because he had ripped the phone apart. And I put the phone back together and I called [my boyfriend's] mother and told her that she need to find him because something was wrong with him. I didn't know what was wrong with him. And I told her, you know, that we had been fighting. So I needed somebody to be with my son while I went to the hospital to make sure that I was okay. And I called my mother and she came over, her and my sisters came over, and she called my aunt. And it turned into a big nasty fight because my aunt had her phone calls forwarded to my house. And her son called, and I answered the phone. And I didn't know that my aunt was on the way. Well, she had transferred her calls, and [my son] could tell that I was upset. And [my cousin] asked me what happened. And I told him and he went to look for [my boyfriend]. You know, he wanted to know why he put his hands on me? Why did he hit me? And he went to my boyfriend's mother's house, but [my boyfriend] wasn't there. So [my cousin] had upset his mother, and his mother called the police. She called the police and she found out where [my boyfriend] was at and asked him to come home because my cousin had made threats against his life, to [my boyfriend's] mother.
>
> And I didn't want it to go that far, you know. But I was so upset at the time, and scared. I didn't know what was really going on as far as my health went. And my mother went back home, and his mother [my boyfriend's] lives down the street from my mother. So, you know, you can look out my mother's house and see down to his mother's house, and the police had stopped my brother and them, my mother and my sisters, they were in two separate cars. The police stopped both cars because his mother said that my cousin had guns, and there was a whole bunch of people looking for her son, and she was scared.

While the original incident involved a woman and her boyfriend, it quickly involved a large number of people: her mother, the boyfriend's mother and son, her sisters, brother, and an aunt. This all took place within less than an hour. Part of this is due to the proximity within which poor and working-class African Americans often live to one another in a medium-size city like Buffalo. Ayisha's mother and the boyfriend's mother, for instance, were neighbors. African Americans are squeezed onto one side of town, and family interconnections are apparent. Also, mothers, daughters, sisters, aunts, and so forth are in and out of one another's houses repeatedly as they trade goods and services, particularly those related to children. Thus the conditions exist for these events to become highly public in a matter of minutes. While they do not trust the police and courts to do the right thing—they have not done so historically and will not do so now—they do call them. In addition, however, family members and friends take it upon themselves to take responsibility in these situations.

Black and White women deal with the reality of domestic violence throughout the life span differently. Black women interviewed here are eager to name the issue and discuss it. White women are eager neither to name the "problem" nor discuss it; however, regarding neighborhood/community, White women are willing and able to name the problem (demise) and hold Blacks and Latinos responsible for current conditions. When it comes to the violence that their own men perpetrate, however, violence that affects them even more directly and frequently than that outside the doors of their home, they are unwilling to engage in a discussion of accountability.

Concluding Remarks

Standpoint theorists (Haraway, 1988; Rosaldo, 1989) argue persuasively that the vantage point from which one sees the world determines what one will see; that one's race, social class, and gendered biography, for example, will position the eye in such a way that individuals from varying standpoints will see the same phenomenon quite differently. In this chapter we have wandered through the divergent perspectives of a group of White and African American women, all poor and/or working class, but all seeing the world with a raced and gendered twist. Poor and working-class White women and African American women do not see the world in the same way at all, in spite of the fact that the economy has been largely inhospitable to both groups since the 1970s. Indeed, while they each share some understandings similar to their menfolk, the divergence by gender is as striking as that by race.

The implications of the findings reported here are deeply troubling.[5] The diminution of manufacturing-based employment, twinned with the shredding of the public safety net and the reduction in student financial aid, produce conditions guaranteed to exacerbate the growing inequality of rich and poor in the United States. Moves in the economic and state sectors will negatively affect *all* the people interviewed for this study, whether Black or White. As former Labor Secretary Robert B. Reich mused in his "parting benediction" to the Clinton administration, contemporary social policy has abandoned "the implicit social contract it has maintained with workers for a half a century" (Reich, 1997). Reich notes that the loss of jobs reverberates in what he calls a "growing benefits gap" in which top executives and their

families receive ever more generous health benefits and their pension benefits are soaring in the form of compensation deferred until retirement. In
contrast, only 14% of workers with incomes ranging from $10,000 to
$20,000 are covered by retirement savings plans, with 34% involved in a
pension plan.

Accompanying this economic trend is a curtailment of public assistance—
limiting who is eligible, for how long, under what conditions, and with
what consequences. In addition, funds available for federal and state
higher education are shrinking.

The consequences of the private and public sphere betraying the poor and
working class, of whatever race, are in clear evidence. Families barely scrape
by, reports of neglect rise, and abuse sweeps through homes. American
women's bodies are being beaten, as our data show, on a rather regular basis.
The tattering of the public safety net does not bode well here. Many of the
women we interviewed were able to leave abusive situations only because they
could receive welfare benefits and/or tuition assistance. Without such benefits, they would have been unable to leave and set out on their own. Under the
fragmenting public safety net, support for battered women's shelters has been
slashed along with a host of programs necessary for women and children to
survive without men.

I detail these points in order to suggest that it is, at the very least, advantageous for women to work across race and ethnic groups in order to press
for change in the economic and state sectors. That working-class and poor
White and Black women offer essentially different versions of social
critique around issues with many of the same root causes has serious
potential political consequences. All the women interviewed for this study
fall victim to the restructuring of the economy and the shredding of the
public safety net. While racist America ensures that the consequences are
not *exactly* the same, to be sure, women working across racial and ethnic
groups offer a stronger voice for change than women working separately.
While standpoint theory offers a way of understanding differences in per-
spectival standpoint, such theory does not suggest ways of preventing the
political paralysis that may result.

Why do White and Black women offer such different versions of social
critique? With respect to the case at hand, I would argue that racist America
encourages White women to see the world filtered through a largely racially
coded lens, through which they position men and women of color as always
inferior. This lens encourages them both to center critique of others moving
into the neighborhood as well as to mute critique of their menfolk, always
preserving the mythology of the good White family. Their own racialized
view of the world inhibits any critique of the violence within their own
homes or, more broadly, of the particular form the nuclear family takes as it

entraps them. The positioning of the racial other is the root of the problem here—and, oddly enough, it is a positioning that is most central to working-class White men's identities, not women's. At the point of feeling threatened in the neighborhood, White working-class women absorb that critique of the constructed racial other so central in men's culture. This absorption serves to contain them in a culture of violence and prevents them from envisioning alliances with African American women around issues that, as discussed above, affect both groups.

African American women, on the other hand, are far more independent in their assessments. Unlike White women, they have not historically been the recipients of economic gains associated with their menfolk and are less likely to protect them. So they speak—about domestic violence, about the neighborhood, about themselves. They are far less likely to mute critique of men than White women, and they do so much more rarely. While this certainly enrages some men in the Black community (Fine & Weis, 1998), it contrasts sharply with the buried emotions and not-so-visible scars of working-class White women, who hold others responsible for their plight while hanging on to the very men who shout to protect them at the same time that they crush them in the confines of the constructed castle.

CHAPTER 3

Civics Lessons:
The Color and Class of Betrayal

*Michelle Fine, April Burns, Yasser Payne, and
María Elena Torre*

Every day, every hour, talented students are being sacrificed. . . . They're
[the schools] destroying lives. (Maritza, college student, speaking about her
urban high school)

Obviously there's no there's . . . there are not enough books [and] there's overcrowding . . . I'm expected to teach a class of 46 to 48 students with only
36 books with only 36 chairs. If those conditions don't improve, education
can't improve. Again, go to any other school—and of course you're going to
see a better academic program because of more resources for more children,
more one-on-one interaction with student to teacher. And again, I'm only one
person. I don't have a TA. I don't have any assistance in the classroom except
the other kids. . . . Overcrowding . . . we're expected to perform miracles, part a
Red Sea, if you will. (Joel Vaca, educator)

In so many hallowed buildings we call public schools, the spirits and souls
of poor and working-class urban youth of color and their educators are
assaulted in ways that bear academic, psychological, social, economic, and
perhaps also criminal justice consequences. We write on the devastation
wrought by alienating public schools (Delpit, 1995; Hilliard, 1990; Kohl,
1994; Kohn, 2000; Woodson, 2000). We write to theorize within and
beyond reproduction theory (Anyon, 1997; Aronowitz & Giroux, 1993;
Bowles & Gintis, 1976) to understand the psychological and social devastation

incited by buildings that are structurally damaged, educators who are undercredentialed, institutions that call themselves schools but have little to offer in the way of books, instructional materials, or rigor.

Poor and working-class youth of color are *reading* these conditions of their schools as evidence of their social disposability and evidence of public betrayal. These young women and men critically analyze social arrangements of class and race stratification and their "place" in the social hierarchy. Like children who learn to love in homes scarred by violence, these young women and men are being asked to learn in contexts of humiliation, betrayal, and disrespect. It would be inaccurate to say that youth are learning nothing in urban schools of concentrated poverty. Neither fully internalizing this evidence nor fully resisting it, these children are learning their perceived worth in the social hierarchy. This profound civics lesson may well burn a hole in their collective soul. In the early part of the 21st century, schools of poverty and alienation transform engaged and enthused youth into young women and men who believe that the nation, adults, and the public sphere have abandoned and betrayed them, denying them quality education, democracy, and equality. Were that not enough, California marks the "cutting edge state" where historic commitments to Affirmative Action in higher education have been retrenched, wrenching even dreams of college and university from generations of African Americans and Latinos. Youth know that the blades of race, class, and ethnicity cut the cloth of public resources and determine who receives, and who is denied, a rich public education.

Many have written eloquently on this perverse realignment of the public sphere to satisfy and engorge elite interests; that is, to gentrify the public sphere. But few have interrogated how poor and working-class youth of color witness, analyze, critique, and mobilize in the face of this state realignment. This is the project we set out to explore in this paper: to interrogate how poor and working-class youth of color view both the distributive injustices that now orchestrate the public education system in California and the procedural injustices by which the state refuses to hear their voices of protest.

In the early 1990s, I (Michelle) wrote *Framing Dropouts*, in which I articulated an analysis of the ways that public urban high schools systematically exile youths of poverty and color, scarring souls and minds in the process. This essay may sound like an echo produced a decade later. But we are concerned that the stakes for undereducated youth, and for dropouts, are today far more severe than they were in the past. In California, in 1998, 11% of California high school graduates were eligible to attend the University of California, but only 3.8% of Latinos and 2.8% of Blacks, compared with 12.7% of Whites and 30% of Asians, reached this standard (Hurtado, Haney,

& Garcia, 1998). For students of color and poor students access is low and stakes for exclusion are high. The long arm of the prison industrial complex reaches deep into communities of color, yanking out youths at alarming rates while the economy remains hostile to young people without high school degrees. Young women and men of color, even with high school diplomas or some college, fare far worse than their White peers; those without high school degrees have little chance of entering the legitimate economy.

We take the California schools in question to be emblematic of a growing set of public schools, located in communities of poverty and color, in which facilities are in desperate disrepair, faculty are undercredentialed and turning over at alarming rates, and instructional materials are fully inadequate to the task of educating for rigor and democracy. These schools are not simply reproducing race and class inequities. Far worse, these schools educate poor and working-class youth, and youth of color, away from academic mastery and democracy toward academic ignorance and civic alienation. Despite the fact that the youth are asking for clean and safe school environments, quality educators, and rigorous instruction, the evidence suggests that the more years they spend in their schools, the more shame, anger, and mistrust they develop, academic engagement declines, and our diverse democratic fabric increasingly frays. We can ill afford to have youth, particularly poor and working-class youth of color so in need of higher education, to decide early in their academic careers that schools are not designed for them.

Reading Problems

In this work we seek to understand how young people "read" existing race and class stratifications, as these stratifications organize the system we call public schooling. There are debates in the justice literature about, for instance, whether persons on the bottom of social hierarchies voice more powerful critique (Collins, 1991; Harding, 1987) than those who are privileged, or instead deny injustice, victim blame, and mimic dominant ideologies (Jost, 1995; Marx & Engels, 1846). The question is often posed: Can those who have been oppressed really "know" what they haven't seen? If they do, does their critique facilitate hope and/or despair?

The data collected suggest that indeed these youth know, see, and speak. And yet they do have "reading problems." Not because of any deficiency in their own literacies, but because the political texts they are asked to read bear brutal consequences for their educational practice, their civic engagements, and their economic trajectories. The text of alienation they read in their school buildings, in the rapid-fire teacher turnover, in the absence of books and materials, and in the administrative refusal to listen and remedy sharpens an acute talent for critical consciousness, and indeed, saddles them with reading problems. For this site of development and learning— the school—is even more profoundly a site for betrayal.

Methodology

To collect data from a broad range of students attending schools in the "plaintiff class," jury research firms were hired to conduct random digit dialing in affected neighborhoods in order to generate the survey and focus group samples. Four criteria were specified: Respondents need to be current students, not dropouts; respondents need to be reached via random digit dialing, no friendship or snowball nominations; respondents should not be connected to, or made explicitly aware of, the litigation until after the interview; and parental consent is essential.

Across a number of communities, jury consultant/research firms conducted random digit dialing surveys in order to generate the sample. On average, approximately 400 calls were placed to generate a focus group of 10 to 12 young adults. Therefore, the focus groups represent students who are educational "survivors" (not dropouts), randomly identified, and not selected from within peer or friendship patterns.

A multimethod research design was undertaken: *Surveys* were completed anonymously by 86 middle and high school focus group members, prior to their involvement in the focus group discussion; 11 *focus groups* were facilitated with 101 youth attending plaintiff schools in the San Francisco, Oakland, and Los Angeles areas, as well as a group (of peers) in Watsonville; and 11 *telephone interviews* were held with graduates of California schools that fall with the plaintiff class. All of these graduates are currently attending college.

Survey-based gender and race/ethnicity data on 86 students indicate 44 females, 42 males, and 4 students who identify White, 1 biracial, 25 Latino/Hispanic, and 56 Black. Parental and student consent were obtained for all focus group participants. In a few cases in which there was no parental consent, participants were turned away. Participants were reimbursed for their participation.

Cumulative Inequity: Schooling Toward Alienation

Counter to stereotype, the poor and working-class youth whom we interviewed want high quality, demanding teachers. They are upset when caring and demanding teachers leave their schools. The evidence from elementary, middle, high school, and college students—cross-sectional for sure—reveals, over time, how pride in self curdles to shame in miseducation, how yearning for quality educators warps to anger about denied access to such educators, and how local civic engagement shrinks away from national commitments to citizenship. These three institutional dynamics are central to this production of *schooling toward alienation*.

As you will read in the focus group material, the elementary school children were filled with enthusiasm and excitement about their schools, math, journals, and the acquisition of knowledge. They envision a world spread open with possibilities. Periodically, in their focus group, a voice of fear would be spoken. When asked what they would like to change about their schools, the young children responded, "Bring a lot of security guards and stop the dogs . . . No big kids . . . Teachers to respect . . . Our teacher says we should stop fights because when we go outside, people just walk up to you and starting throwing bottles at you . . . Stop the big kids from coming to beat up the little . . . Stop grown ups, stop grown men from the little kids, because you never know who's [lying] out there . . . Our teachers to stop kids from throwing balls at your head . . . Good lunches . . . Bathrooms more cleaner . . . Stop people from cussing, trying to beat you up, people telling lies . . . Stop graffiti . . . More books and a bigger library. . . ." Relatively unaware that wealthy or White students receive superior education, they are, for the most part, delightfully enthusiastic about their own academic prospects. They ask simply for adults to protect.

By middle school, children in these schools are somewhat more sophisticated, if skeptical. Aware of the distributive injustices (Deutsch, 1974) they endure—inadequate schools—they are naïve about the procedural injustice. In the middle school focus groups you can hear a voice of innocence: *If only* someone knew about the conditions of their schools, they would respond appropriately. By high school, students voice a deep, well-articulated, painfully sophisticated analysis suggesting that no one cares. The high school students recognize that wealthy and White students are better off educationally. These youth, concerned about distributive and procedural injustices, believe that the federal and state governments, the economy, and some of their teachers represent the interests of the wealthy. While a discourse of possibility and hope survives even here, these older students view educational inequities as simply an extension of social disregard for them.

The longer students stay in schools with structural problems, high levels of uncertified teachers, teacher turnover, and inadequate instructional materials, the wider the academic gaps between White children and children of color, or wealthy children and poor children, grow and the more alienated they become (Ancess, 2000; Boyd-Franklin & Franklin, 1999; Bryk & Driscoll, 1988; Elliott & Dweck, 1988; Fine, 1991; Meier, 1998; Valenzuela,

1999). We track, in this essay, how schools of alienation incite cumulatively a process that warps yearning into anger, pride into shame, and local engagement into civic alienation.

From Yearning to Anger

> I like lab period and algebra teacher . . . he makes you relax, tell you jokes, it kind of calms you off . . . . That's what I like about my teachers, they all basically do that. (Middle school boy)

> Right now I have this one teacher that's like, he's my English teacher and he's like really trying to help the students right now. We're looking into colleges and stuff. He's really trying to help us, like learn things, because it's like, he'll pull you out of class for a reason. It will be like to learn the stuff. (High school girl)

These students know what good education looks like. And they want it. Across focus groups and surveys, the students were very clear that they want teachers who care and demand rigorous work. We asked the students, "What does a teacher who cares look like?" Students described a good teacher as someone who holds high standards and helps students reach those standards. Someone who asks questions and listens to student answers. Students were excited about teachers who want to know what students think. Some praised faculty who assign lots of homework, if they provide support and time to finish.

> **Girl:** Like he said, we got a lot of substitutes right now. . . . Some of them cap [put you down], some of them play football. That's not what we come to school for. So we got our teachers there that are pretty cool. But last year we had all our teachers. I love the good teachers, but the best ones are like . . .
>
> **Boy:** They change the whole school around.
>
> **Girl:** They change the whole school.
>
> **Boy:** My favorite is all the good teachers.

These students know the difference between substitutes who play football and teachers who "change the whole school around." They appreciate a caring teacher who is responsive when they are confused. A good teacher wants to know the students and provides lots of red marks on their papers. Trouble is, few of these students encounter and enjoy good teachers on a regular basis. Most explain that they have had a range of teachers. Too many, however, have disappeared mid-year, are long-term substitutes, or don't know their content areas. In the plaintiff schools, the percentage of fully certified teachers ranges from 13 to 50%. In the state of California, the percentage of undercredentialed teachers is directly related to the percentage of students of color and students eligible for free/reduced price meals, rising to an average of 24% noncredentialed teachers for 91 to 100% of students eligible for free/reduced lunch. Teacher turnover rates are reported by some principals to be as high as 40% in a matter of 2 to 3 years.

By high school, the yearning for quality educators bumps into the realization, by these youth, that they are being denied. At the bump, resignation blends with anger. The optimism of youth seems to drain by high school, when students describe "teachers only there for a pay check" or other adults who "know, they know, they just ignorant and don't care about us." By high school, the youth believe that they are being denied a fair share of educational resources for their education (Fine & Burns, 2003). At this point, the yearning converts to anger:

> When I ask for help, and there's too many kids and I know the teacher can't pay attention to me, I'm ignored. That makes me mad. They blame kids when they can't fix things.

> * * *

> Well, at Tech it's not really that bad because they like—it is bad but they had like another school system inside of it called like Phi Beta, like all the smart kids, whatever and it's like no minorities in there. And they get all the good instruments and all the other stuff like engineering and they got all this stuff. And they like split them up and the like the rest of Tech, they got their own side of the school. So it's just kind of scandalous how they, you know, put everyone else, you know, on the other side of the school or just different classes.

> * * *

> Younger kids coming up in conditions like this, they can bring the problem of racism because most of the quote unquote good schools are majority Caucasian or whatever, like someone brought up about the pictures. There's so, if they look around they school and they say, "Well we basically all minorities. And they look at other schools and say why they getting treated better than us?" Well we, we all humans and we have been treated worse. So then that could bring some anger and then they just start lashing out at people, Caucasian people for no reasons, for all the wrong reasons.

The structural conditions of their schools, combined with the belief that White and wealthy youth receive better, provoke a sense of anger voiced by many youth, particularly high school students whom we interviewed (Boyd-Franklin & Franklin, 2000). Anger flows when the inequities seem "scandalous," targeted at "minorities," or designed to keep "some of us" on the "bottom" (Ward, 2000). The anger is loosely directed at the government, society, or sometimes at "Caucasians." These young women and men express a cumulative and piercing sense of what Crosby, Muehrer, and

Loewenstein (1986) and Leach (forthcoming) call *relative deprivation*: a substantial discrepancy between what they believe they deserve and what they actually receive. Relative deprivation, with associated anger and grievance, derives when individuals experience a discrepancy between what they have and what they want, what they have and what they believe they deserve, and what they don't have and others do.

It is important to be clear. These youths are not simply internalizing the messages that the broader society is targeting at them. Nor are they simply resisting these messages. In a complex montage of internalization, resistance, and transformation, these young women and men clearly and unambivalently read their social disposability and their political dispensability. They know they are viewed as unworthy. With the wisdom of "dual consciousness" (DuBois, 1935), through the hazy gauze of meritocratic ideology and false promises, and with the guillotine of high-stakes testing overhead, they speak through dual registers of yearning and anger, pride and shame, engagement and alienation, fear and desire. They can, at once, critique the dominant ideologies about poor kids, urban youth, and pathology and mimic these same sentiments when asked to evaluate other students who are having difficulties. Perhaps the ultimate sign of their desire to belong, to be citizens with a place at the table, they are *critics, consumers,* and *producers* of a meritocratic ideology. And they are angry that despite their willingness to engage, they are denied:

> **Girl:** I'm in 10th grade. And what I like about my school, or what I don't like about my school is how they teach us like animals, like they cage us up and like they keep putting more gates and more locks and stuff and then they expect us to act like humans and I feel like if you treat us like animals that's how we going to act. . . .

In a series of comments that are difficult to hear, the next set of students are concerned that educators "treat us like inmates" or think they are "coming in to teach killers." In the absence of a community of qualified educators and a rich, intellectually engaging school environment, most youth turn away from the academic and relational features of schooling with a blend of anger, resignation, or despair. Those who graduate feel little loyalty to their high schools, and sometimes even what may sound like survivor guilt (Lifton, 1994):

> Leaving my high school was sad but I didn't do enough at [my high school] to make it better. It pains me to see what my younger brothers and sisters go through at [my high school]. I feel guilty about my opportunities, compared to others in my community and seriously considered dropping out of college several times. . . . You know, it's hard to know that I am getting an education while other people I know aren't. I guess I'm the lucky one, given all of the students who couldn't beat the stacked odds. (Chantal, graduate, now in college)

The anger bleeds toward some educators, privileged youth from other communities, and the broken promise of democracy for all. Within these statements of anger, however, there is still pride, hope, and a yearning for something to change.

Pride to Shame

Across the focus groups with current students, and in individual interviews with graduates, youth express evidence of strong, psychologically positive pride in self and community. Most plan to go to college. They envision careers as doctors, pediatricians, surgeons, nurses, lawyers, teachers, preachers, police, firefighters, foster parents, naval officers, engineers, singers, chefs, bartenders, and other colorful futures. These youth, for the most part, carry a strong sense of self, family, and community. They recognize, proudly, that they have skills that other youth don't have, developed largely through confrontation with adversity. "I think we have more life experience." "We have street knowledge." "We're smarter, we're not just all proper." "We know about struggling, trying to get to the top, and not just, you know bouncing right up there." Some of these same youth comment upon specific, positive aspects of their schools. A number fondly recall teachers who supported them in hard times. One young man praised the school choir, while another delights in the jazz band. One student enjoys the freedom of his school. A group of students from a magnet school appreciate the "teachers, like you can talk to them. Teachers are always trying to encourage you, some of them."

While the students express strong and confident selves *within* their communities, shame, stigma, and fear peppered their talk when they discussed wandering *beyond* the borders of their local worlds (Bronfenbrenner, 1979; Davidson & Phelan, 1999; Eccles et al., 1993; Goffman, 1961; Lewis, 1992). At that point, they describe themselves as academically handicapped by opportunities denied, ill equipped to attend a "real" or "serious" college, embarrassed by limited vocabulary, math skills, and exposure to higher education. Michael Lewis (1992) argues that the experience of shame requires a self-conscious comparison to others or a recognition of failing to live up to a standard. These students know well, and often with shame, the "lacks" that their education has instilled in them. The students speak as if they embody the inferiority of their schooling. As one young woman, now in high school, explains:

> [If kids from a wealthy school came in here right now,] I wouldn't talk because they would be more sophisticated or something, and understand words I don't know and I don't want to be embarrassed. (abbreviated quote in Fine's notes)

Students explain that they have been miseducated because people in government and throughout the state—even some of their teachers—view poor and working-class youth, or urban youth, as unworthy of quality education. One focus group conversation was particularly chilling on this point:

> Yes, that be like putting all the bad kids in one school, that's just like putting, you know, just like putting them in jail. They going to be crazy. . . .

It was painful to listen as some students explained that they believe that schools *want* students to feel ashamed or embarrassed so that the students will leave and classes will become smaller, with no adult responsibility for the loss of student bodies. These interviews reveal a raw sense of social disposability, and as penetrating, the students' sense of helplessness to disrupt these conditions (Burhans & Dweck, 1995; Dweck & Reppucci, 1985; Elliott & Dweck, 1988; Miller, 1985; Rholes et al., 1980; Seligman, Maier, & Solomon, 1971; Stipek & Tannatt, 1984; Zhao & Mueller, 1998). Michael Lewis argues that youth or adults who endure a prolonged experience of shame are likely to express anger, "an emotional substitute for unacknowledged shame . . . a reaction to a frustration of action . . . a reaction to an injury to self" (1992, p. 150).

Filth

Toward the end of each focus group we circled the room, asking each student to suggest one element of their ideal school. It was striking when a young girl whispered, with some initial hesitation but then elegant simplicity: "If I could have my ideal school, I guess I would have seats on the toilets and enough paper in the bathroom to clean yourself" (abbreviated quote in Fine's notes, not transcript). A young man in the focus group said, "If you go to a dirty school, you feel like you're dirty, you know, not clean."

A second form of shame was narrated: the shame of being educated in contexts of filth and decay. Those environmental stressors recognized by psychologists and planners as most threatening to instruction are the very structural conditions found in the plaintiff class and include facilities in disrepair, overcrowding, temperature problems, filthy bathrooms, mice, vermin, animal feces, and noise (Duran, 2002; Kozol, 1991; Lepore & Evans, 1996; Maxwell, 2000; Saegert & Evans, 2003; Spivak, 1973).

Schools, like other contexts of childhood and adolescence, are not simply the places where development happens (Lerner, 2002; Lerner & von Eye, 1998; Werner & Altman, 1998; Wolfe & Rivlin, 1987). They are intimate places where youths construct identities, build a sense of self, read how society views them, develop the capacity to sustain relations, and forge the skills to initiate change. These are the contexts where youth grow or where they shrink. Environmental psychologists Werner and Altman (1998) argue:

[C]hildren are not separate from their actions or feelings, nor are they separate from other child or the physical, social and temporal circumstances that comprise unfolding events. They are so interconnected that one aspect can not be understood without the others. . . . The street . . . is not separate from its inhabitants. (p. 125)

Buildings in disrepair are not, therefore, merely a distraction; they are identity producing and self-defining. Since the early part of the 20th century, psychologists and sociologists (Cooley, 1998; DuBois, 1935; Fanon, 1967; Goffman, 1961; Mead, 1988; Merton, 1987) have argued that children and youth develop a sense of self from the messages they gather from adults, peers, structures, and institutions around them. What the culture says about children, about their families and communities, is internalized, in part, by them. Children who are valued tend to be more positive in self-concept than those who are disparaged (DeLuca & Rosenbaum, 2001). This value may be communicated in what people say about and to them. But just as powerfully, the quality of the contexts in which they are growing "speaks" to youth about how they are viewed and valued. For better or worse, these "voices" come to form part of the core of how children feel about themselves and/or the extent to which they are valued by others (Maxwell, 2000). If surrounded by decay, disrepair, and filth, and no adult intervenes to protect, children may come to see themselves as worthy of little more or at least that adults see them as unworthy.

Student Alondra Jones details the corrosive effects of a negative structural context on the developing selves of young students:

It makes me, you know what, in all honesty, I'm going to break something down to you. It make you feel less about yourself, you know, like you sitting here in a class where you have to stand up because there's not enough chairs and you see rats in the buildings, the bathrooms is nasty, you got to pay. And then you, like I said, I visited Mann Academy, and these students, if they want to sit on the floor, that's because they choose to. And that just makes me feel real less about myself because it's like the state don't care about public schools. If I have to sit there and stand in the class, they can't care about me. It's impossible. So in all honesty, it really makes me feel bad about myself.

Obviously, you probably can't understand where I'm coming from, but it really do. And I'm not the only person who feels that. It really make you feel like you really less than. And I already feel that way because I stay in a group home because of poverty. Why do I have to feel that when I go to school? No, there's some real weak stuff going on."

"It's on Me": Self-Blame and Academic Troubles

Across the focus groups a third form of shame was narrated: a fleeting, infrequent, but emotionally powerful discourse of self-blame for past mistakes (Fanon, 1952, 1967). While most of these youth attribute their miseducation to structural inequities, a strong undercurrent of student blame pierced the focus groups:

> **Girl:** If I sit in that class and choose to talk, then, hey, that's me. That's what I mean, I ain't going to be nothing in life. So if that teacher, even if she teaching a little bit of stuff, I know to sit down and listen to it because I mean, this all I'm going to learn. When I leave high school, I mean what else is there? I mean, on my transcript I'm not going to make it into a university. I could tell that now. I mean, all I got is a two-year college or one of them things that come on TV for computer class or Job Corps or something like that. . . .

* * *

> **Girl:** When I was in middle school . . . I skipped that grade, went right to the 9th grade from 7th grade. I chose to mess that 9th grade year up. I chose to cut and shoot dice and be doing other things that I'm not supposed to do, you know. So that was my mistake, my fault. You know, in my 10th grade year, I destroyed it, you know. I made nothing of it all, nothing. I passed, I don't know how I passed, you know. So when I look at my transcript, I look at it and say this is where I failed. I know I won't be able to make it into a university because of me, not because of what peer pressure or what this principal said or what this teacher was teaching me.

While the students discussed, in the aggregate, structural problems of teacher turnover, overcrowding, absence of books, ineffective guidance counselors, and so on, they also accepted much responsibility for their own behaviors. Speaking as critics, consumers, and producers of meritocratic ideology, a whispered or shadow discourse flows through the groups, revealing self-blame for past behaviors. Students who offered such analyses typically asserted very punitive, superego-like perspectives on their own biographies: Past mistakes do and should dictate lives of impoverished educational, social, and economic opportunities.

Students who view educational difficulties as largely their own fault also tend to hold very low expectations for personal change or for the effective intervention of adult educators. There is little sense that school can or will help them achieve positive educational outcomes (Fine & Powell, 2001). Low expectations for adults convert into self-defeating attitudes by which students hesitate to ask for help they need. One young man expressed it well: "*I don't ask the teacher for nothing.* I do it all on my own, or ask my friends for help." At just the age, and in just the schools, in which youth desperately need (and want) adult guidance and support, they are learning not to ask. "I don't ask the teacher for nothing" is of course a defensive posture, rejecting educators' help before educators refuse his request. These students then convert this defense into an internalized and unrealistic belief in personal responsibility. In the end, these students do not learn how to ask for or receive help, do not get the help and, in the likely event of failure, they conclude that it is "my fault."

Further, there is little recognition by these youths that the structural and academic conditions of their schools actually contribute, in large measure, to the disruptive behaviors that they and their peers engage in and witness. As the exchange between the 9th grade boy in chemistry and the other students reveals, youth are well socialized to blame school problems on youth or poor parenting. By blaming students, the structural sources of these problems are "whited out."

Although not asking for help is a defensive posture to protect against adult apathy and persistent refusals to help, it can transform into a belief that success is always achieved against the odds and despite the intention of adults whom they believe would rather see them fail or drop out. If asking for help is ignored and held against students, read by adults as a sign of weakness, then such support is unacceptable to young people maintaining a sense of pride. Consequently, the disproportional success of White and middle-class youth is further legitimated as the privatized supports that wealthier students are able to enlist are further erased from view.

Perhaps most damaging with respect to future outcomes, some of the youth have elaborated a very punitive ideology that mistakes they have made in the past will and should predict negative future outcomes. These youth have committed what psychologists would call a "characterological personal attribution" or "fundamental attribution error" for past mistakes. When people attribute bad outcomes to a moral flaw in themselves, it tends to be difficult to shed the shame, change behavior, and/or believe that they are entitled to future positive outcomes. They have internalized the broader societal message about poor youth: that they *deserve* bad outcomes from the time of their "mistakes" forward (Janoff-Bulman, 1992). Poor children, especially poor children and youth of color, in contrast, tend to be held personally accountable for mistakes for which other children are given second chances (see Lefkowitz, 1998; Poe-Yamagata & Jones, 2000). This often has dire consequences that can last a lifetime (see Ayers, Ayers, Dohrn, & Jackson, 2001).

Liberty and Justice—For Whom?
From Local Engagements to Civic Alienation

In focus groups and surveys, the California youths express refreshing, deep, strong, and committed social engagements *toward* family, community, and cultural groups. As Bowen and Bok (1998) demonstrate with youth of color who graduate from college, these are the very young adults most likely to display a commitment to give back to the community and to serve and model an ethic of community spirit. The poor and working-class youth who were interviewed described vividly this spirit of citizenship.

When asked about their future goals on the survey, high school students rated the following goals as very important: 92% helping family, 89% getting more education, 58% improving race relations, 56% helping those less fortunate, and 41% making the community better. As their conversations suggest, these youths exhibit a desire and capacity to care, connect, and be responsible.

Constance Flanagan and colleagues, who have studied youths' political attitudes in seven countries, have found that "schools are like mini polities where children can explore what it means to be a member of a community beyond their families, where they learn they are the equal of other citizens, and where they can learn how to negotiate their differences in a civil fashion. . . . [S]chools are settings where children develop ideas about the rights and obligations of citizenship" (Flanagan, Bowes, Jonsson, Csapo, & Sheblanova, 1998, p. 462; see also Boyd-Franklin & Franklin, 1999; Fallis & Opotow, 2002; Haney & Zimbardo, 1973; Miller, 2001). We, too, were interested in the attitudes of these youths as citizens of a democracy, and so we interrogated their commitments to kin and social issues.

While voicing strong commitments to family, community, those less fortunate, and race relations, the young men and women from California simultaneously reveal a stinging anger at schools that spreads outward toward other governmental institutions and the nation. While 92% consider it very important to help family, only 23% consider it very important to serve their country. Their willingness to extend their caring and commitments to the country, to beliefs in democracy, and to a broad moral community called America, has been jeopardized (Flanagan et al., 1998; Yates & Youniss, 1998). Frustrated, their alienation stretches from schooling denied to governments that betray and democratic promises that remain unfulfilled:

> It's like what is the Board getting paid for and they can't even come fix our bathroom. They can't even mop our halls. So what they doing with that money?

* * *

> They [government] fake like they are [trying to change things]. Because they go to the board meetings and they talk to Willie Brown and everything. And one of my friends is on the committee. And all the [inaudible], Willie Brown says oh, this is what, we're going to do this and everything and he's always talking about how San Francisco is one of the cleanest cities. And he's a wolf ticket seller. I mean, he lies, sorry.

As these comments reveal, the youth want nothing more than what most adults ask for today: *public accountability.* They want someone to ensure that the state and adults will fulfill their legal obligations to educate. They want someone to monitor inequities, intervene, and remedy. The focus group and survey data suggest that poor and working-class youth and youth of color in California's most disadvantaged schools are being educated away from these "obligations of citizenship" and toward civic alienation. They are learning that their needs, as poor and working-class children and as children of color, are irrelevant to policy makers and government leaders. They speak through a sophisticated discourse of public critique, but do not believe that anyone is listening.

The survey data reveal the suspicions these youth also hold of the economy and the government. Forty-two percent of the surveyed high school students and 25% of the interviewed middle school students believe that labor market prospects will *always* be hard for them and their families. Forty percent of the high school students, and half of the middle school students, believe that government is designed to serve the "rich." Only one third of the high school students and 20% of the middle school students think they can make a change in the workings of government. Finally, although 65% of the middle school youth view America as "basically fair and everyone has an equal chance to get ahead," this figure drops to 23% by high school.

These youth reveal a broad-based, sophisticated, and critical understanding of social structures, the immobility of inequity, and their "place." Researchers have documented how youth across race, ethnicity, and class reveal the ways in which schools teach them about social stratifications and their place within social hierarchies (Cookson & Persell, 1985; Fine, 1991; Fine, Weis, & Addelston, 1997). What is remarkable in the California youth, however, was the combination of their strong commitments to give back and engage as citizens in local contexts, and their systematic recoiling from and refusal to engage as citizens in the state and nation. Eager to participate actively and generously with family, neighborhood, and those less fortunate, many of these young women and men refuse to serve as neglected or disrespected citizens of the state.

Hearing Problems

Many have heard poor youth and youth of color who attend inadequate public schools talk about some teachers who do not care, schools that do not educate, and the resultant anger, shame, stress, and anxiety (Fine, 1990, 1991, 1994; Fine & Powell, 2001; Fine & Somerville, 1998; Valenzuela, 1999; Wasley et al., 1999). These California youth were no exception. As one young man described his concern:

> Because before we had a teacher for like the first 3 weeks of our multi-culture class and then the teacher didn't have all her credentials so she couldn't continue to teach. And since then we've had like 10 different substitutes. And none of them have taught us anything. We just basically do what we wanted in

class. We wrote letters, all the class wrote letters to people and they never responded. We still don't have a teacher.

What was striking and distinct about the California focus groups was the powerful voice of institutional betrayal that these youths expressed to audiences who refused to listen. It was not simply the case that these youth, like so many youth across America in under-resourced schools, were denied adequate education and felt helpless. Many of the youth had, in the face of overwhelming odds, tried to secure help. They had spoken up, protested, asked for a "real" teacher or raised an academic concern. What broke their hearts and their spirits was that few adults listened. Even fewer acted. As one young woman in a focus group offered:

> The teachers, they are there and then they are not there. One minute they're there, they're there for a whole week, and then they gone next week. And you try to find out where the teacher, and they say, "We don't have a teacher." We outside the whole day, you just sit outside because there ain't nobody going to come through. We ask the security guards to bring us the principal over there. They tell us to wait and they leave. And don't come back. They forget about us. We ain't getting no education by sitting outside.

Students in another high school focus group were most agitated as they contrasted how their schools ignored their requests for quality education, but responded (if superficially) when the state investigated school policies and practices:

> We all walked out 'cause of the conditions, but they didn't care. They didn't even come out. They sent the police. The police made a line and pushed us back in. Don't you think the principal should have come out to hear what we were upset over? But when the state is coming in, they paint, they fix up the building. They don't care about us, the students, just the state or the city.

These youth describe a doubled experience of disappointment and betrayal. Disappointed by the relative absence of quality faculty and materials, they feel helpless to master rigorous academic material and powerless to solicit effective help. Were that not enough, when these youth do complain, grieve, or challenge the educational inequities they endure, they confront a wall of silence, an institutional "hearing problem." On surveys, only 34% agreed or strongly agreed with the item "People like me have the ability to change government if we don't like what is happening." These schools are preparing a generation of youth who sustain ethical commitments to family, kin, and community but believe that the government and the nation view them as unworthy and disposable. In such settings, youth report high levels of perceived betrayal by, resistance to, and withdrawal from persons in positions and institutions of public authority (Fine et al., 2002). These schools are helping to blunt civic engagement and produce, instead, civic alienation.

The Impact on Academic Performance

A high school graduate, now at UC Berkeley, explains:

> I just wasn't at all prepared, like compared to my sister. She's at UC Berkeley now but she went to Lowell. She was really prepared for college. Her school had lots of AP classes, she took five AP exams and passed four. My school only had two that I could take . . . I didn't know what to expect or about picking majors or anything. I got really discouraged when everyone around me was doing so well and knew what was going on. It was really hard for me. I had to drop out of more than half of my classes my first year. I thought about dropping out of school altogether. Luckily I had the support of my friends—other students who graduated from [my school] who told me to stick it out, to just try to go slower . . . I was feeling like everyone else was doing so well—why did Berkeley accept me?

One young man, a high school student, explained poignantly his view of teachers' low expectations of him:

> Teachers and just people in general underestimate youth, black youth. And they think I'm supposed to be speaking ebonics, hanging out on the streets, dealing drugs and stuff. But and then when you get in schools and then you go overboard with your assignments because when you first go to school, you really don't know how the teachers grade, even though they give you their rubrics and their plain things to tell you how they score and grade you. With me, I always want to do the best I can. So if they tell me to write a three-page essay, I write a 15-page essay. So I do and then it's like, well, where'd you get this from? Did you copy out of a book? . . . They're always underestimating your ability to work. . . .

This young man is expressing a searing assault on his dignity—imposed, according to him, by teachers' underestimations of his abilities and challenges to the work he had produced. Research by Delpit (1995), McDermott (1987), Merton (1987), Rosenthal and Jacobson (1968), Steele (1997), and most recently DeLuca and Rosenbaum (2001) conclude that teacher expectations and treatment of youth are critical predictors of academic performance. Meredith Phillips (1997) demonstrates empirically that students perform at significantly higher levels in schools with a strong "academic press," even more so than schools in which there is primarily a "caring orientation."

In addition to the impact of low teacher expectations and interrupted relations with teachers, a number of studies demonstrate the specific psychological and physiological effects of environmental stressors such as crowding, noise, heat, and other structural factors on students' capacities to concentrate and produce academic work and to induce high levels of negative interactions and anger among and within the youth. Robert S. McCord, in a systematic analysis of schools in San Francisco Unified School District, concludes:

> The findings of my school facility appraisal reported in this Declaration point to a pattern of disparate facility conditions associated with the racial and ethnic identity of SFUSD schools. This pattern of disparate conditions is likely to convey the message of racial inferiority that is implicit in a policy of segregation. (2002, p. 12)

Susan Saegert and Gary Evans have studied the academic consequences of such environmental conditions, with a particular focus on overcrowding. They conclude that higher density environments yield physical, cognitive, and emotional effects. A recent study conducted by Valkiria Duran (2002) systematically examines academic performance among children in 95 New York City elementary schools, with architects' assessments of building quality as the predictor of academic achievement. In a sophisticated statistical analysis controlling for race, ethnicity, and poverty, Duran found that structural building quality predicts students' attendance which, in turn, bears directly on academic achievement. The links are significant. The youth concurred. In one focus group, a series of comments reveals how overcrowding affects learning:

> **Boy:** I just feel like it's deep—right now it's like 5,000 overcrowded. It's way overcrowded. And it's like, you know, you don't even have to go there [inaudible], because basically they don't know if we go there, you can just come on campus or whatever. Like right now, we got three different tracks, and they don't know, like, if you don't have an ID, you just, like, you can tell them you have to take your ID picture of whatever and just go on in, and they'll believe you, because they don't really know who go there, because they've got so many kids in that school.
>
> **Interviewer:** But how does that affect you as a student?
>
> **Boy:** Because, like, they could let the wrong person on campus or whatever or, like [inaudible], and it's really too many people, just . . . last year, I had 42 kids in my algebra class.
>
> **Girl:** That's a lot.
>
> **Boy:** And people were standing up and . . .
>
> **Girl:** Sitting on the floor.
>
> **Boy:** Sitting on the cabinets and stuff and [inaudible].

Krenichyn, Saegert, and Evans (2001) document the psychological and physiological impact of crowding and other environmental stressors on youth. Evans, Kliewan, and Martin (1991) report that youth blood pressure rises, concentration diminishes, and errors on difficult tasks multiply in the presence of noise. Edwards (1979) found that educational building conditions can hurt student performance, accounting for 5 to 11% of student performance on standardized tests.

Andrew Baum, Jerome Singer, and Carlene Baum (1981) conclude that:

> Perhaps most important among aftereffects [of environmental stress] is the simple effect stress seems to have on the ability to adapt in the future. . . . If the amount of adjustment required is large enough, it may render the individual unable to cope and lead to severe consequences. (p. 26)

Stephen Lepore and Gary Evans (1996) document the *cumulative* consequences of multiple environmental stressors on individuals' physiological and psychological resources, over time. They conclude that: "Exposure to one stressor, particularly a chronic stressor, can reduce an individual's ability to adapt to another stressor and even increase vulnerability to subsequent stressors" (p. 359).

These schools not only stress youth and educators. The evidence suggests that they also fail to buffer poor and working-class youth from stressors they experience outside of school (Ancess & Ort, 2001; Meier, 1998). As Lepore, Saegert, and others have documented, working and learning in conditions of environmental stress not only undermines the capacity to concentrate and complete difficult tasks, but may compromise students' and educators' abilities to adapt to the many stressors they confront. Like other environmental conditions that compromise one's psychological "immunity" system, working or attending an environmentally stressful institution may compromise youths' and educators' abilities to cope in these and other circumstances.

Going to College?

Researchers Hanson (1994) and Trusty and Colvin (1999) suggest that adverse educational conditions produce cohorts of "lost talent." In the California data, the lost talent is measured with schools' dropout rates, percentage of graduates ineligible for the UC/CSU system, and students' rightful concerns about academic underpreparation.

As the surveys reveal, almost all of these youth expect to graduate from high school and attend college. A full 85% of surveyed high school students consider it likely that they will graduate from their present school, and 91% indicate that they would like to attend college after graduation. However, a full 50% feel that they are less well prepared for college than peers throughout the state of California. This represents a serious rise from the 15% of middle school students who report that they feel less well prepared for college than peers. The high school students appear to hold high aspirations for college, but are filled with anxiety about inadequate preparation.

In addition to the high school students who worried about underpreparation, a small group of graduates from these schools who are now attending college were interviewed. Given the high dropout rates of these schools and the few who go on to college, this sample of college-going students represents some of the most academically successful graduates of their schools. Most were surprised to feel less competent than peers. A number admitted to thoughts of dropping a course or dropping out of college. A female graduate, now at UC Berkeley, relates that:

> I kept thinking they know more than I do. It seems like I had to do more than them, like I have to go to a lot of tutorial classes. What [my school] has offered me has made my transition to college really difficult. I'm pretty much intimidated in college . . . I keep thinking, "Am I going to make it?"

The reflections of these graduates reveal the academic and psychological consequences of academic under-preparation, even for the "stars" of these schools. As a male graduate of the class of 2000 at UC Berkeley attests:

> High school didn't provide me with any AP or honors classes so I was never exposed to college level work. When I took calculus my first year in college, I couldn't compete. I ended up having to drop the class and take an easier math course. The expectations and standards at [school] were too low. Many students felt like they weren't being exposed to the education they needed. We could see what students at Lowell High were getting, all the AP classes and textbooks. But we had to share most of our books and some we couldn't even take home.

These young women and men *thought* they were top students at their California high schools. Reflecting back on their high school years, these college students all admit that they were underchallenged. While they credit teachers and/or counselors who "really pushed me . . . taught me to keep an open mind and not to quit," all agree that teachers "could have given more work, they could have been harder on us." When asked, "What did you get from your high schools?" these young women and men reported that high school was a context in which they developed a sense of persistence, learning to beat the odds, to struggle, even when no one was in their corner. One young woman, now attending community college, explains, "In high school, I didn't feel any support, especially in terms of college going. I got some basics . . . but I don't feel prepared for college."

Another young woman was clear about what she learned in high school: that her school was not designed to help poor, immigrant children. When asked, at the end of the interview, "What would you want to tell a judge about your high school experiences?" this young woman, a graduate of a plaintiff school currently attending community college, spoke eloquently: "Every day, every hour, talented students are being sacrificed. . . . They're [the schools] destroying lives."

Civics Lessons

The schools in question are educating youth toward intellectual mediocrity and alienation, and away from academic mastery and democracy. The youth whom we surveyed and interviewed are the academic success stories of impoverished neighborhoods. These are not young women or men who have dropped out. They have not been selected for their critique, alienation, or knowledge of the lawsuit.

Despite the fact that the youth are asking, desperately, for quality educators and rigorous curricula, the evidence suggests that the more years these youth spend in plaintiff schools, the more shame, anger, and mistrust they develop, the fewer academic skills they acquire, and the more our diverse democratic fabric frays.

Given the political economy of the United States, the racial stratifications, and the broad base of social inequities that confront poor and working-class youth, and youth of color, the question for this case asks: To what extent do these schools reproduce broad social inequities, worsen them, or reduce their adverse impact? (See Anyon, 1997.) The evidence presented here suggests that these California schools substantially worsen already existent social inequities with psychological, academic, and ultimately economic consequences. One may ask, further, isn't it the case that all public schools serving poor and working-class youth, and youth of color, suffer these conditions and produce these outcomes? To this question, the answer is a resounding no.

There is now a well-established body of evidence, drawn from systematic studies of small schools in Philadelphia, New York City, Chicago, and elsewhere, that demonstrates that public schools can be effectively organized for poor and working-class youth of color, to open opportunities, support their pride, satisfy their yearnings for quality education, prepare for higher education, and cultivate a strong ethic of community engagement. Alienation is neither natural nor healthy. There is substantial evidence that schools can interrupt the damage of larger social forces (see Ancess, 2000; Cook, Cunningham, & Tashlik, 2000; Fine & Powell, 2001; Haycock, 2001; Meier, 1998). In the last 10 years I (Michelle) have been fortunate to conduct research with a series of such schools in New York, Philadelphia, Chicago, and New Jersey. These are public schools with quality faculty and instructional materials, dedicated to rigorous education for all students, including poor and working-class youth and youth of color. In these schools, all students are exposed to high-quality educators and rigorous instructional materials. These schools work hard to create intellectual contexts of equity and excellence. Students learn about social stratification by researching history, economics, and social movements. In contrast to the interviewed students in California, students in these schools learn about the possibilities and movements for social change and their responsibilities to participate in creating change (see Anand, Fine, Perkins, & Surrey, 2002; Ancess, 2000). Their social critique moves to hope and action, not despair and alienation.

In the California schools in the plaintiff class, students are indeed getting "civics lessons" in which they are learning to feel powerless, alienated, shameful, angry, and betrayed. The likelihood of democratic engagement by these youths and young adults is fundamentally threatened by their experiences in these schools (Flanagan et al., 1998). Even so, some have tried to speak out about these educational inequities, only to be ignored again. With this lawsuit, they are asking adults to be allies in the struggle for racial and class justice.

SECTION 3

Designs for Historic Analysis

CHAPTER **4**

Gender, Masculinity, and the New Economy
Lois Weis

Amid cries of "farewell to the working class" (Gorz, 1982) and the assertion of the complete eclipse of this class given the lack of "direct representations of the interaction among workers on American television" (Aronowitz, 1992, p. 194), I offer *Class Reunion* (2004b)—a volume aimed at targeting and explicating the remaking of the American White working class in the latter quarter of the 20th century. Arguing that we cannot write off the White working class simply because White men no longer have access to well-paying laboring jobs in the primary labor market (Edwards, 1979), jobs that spawned a distinctive place for labor in the capital-labor accord (Apple, 2001; Hunter, 1987), or assume that this class can be understood only as a tapestry that works easily across ethnicity, race, and gender (Bettie, 2003), I explore empirically and longitudinally the remaking of this class both discursively and behaviorally inside radical, globally based economic restructuring (Reich, 1991, 2002).

Beginning in 1985 with my ethnographic investigation of Freeway High (*Working Class Without Work: High School Students in a De-Industrializing Economy*, 1990), and culminating in intensive follow-up interviews with these same students in 2000–2001, I track a group of the sons and daughters of the workers of Freeway Steel over a 15-year period. The original volume—*Working Class Without Work*—explores identity formation among American White working-class male and female students in relation to schools, the economy, and family of origin, capturing the complex

77

relations among secondary schooling, human agency, and the formation of collective consciousness within a radically changing economic and social context. I suggest in the volume that young women exhibit a "glimmer of critique" regarding traditional gender roles in the working-class family, and that young men are ripe for the New Right consciousness given their strident racism and male dominant stance in an economy that, like that immortalized in the justly celebrated movie *The Full Monty* and the BBC serial "The Missing Postman" (Walkerdine, Lacey, & Melody, 2001), offers them little.

Now, 15 years later, I return to these same students in *Class Reunion*, a study firmly lodged in what Michelle Fine and I call "compositional studies"—a theory of method in which analyses of public and private institutions, groups, and lives are lodged in relation to key economic and social structures. Through a careful look at the high school and young adult years (ages 18–31) of the sons and daughters of the industrial proletariat in the northeast Rust Belt of the United States, I track the remaking of this class through careful and explicit attention to issues that swirl around theories of Whiteness, masculinity, representations, and the new economy. Reflective of the triplet of theoretical and analytic moves that we put forward as signature of our work—deep work within one group (over a 15-year time period in this case); serious relational analyses between and among relevant bordering groups; and broad structural connections to social, economic, and political arrangements—I argue that the remaking of the White working class can be understood only in relation to gendered constructions within itself, the construction of relevant "others"—in this case African Americans and Yemenites—as well as deep shifts in large social formations.

Changing Economies, Changing Gender

Here I focus on a slice of the larger study—the varying ways in which White working-class men remake class and masculinity in the context of massive changes in the global economy. Data gathered at two points in time—during the men's third year of secondary school in 1985 and again at the age of 30–31 in 2000–2001—enable me to interrogate the relation of macroeconomic and social relations on individual and group identities; to excavate the social psychological relations "between" genders and races, as narrated by White working-class men; and to explore the nuanced variations among these men. Here we see identities carved in relation, in solidarity, and in opposition to other marked groups and, most important, in relation to what the economy "offers up" over time. It is in the push and pull of these men, within both hegemonic high school-valued masculinist forms and the currency of such forms in the economy, that we can begin to understand the remaking of the White working class. Significantly, for White working-class males in the United States, struggles to assume symbolic dominance in an ever-fragile economy sit perched on the unsteady fulcrum of racial and gender hierarchy (Weis, 2004b).

Stretching to situate themselves within the postindustrial world, young White working-class Freeway men continue to forge their selves in relation to the three primary definitional axes that are defining characteristics of their youth identities: (a) an emerging contradictory code of respect toward school knowledge and culture not in evidence in key previous studies of this group, but one that rests fundamentally on the form of school-based knowledge rather than its substance; (b) a set of virulently patriarchal constructions of home/family life that position future wives in particular kinds of subordinate relationships; and (c) constructed notions of racial "others" (Weis, 1990). I argue here that the ways in which individual White working-class men position themselves and are positioned vis-à-vis these three major axes over time determine, to some extent at least, both where they individually land 15 years after high school and the broader contours of the White working class. Specifically, in the case of the men, it is in the pulling away from what is defined within high school peer groups as normative or hegemonic masculine cultural forms that we begin to see how young men move toward adulthood. Tracing the push and pull of hegemonic masculine cultural forms as defined in high school, I suggest here that it is within this push and pull as lived inside the new global economy and accompanying tighter sorting mechanisms that we can begin to understand both the generalized shape of what I call the new working class and individual positions within this class as well as potentially outside of it.

Work on masculinities has become increasingly popular into the 21st century (Jackson, 2002) and, as Connell notes, there has been a "great flowering of empirical research on masculinities" (2000, p. 24). Central to this work, according to Jackson, are "four tenets: 1) masculine identities are historically and culturally situated, 2) multiple masculinities exist, 3) there are dominant hegemonic and subordinate forms of masculinities, and 4) masculinities are actively constructed in social settings" (pp. 39–40). As Kenway and Fitzclarence (1997) argue, "Hegemonic masculinity is the standard-bearer of what it means to be a 'real' man or boy and many males draw inspiration from its cultural library of resources" (pp. 119–120, as cited in Jackson, 2002, p. 40). Jackson further states:

> Hegemonic masculinities are located in a structure of gender/sexual power relations, and within these, boys define their identities against the Other (Epstein, 1998). Gay masculinities feature in the "Other" category as does an attachment to "the feminine" (Kenway and Fitzclarence, 1997). Evidence suggests

(see for example Epstein, 1998) that undertaking academic work is perceived by young people as "feminine" and therefore, if boys want to avoid the verbal and physical "abuse" attached to being labeled as "feminine" or "queer," they must avoid academic work or at least they must appear to avoid academic work (academic achievement itself is not necessarily a problem for boys, but being seen to work is a problem). (pp. 39–40)

The young men I worked with in the mid-1980s are no exception here, although, as I argue in *Working Class Without Work*, there is no overtly oppositional behavior lodged against school knowledge and culture as is the case in previous investigations of this population (Everhart, 1983; Willis, 1977). Nevertheless, while the young Freeway boys exhibit an emerging contradictory attitude toward schooling and school culture (in other words, they think they "need it"), they embrace only the form of such knowledge and culture rather than its substance. In point of fact, young men who embraced the valued masculine form in the mid-1980s did little to no school-based work, either in school or out, but just enough to "get by" or "pass" (Weis, 1990). This, paralleled with deep assertions of both White and male superiority in relation to a constructed "other" (all women, Yemenites, and African American males, gay men in particular), were defining characteristics of the hegemonic masculine form in this White working-class community and school in the mid-1980s (Weis, 1990). Reflecting on the lads, Willis offers:

> It is important to appreciate that the anti-mental animus of the counter-school culture, while highly relevant in opposing and penetrating the demands of the school, also continues to orient and help direct the attitudes of "the lads"—like a soldier's courage in the absence of war—long after the transition and across the board. This "locking" impels them towards a certain kind of culturally me-diated experiential set of meanings throughout their lives. There will certainly be future situations in which these attitudes and practices produce worthwhile "payoffs," but the danger is that the whole world might henceforth, be divided into two—the mental and the manual. (2000, p. 42)

Drawing upon his well-known notion of cross-valorization, Willis notes "a further twist":

> The anti-mentalism and masculinity of the lads become intertwined, fused, in their sense of themselves. A manual way of acting in the world is also a manly way; a mental way is effeminate. These two things reinforce and lock each other into, if you like, "a market masculinity" on the one hand and a "patriarchal manualism" on the other—mutually producing a locking of dispositions and sensibility, which may quite literally, last a lifetime. (2000, p. 44)

Whether the "locking" of masculinity and anti-mentalism lasts a lifetime is, of course, an empirical question, one that relates directly to *Class Reunion*. While not designed explicitly as a study in masculinity per se, and therefore not centrally located in all current debates on masculinity, my work is informed by recent scholarship in key ways. Given kaleidoscopic changes in the global economy, changes that hit the former industrial proletariat the hardest (read, largely White men), the remaking of the class is tied in critical ways to issues that swirl fundamentally around masculinity as well as the wages of Whiteness and a remaking of the feminine, which is treated elsewhere (Weis, as cited in Dolby & Dimitriadis, 2004a). Like the "missing postman" in the BBC serial of the same name who wanders about delivering his last letter before being laid off, "many men can only see loss ahead of them and cannot face what feels like a loss of manhood and feminization, or, what Cohen and Ainley (2000, p. 83) call the loss of 'musculatures of the labouring body'" (Walkerdine, Lucey, & Melody, 2001). It is within this context that I see and hear the Freeway youth, with whom I worked in the 1980s, grow up.

Here, for illustrative purposes, we meet two men who stay in Freeway or the immediately adjoining working-class suburb (other patterns will be explored in *Class Reunion*). Emblematic of the majority of Freeway men, they work in what might be thought of as an assemblage of both new and traditional working-class jobs, such as paralegal, electrician, warehouse worker, highway toll booth collector, foreman of the high school maintenance department, hospital technician, credit card collector, pizza supplies delivery man, and worker at a muffler shop. Some of these men, those who remain closest to normative White working-class masculinity as constructed in high school, fall more centrally in the "hard living" category flagged by investigators several decades ago (Howell, 1973). Others, those who tend to move off the space of hegemonically constructed White masculinity, fare better, establishing for themselves more stable, or, to use Howell's term, "settled" lives.

Significantly, the movement off the space of White working-class hegemonic masculinity—which emerged in relation to the old industrial economy—now encourages this stability since "settled" jobs tend to be those associated with schooling (read feminine) and those traditionally coded as feminine (such as nurse, paralegal, and hospital technician). Such jobs also demand, to a great extent, a partner who earns nearly comparable money if one wishes an economically nonmarginal lifestyle under terms generally offered to children of the former industrial proletariat in the new economy.

In addition, under this scenario, child rearing requires the ongoing time and attention of both parents since both men and women are working full time in the paid labor force and, generally speaking, because working-class families cannot afford day care and simultaneously do not trust it, feeling that the children should be reared in the home, "not by some stranger"

(Zinsser, 1991). Arguably, this feeling reflects the type of paid child care available in working-class communities as well as the fact that working-class women have staked out child rearing as something that is their responsibility and that they "do well"—claiming it as their own gender-bounded creative space.

Under the current economy, and assuming that child rearing is still largely lodged in the home (even if it is not, the same point holds for day care arrangements), such child care must be patched together and carved out of the nonpaid labor time of both parents, including who drops the children off at school, tends to younger children in the home, picks them up at grandma's, takes them to afterschool hockey (a very popular luxury, particularly for male children in cold climate working-class communities), and so forth, depending on the age of the children. Stay-at-home mothers can no longer be counted on to perform all of this unpaid labor. Thus the carefully imagined rendition of a wife's future domesticity as lodged in high school White working-class hegemonic masculinity must be held in check at some point and rearticulated in action if "settled" working-class lives are to be attained under the restructured economy.

At the heart of this repositioning and, I would argue, remaking of the entire White working class, is the reconstruction of male/female relations and, most important in light of high school desires in the case of young men, the rearticulation of appropriate and valued masculinity. It is, though, not simply the verbal rearticulation of masculinity that is at issue here, as virtually all of the men *verbally* express a desired form of gender roles and relations that are wholly different from those expressed as desired in high school (Weis, 1990). Virtually no man reinterviewed in 2000–2001 suggests the gender regime he envisioned in 1985 as one that is currently valued. The important question here is the extent to which these men actually *live* gendered relations that enable a "settled" new working-class lifestyle. Those who are unable to live and accomplish gender as a set of relations vastly different from those of their parents and grandparents are, I argue, the new "hard livers" in a restructured world economy that, as noted earlier, hits the former industrial laboring class in particular kinds of ways (Reich, 1991, 2001).

Women, and even some men, tend to conceptualize this lived rearticulation of gender as a giving up of "the partying kind of life." In other words, in much the same way that respondents in Lilian Rubin's 1976 classic *Worlds of Pain* verbalize, those who are able to settle down are seen as those for whom the new economy will work. Settled living, though, is far more complex than just giving up the partying life; rather, settled living is now fundamentally bound to lived rearticulations of gendered forms and the ways in which such forms enable what becomes a stable and valued working-class existence. Ironically then, gender once again is the fulcrum on which forms of working-class life balance, but in ways wholly different from how it was enacted under the old industrial economy. It is those men who are willing and able to transgress the constructed working-class gender categories and valued masculinity of their youth for whom the new economy can produce settled lives. In point of fact, in this newly minted class fraction, settled men are those individuals who engage in school, coded as compliant and feminine (Arnot, 2004; Connell, 1989; Jackson, 2002; Mac an Ghaill, 1994, 1996; Martino, 1999; Martino & Meyenn, 2001; Reay, 2002; Willis, 2000), and who enter into and maintain partnerships or marriages with individuals who earn at least as much money as they do. In this latter regard, a domestic partner need not necessarily be a lover. For example, one of the interviewed men has formed a working domestic liaison with his sister. They live together, pooling human and economic resources to raise their children, ages 3 (his, who he is devoted to and sees constantly although the boy lives primarily with his former girlfriend) and 9 (hers; her boyfriend left her before the child was born and he has no contact with the daughter). My point here is that the thorough colonization of the public sphere by men, as well as men's imagined total domination of women in the home/family sphere as envisioned by Freeway working-class boys in the mid-1980s, must be reworked if men are to be among the settled working class.

This was not true in the past since the male family wage could, at least in principle, support and maintain settled family life. If nothing else, men and women could imagine and behave in terms of the possibility of family life as tagged to male earning power wherein men could obtain the secret guarantees of earning the family wage: "sacrifice–reward–dignity" (Willis, 2000, p. 93). Embedded in this past, of course, is the fact that women had few options in the paid labor force, a situation that is markedly different today. Neither the available family wage for men nor the relative lack of paid work for women characterizes today's economy, and not a single man in the early 2000s whom I interviewed suggests that it does.

Some men, however, behave as "new" or radically altered working-class men, irrespective of their private thoughts, thus transgressing gendered borders articulated in previous generations. Others do not, and these men may or may not have additional deeply rooted problems, such as alcoholism or drug addiction, which may or may not lie at the heart of their inability to enact a necessary new masculinity. Those who enact this reformatted masculinity may also have problems with drinking and drugs. Nevertheless, their lived and reformulated masculinity at this moment in time, irrespective of such problems, allows them to purchase a home, raise their children, earn part of a living family wage, purchase a car or two, buy hockey skates for their sons, and even have extra money with which they can add an outdoor deck or a fireplace to their home by doing the manual labor themselves with help from their similarly positioned new working-class buddies—buddies who often have the manual skills of the old working class (carpentry, cement pouring, electrical wiring, and so forth).

All of this, however, is wholly dependent on having a partner with whom they can merge money—a partner with whom they also share the day-to-day, minute-by-minute work of parenting on the birth of children. Without this duality of male/female public sphere–generated income as well as work around the domestic sphere, the settled life with its accompanying and valued (partially class-coded) material and social goods—including homes, wet bars, motorcycles, recreational vehicles (RVs), dirt bikes, cabins for hunting, professional football and hockey tickets, and so forth—simply could not be accomplished. The "settled livers"—those men who are able to stake out stability in the new working class—thus challenge, through their day-to-day lives, traditional gendered boundaries and definitions deeply etched in prior working-class hegemonic masculinity and working-class family life more generally, as well articulated by the young men in the mid-1980s when I first worked with them.

This does not mean that all is well with gendered relations in the family and community, a point that I explore at great length elsewhere (Weis, 2004a, 2004b). What it does mean, though, is that in the traditional White working class, hegemonically forged masculinity offers a linchpin around which individual men with whom I worked swirl as they grow into adulthood. Thus the located 1980s cultural form of masculinity, one tied in specific ways to the industrial economy, offers a point of departure as men move forward in a wholly restructured world economy. In the movement forward—the nature of departure and/or stability *in relation* to the original form rather than the original form per se—we can see a template for future lives. This set of departures/stability must, though, be theorized in relation to what the economy has to offer men and women in the late 20th century and into the 21st. It is, then, the collective youth cultural form (here the hegemonic form of masculinity that many others have noted as well) and, later, individual movement in relation to this form (one forged dialectically in relation to the old industrial economy and the gender-based bargains within this old economy for the working class) that offers powerful material as we work to understand the world of the new working class. More important, of course, this all sits underneath and in relation to massive realignment of the global economy, which touched off this entire set of negotiations to begin with, as well as tighter and more clearly articulated sorting mechanisms related to formal schooling. That formal schooling in this class fraction is traditionally coded as feminine speaks volumes about the gendered fulcrum on which so much of the remaking of the White working class rests.

Here we meet two men who are emblematic of the split detailed above. Unlike some of the other men reinterviewed in 2000–2001 (Weis, 2004b), both remain in and around the Freeway environs, and it is arguably the case that both are part of the "new" White working class, a class descended from the traditional proletariat but no longer embodying its same features. Clint is currently a "hard liver" and John is not. Although they were very similar in high school in terms of their attitudes toward school, school-based behavior, academic track location, daily activities, and expressed masculinity, John now lives a new masculine form, one that enables and promotes both the shared form of a family living wage and the accomplishment of child rearing. Clint, in contrast, embodies the opposite. While giving lip service to a desire for women to work outside the home (in contradiction with what he said in high school), and seeing himself as thoroughly on board with respect to new gendered locations and relations, Clint does not live his verbally expressed new masculine form. We hear from John first:

> **John:** I own this home. My sister-in-law actually lives upstairs. Last year, my wife worked full time. So we needed a baby-sitter. And she [sister-in-law] was living rent-free, but she's babysitting for us. That's as much as you're going to pay for day care. Sam's in school, so now we don't need a babysitter. . . .
>
> I'm an O.R. [operating room] tech. I work at St. Paul's Hospital in surgery. I set up cases—cases as in surgery. And assist the doctors, and then when we're done, you clean up. Yesterday I was in a craniotomy from eleven until six. And okay, it's five-thirty, I'll go to lunch now. Or like, when we do total joint, do a total knee replacement, or a total hip replacement, and there are people that have been working there for 20 years that don't know how to do those. When I started, I was ambitious, I guess. I mean I would be bored just doing little piddley stuff all day long, you know, that's the downside of it, is that I'm always busy.
>
> **Lois:** And how about your wife? What does she do?
>
> **John:** My wife is an ultrasound technologist at St. Paul's also. She started working . . . actually, I found out that there was an opening, and I told her about it. She got the job. I used to work with her other sister, her eldest sister. I used to work with her. Ultrasound is part of x-ray. . . . [When I got out of high school] I joined the Air Force. I was in the Air Force for about 3 years, and I did this in the Air Force. . . . I was on the one hospital with the one doctor. So I went back to school at Midway [a local 2-year school] to broaden my base. My brother-in-law's trying to get me into GM [General Motors]. Hopefully around Thanksgiving I'll know what my chances are. It'll be a skilled trade, which I'll start off making seven dollars more an hour. I mean, I like what I do; I'm good at what I do: I don't get paid for what I'm worth. You know, especially the way I get abused every day. You

know, there's six, seven people sitting around doing nothing. And I just get done with this big case, and "Okay, John, go do this now. And John, can you stay later? John, can you come in earlier?" It's not worth it. . . .

I'm really underpaid. I mean, when I help this doctor, he's going to make, you know, they earn their money from all the training and the years and years and years they had to do this stuff. I understand that. I mean, the nurse's making, you know, 20, 24 dollars an hour. She's sitting on her ass. She didn't check the case. She didn't set up the case. She opens it up and sits down. She preps the patient. I understand that. And then, she does nothing until the case is over unless I tell her to give me something. She makes 24 dollars an hour and I'm making 14 dollars an hour. . . . If I get into GM I'm hoping that my wife can go part time. I can only work so much, you know, so she went full time. Yeah, she wants a car . . . and I got my little car out front.

Lois: Is it fair to say it's been tough financially?

John: Well, I can't say that because I've been a lot worse off. You know, when my parents first got divorced [when he was 14], living with my mom, I mean, she couldn't do for me what I can do for my kids now. I started working when I was 14 years old so I could buy my school clothes, so I could get a new pair of sneakers. These kids don't have to worry about that. We just spent 300 dollars on Tom on his hockey. And then it's like another 150 so he can join this league he's in now. You know, that's expensive. But, whatever.

Lois: Can you describe a typical weekday in your house? Like, you get up in the morning . . .

John: You know, Sue gets up about six; gets in the shower. She gets up, wakes up Tom [13-year-old stepson]. Tom gets in the shower. Me and Sam [son, age 5] get up at seven. And Sam will watch Pokemon until seven-thirty. By that time, Sue's gone and Tom is gone. I make him [Tom] lunch, and they go. You know, Tom catches his bus at seven-thirty. Sue has to be at the hospital at seven-thirty. And then I'm with Sam, you know, feed him, get him dressed, brush his teeth, make him lunch, go sit out on the porch at eight o'clock, wait for the bus. Then I come back after he goes on the bus. I come back and then I'll shower, and, you know, make the beds and eat something, make myself lunch, do the dishes; basically clean up the house before I go to work. And I get home at six o'clock, you know, if there is no real dinner made, I'll just scrounge around for whatever. And Tuesdays and Thursdays, Sue's at the gym working out. She belongs to Jack [Jack's Gym]. I find something to eat. And then, you know, do what needs to be done, got to do laundry; I mean, clean up the house, give him [Sam] a bath, whatever. When it was summertime, cut the grass, go outside, screw around with the kids for a couple hours, you know. Depends on what's going on. I have to go out and do whatever.

Lois: Were you raised in one of those homes where the dad kind of expected . . .

John: [He interrupts me] The dinner every night? Yeah, that's what it was. My mom never worked up until my dad got laid off. You know, my mom stayed home and cooked and cleaned or did the laundry. Ironed the clothes and made dinner every night; yeah.

John had some hard years; when he was in high school, he lived in a now condemned building after his parents divorced. Soon after the divorce, his 17-year-old sister became pregnant and lived with them until the baby was born. Working at a pizzeria below his apartment throughout all of his teenage years, John had no illusions about what the future held. In 1985, he told me that "college prep is the only thing to do. Well, around here, cause there's nothing else. Everything's going down south. Like any kind of good jobs, a better education's what you're gonna hafta need unless you plan to sweep the floors someplace the rest of your life. And that ain't really gonna be my style."

Most of the 15- to 16-year-old Freeway boys expressed similar notions about the value of schooling when I knew them in the mid-1980s. They did not, though, act on this new valuation, as most did virtually nothing in high school except get by through minimal studying and copying one another's homework, engaging in the most low-level form of education and certainly not its substance. (Yet, neither did they demonstrate, at that moment, the overt and boisterous opposition to school noted by previous investigators of this group.) This split valuation of school, then, emerged in sharp evidence during high school years and is a core element of valued White working-class masculinity in the 1980s. In this sense, White working-class young men mirror what we find in many studies of African Americans, wherein schooling is valued and not valued at one and the same time (Ogbu, 1974, 2002). White working-class youth in high school at least verbally valued schooling for what they thought it could get them. They did not, though, *act* on the positive end of this set of understandings. In fact, most participated in the bare form of schooling, rather than engaging in its substance.

As a young adult, John is among the new working class. He owns his home and has one son and one stepson. He no longer lives in Freeway, but in a White working-class suburb immediately adjacent to Freeway, having bought a home four blocks from the Freeway border, a home that puts his children in a different set of schools. As we see though, his stable or settled new working-class existence, which he values highly, is wholly dependent upon his breaking away from the hegemonically constructed White male masculinity. He went into the service, gained some skills, and, upon leaving the Air Force, immediately went to a 2-year college for an Associate's degree, engaging finally in the substance side of the form/substance split with respect to education, which neither he nor the vast majority of White working-class male youth did while they were in high school. In this sense, he crosses over what Willis calls the "anti-mental animus" embedded within White working-class masculinity, reaching over the mental/manual split as it cross-valorizes the feminine/masculine. It is significant that John is in what might be seen as a traditionally female field—hospital technician—although he carefully differentiates himself discursively from the female-coded nursing arena. Although skilled, he earns only fourteen dollars an hour—substantially less, in his mind at least, from what he could earn at General Motors. His settled life is thus wholly dependent on his own job (which can be coded as traditionally female) coupled with that of his wife (ultrasound technologist). It can be assumed that she earns approximately the same money as he does, or perhaps even more, having earned an Associate's degree the same year he did from the same college.

Most noteworthy are his responses to questions about domestic labor. Unlike his father, "who expected dinner on the table every night at five P.M.," John takes full responsibility for much of the household-related work, stating that his wife "works too." John gets his son ready every morning for school, makes lunch for his 13-year-old stepson and himself, makes the beds, does the dishes, cleans the house before he goes to work, and often makes dinner because Sue is not yet home. Instead of expecting to be waited on after sacrificing himself through continual giving of his labor power (the secret guarantee of the family wage—sacrifice, reward, dignity), John lives domestic life as a partnership wherein both adults need to participate if they are to purchase a house, maintain a home, encourage the children to play hockey, own two cars, and belong to Jack's Gym. While all this is not, of course, necessarily what his wife would say about the domestic arrangements (a great deal of research notes the double burden of women as they enter the paid labor force), it is nevertheless obvious that John moved off centrally located working-class masculine space in order for this all to be accomplished, although he used traditionally masculine space in the form of the armed services to catapult himself out of Freeway and into a new settled working-class life. Ironically then, traditionally hegemonic male space (the armed forces) can act as a bridge to the enactment of a new masculine form—a masculine form different from the old working-class hegemonic masculinity and one that is demanded in this class fraction if a man is to be other than "hard living" in the restructured economy.[1]

John knows that his settled life is still highly precarious. Life is incredibly expensive and he senses the fragility of his current domestic arrangement. Most important, though, he had to invest in a new form of masculinity in order to make this all work. Stretching beyond talk about shared responsibly, John engages in the day-to-day labor associated with his settled working classness—a set of arrangements far from centrally located and valued masculinity forged under conditions of the capital-labor accord.

In stark contrast to John, Clint lives largely the same life he did in high school, never straying far from the masculine space occupied and expressed as one valued for the future during his secondary school years:

Clint: My parents basically still live there [house where he grew up]. Well, I still live there too. And back and forth between there and my girlfriend's. . . . Now I'm working on cars, doing the same thing [that I did in high school]; that's what I'm doing for a living. I'm running a Deltasonic [car wash] now. I'm on contract with them.

Lois: I'm going to show you a picture of yourself from high school.

Clint: Man, that was a long time ago. Guess my hair was kind of short [now it is in a pony tail]. Kept in touch with a lot of the same people I got there [written down underneath the blurb in his senior yearbook picture]. . . . I was in trouble in high school. We always had a good time. Out partying all the time. Not going to class. We were good at that. Ah, we might have gotten thrown out of the parking lot a couple of times [for smoking cigarettes or marijuana]. We had a lot of good times though. Man, I haven't looked at these books in years. Actually, we all still do the same thing when I see all these guys. Go out and party. Especially Bruce [who I interviewed also] and T.J. Bruce more than anybody though. We just go out drinking, go to a ball game, whatever. Watch a [car] race. We went to a wedding a couple of weeks ago. That was a wild one. Bruce couldn't go though. His girlfriend was there. He couldn't go. He was watching the kid. That's an iffy situation there. . . .

I just did what I had to do to graduate. That's about it. One of them "get it done, get out of here" kind of things. Everybody just wanted to graduate, get it over and done with and get out of here. That's the way we all ended up being. They [the school] wanted you to stay in school though. . . . You think about it now and maybe I shouldn't have rushed that much. And then you look back now and see all you do is get up and go to work, go home, go to sleep, get up, and go to work, go home. Especially the way I work, 10 hours a day. Seven-thirty to five thirty, Monday through Friday, and seven-thirty to two on Saturday. I don't necessarily stay all those hours, but it's the hours we're open. Right now I just manage it. The last 8 years I was doing it; the last 2 years I haven't been really doing it that much. Since I screwed up my back, I haven't done it at all. I did that back thing in April [this is November]. I blew out a disk. Lifting something. And then I went to work back in June and then I pinched a nerve like 2 weeks ago. I was going to take some night course just for—I was going to go into welding. . . . I don't know. It was a thought. I'm going to have to see what happens with my back. If I don't go back to work soon, it's possible I might lose this job. That's why I'm going back after I go to the doctor tomorrow. I'm gonna go back Monday just for the fact I don't want to lose my job.

Lois: Can you describe your money situation now compared to when you grew up?

Clint: Right now, not very good without me working. I'm still waiting for a Comp check. I do all right. I live with my girlfriend, but like I said, it's back and forth. I don't own a house. I didn't buy a house yet. My girlfriend has an apartment. Her 17-year-old daughter lives with her. She's divorced . . . I go wherever I want, whenever I want. She don't like the fact that I just bought a 15,000 dollar motorcycle. She likes the bike. It's just she thinks I should've bought a house instead. I wanted it [the bike] so I went and bought it. . . . We been fighting a lot

lately, so I don't know how much longer this is going to last. Just the fact that
I come and go wherever I please, do whatever I want. Nobody tells me what to do.
I just do what I want is what it comes down to. You know, like that. The last straw
will be, let's see, what is today, the second? I give it another week when I tell her
I'm leaving for Atlanta to go to the race [car race]. That'll probably be the icing
on the cake. But, that's one of them things. Nascar race. Winston Cup car race.
Last race of the year in Atlanta. Me and a couple other guys are going. We were at
a friend's house. The guy who got married—we were at a friend's house and
everybody started talking about it and the next thing I knew my phone rang and
[he said] "I already called, I looked it up on the computer. I called [for] tickets
and we're going. You going?" And I said "sure." So she don't know about it yet.
She's not going to be happy. We've been together since '92. She works at Unibase,
a uniform company. She works in the warehouse.

Unlike John, who was very similar to Clint in high school, Clint remains
largely on high school constructed masculine space. He spends most of his
time with the same individuals he partied with in high school and, by his
own admission, engages in largely the same activities—drinking and
smoking grass. "Out partying all the time" as a teenager, his life has not
changed much except for the fact that he can now legally drink and he puts
in many hours working at the local Deltasonic car wash. Sounding much
like men of the old industrial working class (Sennett & Cobb, 1972; Willis,
1977), he now regrets not putting more time into school, suggesting that
"Maybe I shouldn't have rushed so much." Clint rests within what I call the
new working-class "hard livers"—bouncing back and forth between his
parents' house and that of his girlfriend, not sure how long he will have a
job, spending a great deal of time in bars with his buddies from high school
(who I also interviewed and who are in the same sketchy position both in
wage labor terms and in terms of their domestic lives), and just generally
doing "whatever [he] wants," not feeling accountable to anyone or anything. Clint certainly does not valorize patriarchal gender relations in
the same way he and virtually every other Freeway young man in the mid-
1980s did when I knew them, and he indeed recognizes that his sister
works at American Axle on the assembly line and "works harder than most
guys I know," thereby contributing to a settled working-class lifestyle in her
own family. However, Clint has been unable and/or unwilling to move
himself into that space that would allow him a settled working-class lifestyle. He has not gone on to school, still coding it as boring, repetitive, and
docile (in other words, feminine); is firmly planted in the anti-mental
animus with regard to his own labor, thereby living a form of "patriarchal
manualism"; and does not participate in a particular kind of domestic life
in which resources, both human and material, are pooled. Clint, then, has
stayed largely within masculine space forged and valued in high school,
unable and unwilling perhaps to facilitate an alternative trajectory—a

trajectory that demands a different lived stance vis-à-vis gender than that fantasized about and enacted in secondary school.

Concluding Remarks

I am suggesting here that the reconstituted working class in America is living a newly created split between "hard" and "settled" livers, one resting on the fulcrum of gender definitions and relations. Like Connell (1995), then, I am affirming different masculinities, but noting that the nature of such masculinities can shift markedly over time. Looking at the same individuals in 1985 and again in 2000–2001, we see that the ways in which they position themselves in relation to high school hegemonic masculinity has a great deal to do with where they end up 15 years later. All the young White men meet the harsh economy they feared they would while in high school—just 5 or so years after the major steel plant closed in Freeway, a closing that hit hard the White working class in the area. As Reich (1991, 2001) and others argue, the old industrial sector is gone, and with it the kinds of jobs that pit working-class males in a routine manner against the brutality of heavy industry. It is in the push and pull with adolescent axes of identity development that Freeway men stake out and are able to stake out adulthood. It is the combination of structural forces "determining," to some extent, the shape and form of the economy and culture with the ways in which individual men take up positions within this set of structural pushes and pulls that both "determines" future individual place and, as I argue at length in *Class Reunion* (2004b), the perimeters of the class fraction itself.

This set of theoretical understandings challenges both structural and culturally rooted theories of reproduction. Mechanistic notions of reproduction of the economy, culture, and the individual obviously will not do here given massive economic realignment. But neither do more culturally based theoretical understandings. I am suggesting here that not only do collective cultures emerge dialectically in relation to structures, as Paul Willis (1977) suggests, but that there are elements within these collectively based cultures, in this case masculinity, as well as individual negotiation of the elements over the years that set the stage for later relations and sensibilities. It is in the struggle with such collectively based cultures on a more individual level that adult lives begin to play out in a drastically changed economy.

In this way, too, we can begin to understand the lived reconfiguration of the entire class. This is not to say that large structural determinations are not there. Surely they are, as I have noted repeatedly with respect to the changing global economy. It is equally not the case that collectively based youth cultures are irrelevant to future life possibilities and the broader shape of society. I agree with Paul Willis that we cannot assume a "continuous line of ability in the occupational/class structures," but rather "must conceive of radical breaks represented by the interface of cultural forms" (p. 1)—cultural forms that are, to some extent at least, under the control of those who produce them. Nevertheless, it is in the ongoing and ever-changing interaction with these two major sets of forces (structural and cultural) that individuals ultimately begin to stake out their futures. In the case at hand, it is in the reinforcement and/or pulling away from what is defined within high school peer groups as hegemonic White working-class masculine form that we begin to see how young people, in this case young men, move toward adulthood. Ultimately this enables us to trace the movement and emerging contours of the new White working class under a wholly restructured global economy. Ironically, as we see here, while the old industrial order rested on a stable gender regime, it is the unsteady fulcrum of gender (roles, definitions, and hierarchy) that lies at the very heart of reconstituted White working-class life.

Designs to Document Sites of Possibility

CHAPTER 5

Participatory Action Research: From Within and Beyond Prison Bars

*Michelle Fine, María Elena Torre, Kathy Boudin,
Iris Bowen, Judith Clark, Donna Hylton, Migdalia
Martinez, "Missy," Melissa Rivera, Rosemarie A. Roberts,
Pamela Smart, and Debora Upegui[1]*

Participatory action research (PAR) represents a stance within qualitative research methods, an epistemology that assumes knowledge is rooted in social relations and most powerful when produced collaboratively through action. With a long and global history, participatory action research has typically been practiced within community-based social action projects with a commitment to understanding, documenting, and/or evaluating the impact that social programs, social problems, and/or social movements bear on individuals and communities. PAR draws on multiple methods, some quantitative and some qualitative, but at its core it articulates a recognition that knowledge is produced in collaboration and in action.

With this essay, we aim to accomplish four ends. First, we provide a cursory history of PAR, beginning with Kurt Lewin (1951) and traveling briskly through the feminist and postcolonial writings of critical theorists. Second, we introduce readers to a PAR project that we have undertaken in a women's prison in New York State, documenting the impact of college on women in prison, the prison environment, and on the women's post-release outcomes. Third, we present a glimpse at our findings and offer an

95

instance of analysis, demonstrating closely how we thematically and discursively analyzed data about "transformation" as a research collective of inmate and university-based researchers. Fourth, we articulate a set of reflections on our work as a PAR collective and the dilemmas of writing openly under surveillance.

The roles and responsibilities of outside scholars in relation with inside scholars have long been a question for theorists and researchers of social injustice. Many have agitated for a form of participation, but few have articulated the nature of the work-together (see Chataway, 1997, for an exception; also McIntyre, 1997). This essay invites readers into a prison-based PAR project, in which a team of university-based researchers and inmate researchers collaborated to document and theorize the impact of college within and beyond the prison environment. Like many before us, we sought to organize all aspects of the intervention and the research through democratic participation. And like those, our practice did not always live up to the design. We do not see insiders or outsiders as the "true" bearers of truth or knowledge, but like M. Brinton Lykes (2001), Linda Tuhiwai Smith (1999) and Ignacio Martín-Baró (1994), we recognize in our souls the relative freedom and, therefore, responsibility of outside researchers to speak critically and constructively with insiders about the possibilities and limits of participatory research within the walls of prison.

A Too-Brief History of PAR

Kurt Lewin has long been the name attached to the "genesis" of action research in the United States. From the 1940s forward, with vision, critique, and intellectual courage, Lewin dared to assert participant knowledge as foundational to validity and democratic and participatory research as foundational to social change. Working very much within a psychological paradigm for a greater social good, Lewin carved a space for "the development of reflective thought, discussion, decision and action by ordinary people participating in collective research on 'private troubles' (Mills, 1959) which they have in common" (as cited in Adelman, 1997, p. 87). Lewin challenged the artificial borders separating theory, research, and action, insisting, "no action without research; no research without action" (as cited in Adelman, 1997, p. 90). At the core of Lewin's project was, like with John Dewey, a refusal to separate thought from action, an insistence on the integration of science and practice, and a recognition that social processes could be understood only when they were changed (see Cherry & Borshuk, 1998).

Frances Cherry and Catherine Borshuk place in historic context the power of Lewin's work while he was director at the Commission for Community Interrelations (CCI) of the American Jewish Committee. According to Cherry:

Perhaps closest to contemporary participatory action research would be the category of research conducted by CCI: a community self survey of civil rights in which the importance of members of the community conducting the research was stressed as essential. . . . Lewinian thinking [recognized] that science and social problem-solving should be intimately connected, and that action research was inevitably participatory. (personal communication, 2000)

The community self-survey of civil rights, initiated under Lewin's leadership, exemplifies the kind of democratic progressive community projects CCI advocated, "attempting to move beyond academic expertise and to place the tools of research in the hands of concerned citizens" (Cherry & Borshuk, 1998, p. 129). Lewin's vision of democratic social research was compromised significantly over time, by the increasing conservatism of U.S. psychology, McCarthyism, and scientism, and was converted into a set of techniques and axioms, rather than a radical challenge to science as practiced.

Central and South American theorists and practitioners, including Orlando Fals Borda (1979), Paulo Freire (1982), and Ignacio Martín-Baró (1994), have, more recently, structured a set of commitments to PAR that move Lewin well beyond the borders of psychology, into an explicit analysis of the relation of science to social inequality, community life, and radical social change. As Martín-Baró explicated:

If our objective is to serve the liberation needs of the people [of Latin America] . . . [We must] involve ourselves in a new praxis, an act of transforming reality that will let us know not only about what is but also about what is not, and by which we may try to orient ourselves toward what ought to be. (1994, pp. 27–29)

Like Martín-Baró, Fals Borda (1979) and colleagues sought a set of practices that would reveal "facts" as processes, "causality" as circular or "spiral in nature," and "multiple determinations" rather than "immediate antecedents." For Fals Borda, like Lewin, a dynamic or dialectical confrontation between common sense and systematic observations, followed by intensive reflection and action, engaged at the provocative borders between insiders and outsiders, were the recursive steps of participatory action research.

Deeply critical of the relation of science to social inequity, and equally hopeful about using science for radical social change, Fals Borda and colleagues recognized

the possibility for the masses of workers themselves to create and possess scientific knowledge; that social research and political action can be synthesized and mutually influential so as to increase the level of efficiency of action as well as the understanding of reality. (1979, p. 41)

Across history and current texts, these PAR scholars have worked to articulate specific principles of PAR. At root, participatory research recognizes what Antonio Gramsci (1971) described from a prison cell in Italy, the intellectual and political power of "organic intellectuals" from whom counter-hegemonic notions derive, whose lives are deeply grounded in class struggles. Herein lies the fundamental challenge to what Habermas called "scientism" or what John Gaventa called "official knowledge" as the sole legitimate claim to truth (Gaventa, 1993; Habermas, 1971; Hall, 1993; Kemmis & McTaggart, 2000; McIntyre, 2000). With similar commitments, Hans Toch authored a powerful article in September 1967 that spoke about PAR in prison, the knowledge of convicts, and the humility of outside researchers; it was an article well ahead of its time. We owe much, in this essay and this work, to the wisdom and foresight of Hans Toch.

Relationships, Responsibilities, and Action at the Heart of Participatory Research

> In the participatory research propounded here, the silenced are not just incidental to the curiosity of the researcher but are the masters of inquiry into the underlying causes of the events in their world. In this context research becomes a means of moving them beyond silence into a quest to proclaim the world. (Freire, 1982)

In the last 5 years, with both feminist and explicitly critical turns, the writings on the stance of participatory researchers have broken important new ground. Our work has been enormously influenced by five such turns. First, there has been a sharp recognition of participation *with*, not only *for*, community. Psychologist Brinton Lykes marks this move in her language, reflecting her stance on a project in which she

> agreed to *accompany* a friend to her community of origin in the Highlands of Guatemala. . . . [Recognizing myself] as a "situated other" within a *praxis of solidarity* [which] informs my ongoing efforts to develop alternative methods for "standing under" these realities and participating with local actors in responding to problems in daily living. (2001, p. 1)

Second, we are inspired by participatory action researchers, who, drawing from critical race and legal theories, have recognized the intellectual power and searing social commentary developed at the bottom of social hierarchies (Ladson-Billings, 2000). Mari Matsuda (1995), a critical legal scholar writing for an "outsider's jurisprudence," writes:

> When notions of right and wrong, justice and injustice, are explained not from an abstract position from the position of groups who have suffered through history, moral relativism recedes . . . [toward] a new epistemological source for critical scholars looking to the bottom. (p. 6)

Third, from the growing literature on research for and by indigenous peoples, some participatory researchers, ourselves among them, draw from the writings of Maori theorist and researcher Linda Tuhiwai Smith (1999), who recognizes not only the knowledge accumulated in indigenous communities, but also that indigenous values, beliefs, and behaviors must be incorporated into the praxis of participatory research. From Tuhiwai Smith we take profound insights about respect for local custom and practices, not as an obstacle to research, but as a site for possible learning, shared engagement, and long-term social change.

Fourth, we have been inspired and moved by the writings of critical psychologist Kum Kum Bhavnani (1994), who has authored an essay in which she struggles aloud with questions of objectivity; that is, feminist objectivity, in her self-consciously political research. Holding herself responsible to satisfy high standards for quality work, Bhavnani writes about three criteria for "feminist objectivity": inscription, micropolitics, and difference. Inscription entails holding herself accountable to produce stories about young women and men that counter—and do not reinforce—dominant, stereotypic scripts. Micropolitics demands that she explicitly analyze, in her empirical texts, her relation to and with the "subjects" of her research. And difference reminds her that she must theorize not only the strong trends that sweep across her data, but interrogate, as well and with equal rigor, the subtle and significant differences within.

Fifth, Glenda Russell and Janis Bohan (1999) argue that it is crucial to theorize and strategize how PAR gives back to communities good enough to open themselves up for intellectual scrutiny. Russell and Bohan are two of the very few scholars who deliberate on the questions of audience, product, and what is left behind. For these activist scholars, creating a legacy of inquiry, a process of change, and material resources to enable transformation are crucial to the PAR project.

These five turns—toward working with a community, recognizing local knowledge, respecting local practices, stretching toward a grounded feminist objectivity, and giving back—emerge for us as guiding refinements in the practice of PAR (see also Brydon-Miller, 2001; Olesen, 2000).

A Note on Limits and Responsibility

While many scholars have begun to write on the power of PAR, a number of feminist and critical race theorists have wandered into the other side of the conversation, daring to reveal what Venezuelan community psychologist Esther Weisenfeld (1999) has called the "unfulfilled promises of PAR." We are indebted to these writers, for it is in their firm belief about the power of participation that they feel compelled to write honestly with caution. Thus, Patricia Maguire (2001) reflects on her training of participatory researchers in the new South Africa and reports a low-level but pervasive resistance to the dialogic, nonauthoritarian nature of the work, such that participants were eager to contribute fully when they were taught or led in traditional relations of authority, but were disappointed when they were not. Anne Bettencourt, George Dillman, and Neil Wollman (1996) write on participatory research as a form of grassroots organizing, and note with concern that once a compelling project is stirred up, participatory researchers have an obligation to find, build, and then pass the torch onto an interior leadership structure to move the action forward, and resist taking up that role themselves. Cynthia Chataway (2001) offers a very careful analysis of her work with a Native American community, respectfully recognizing that although equal and public participation may be the goal of outside researchers, those who work and dwell in communities that are oppressed and surveilled may, indeed, be grateful for the research and yet prefer privacy as a form of public responsibility. John Stanfield II (1994) notes that participatory research has become a "partial solution" to the historic oppression of people of color in social sciences but, he continues, "rarely do researchers share career rewards with 'subjects' of color, such as coauthorships and access to authoritative credentializing processes" (p. 336).

In a very useful move, Brinton Lykes, who has worked, read, and thought carefully about the delicate praxis of participatory methods in Guatemala, Ireland, South Africa, and Boston, Massachusetts, offers a crucial and generous set of reflections on working criteria for evaluating participatory methods, including

> the method's compatibility and/or complementarity with other existing resources in local communities with a majority population living in extreme poverty, thereby enhancing sustainability of the project . . . [and] the method's capacity to facilitate an action/reflection dialectic when new ways of thinking and/or alternative cultural practices emerge within and among local participants and their communities in response to the PAR process. (2001, pp. 195–196)

We hear all of these cautions as wisdom. Although we are privileged to be working within a maximum security prison with a supportive superintendent and correctional staff, and prison-based researchers and respondents, the stakes for these inmates, should they broach some forms of honesty or critical action, could be devastating. We have learned, as Linda Tuhiwai Smith would warn us, that what appears to be paranoia may just be local wisdom, and not to confuse "finding your voice" and "speaking out" with courage. Thus we have learned that "equal" participation and responsibility does not mean the "same." Instead, it means endless ongoing conversations among ourselves, always revisiting every decision about who can take risks, who dares to speak, who must remain quiet, and what topics need never see the light of day. As Linda Martín Alcoff (1995) has written, we are painfully aware that we always need to "analyze the probable or actual effects of [our] words on the [many, contradictory] discursive and material contexts [both within and beyond the prison]" (p. 111).

The Context for the Project

The 1980s and 1990s in the United States were decades of substantial public and political outcry about crime and about criminals. During these years, stiffer penalties were enforced for crimes, prisons were built at unprecedented rates, parole was tougher to achieve, "three strikes and you're out" bills were passed, and college was no longer publicly funded for women and men in prison. Indeed, with the signing of the Violent Crime Control and Law Enforcement Act, President Bill Clinton stopped the flow of all federal dollars (in the form of Pell Grants) that had enabled women and men in prison to attend college. It was then up to the states, simply, to finalize the closing of most prison-based college programs around the nation. At Bedford Hills Correctional Facility, a vibrant college program had been coordinated by Mercy College for more than 15 years. In 1995, this program, like over 340 others nationwide, was closed. This decision provoked a sea of disappointment, despair, and outrage from the women at Bedford Hills who had been actively engaged in higher education and in GED/ABE preparation. Within months, a group of inmates met with the superintendent and, later, an active community volunteer, Thea Jackson; soon they, with Marymount Manhattan College president Regina Peruggi, resurrected college in the prison as a private, voluntary consortium of colleges and universities dedicated to inmate education.

The design of the college was conceptualized through pillars of strong, ongoing participation by the prison administration, staff, inmates, faculty, and volunteers. Students, in particular, are expected to give back in any number of ways. For example, they teach, mentor, pay the equivalent of a month's wages for tuition, and demonstrate high levels of community engagement once they are released (see Fine et al., 2001). Structurally, the design of the college program called for the college administrators at Bedford to meet regularly with the prison administration, the inmate committee, and a representative of the board to create and sustain a "safe" context for serious conversation—reflection, revision, and reimagining of the college program. Those involved felt it important to design the program with core participation from every constituency because many, including the long-termers who witnessed the loss of college, did not want the younger women to ever take the program for granted, assume its permanence, forget its fragility, or view it as an entitlement. Little did we know that the forms of participation within the college would emerge, powerfully, as one of the central positive outcomes of the college program. That is, women who have for the most part spent the better (or worst) part of their lives under the thumbs of poverty, racism, and men could, in college, "hear my own voice" or "see my own signature" or "make my own decisions"— reimagine themselves as agents who make choices, take responsibility, create change for themselves and others (e.g., family, children, and younger women at Bedford), and design a future not overdetermined by the past.

At its heart, this college program has not simply been about taking courses, but about deep immersion in an intellectual and ethical community of scholars. The physical space of the Learning Center—equipped with non-networked computers (no Internet), contributed books, magazines, newspapers, and flags from colleges and universities in the consortium— holds what Seymour Sarason (1974) would call the "sense of community," a place where, the women will attest, "if I need help I can find it—even if that means someone to kick me in the ass to get back to work and finish my papers." This intellectual community also spills out onto the "yard" where you can overhear study groups on Michel Foucault, qualitative research, and Alice Walker, or in the cell block where the ticking of typewriter keys can be heard late into the night or a "young inmate may knock softly on [my] wall, at midnight, asking how to spell or punctuate. . . ." For the women at Bedford Hills, 80% of whom carry scars of childhood sexual abuse, biographies of miseducation, tough family and community backgrounds, and long lists of social and personal betrayals, growing back the capacity to join a community, engage with a community, give back, and trust are remarkable social and psychological accomplishments.

Thus, when Michelle Fine was asked to conduct the empirical documentation of the impact of college on the women, the prison environment, and the world outside the prison, it seemed all too obvious that a participatory design behind bars would be nearly impossible—and essential.

Research Design

In 1997, the Leslie Glass Foundation offered to fund the documentation of the impact of college on the prison community. Michelle Fine, professor of psychology at the Graduate Center of the City University of New York, agreed to become the principal investigator of the project and hired a team of graduate students to help conduct the study. It was determined, early in the design phase, that the project would be maximally informed, useful, and productive if there were a set of inmate researchers on the team as well (see Toch, 1967). We consulted with the superintendent, who agreed with the design, after the New York State Department of Correctional Services (NYSDOCS) provided official approval. The following inmate researchers joined the team: Kathy Boudin, Iris Bowen,[2] Judith Clark, Aisha Elliot,[3] Donna Hylton, Migdalia Martinez,[4] "Missy," and Pamela Smart. Over time, NYSDOCS, through the efforts of E. Michele Staley, grew to be a crucial member of our research team, computing the post-release reincarceration rates for women who enrolled in, graduated from, and/or did not participate in the college program.

Study Design

The design of the research called for both quantitative and qualitative methods. The research questions required that a quantitative analysis be undertaken to assess the extent to which college, in fact, reduced recidivism and disciplinary incidents. A qualitative analysis was needed to determine the psychosocial effects of college on the women, the prison environment, their children, and the women's lives after release. See Table 5.1 and Table 5.2.

A Glimpse of the Findings

Using very different methods, we were able to research intensively a number of questions about the impact of college on women in, and released from, prison. Integrating both quantitative and qualitative methods allowed us to further probe questions that needed additional explication.

To What Extent Does Involvement in College Affect Women's Reincarceration Rates?

In the fall of 1999, the research team approached the NYSDOCS, requesting that a longitudinal analysis of reincarceration rates be conducted on those women from Bedford Hills Correctional Facility who had attended the Mercy College Program and had subsequently been released. E. Michele Staley, program research specialist III, conducted the analyses for the project and provided data on return-to-custody rates for all participants at any time since release, and then return-to-custody rates for all participants within 36 months of release.[5]

Using the standard NYSDOCS measure of 36 months, researchers noted that out of the 274 women tracked longitudinally, 21 college participants returned to custody. Thus, women who participated in college while in prison had a 7.7% return-to-custody rate. In contrast, an analysis tracking all female offenders released between 1985 and 1995 revealed a 29.9% return-to-custody rate, within 36 months. Women without college are almost four times more likely to be returned to custody than comparable women who participated in college while in prison. Women with no college are twice as likely to be rearrested for a "new term commitment" (a new crime) than women with at least some college. Further, women

TABLE 5.1. Research Questions, Methods, Samples, and Outcomes

Research Questions	Methods	Samples*	Outcomes
What is the impact of the college experience on inmate students?	• Archival analysis of college since inception		• Sense of academic achievement • Personal transformation
	• One-on-one interviews conducted by inmate-researchers	N = 65	• Expression of responsibility for crime and for future decisions • Reflection on choices made in the past and decisions to be made in the future
	• Focus groups: with inmates, faculty, children, and college presidents	10 focus groups: N = 43 (inmates) N = 20 (faculty) N = 9 (children) N = 7 (presidents)	• Civic engagement and participation in prison and outside
What is the impact of the college experience on the prison environment?	• Interviews with corrections officers and administrators	N = 5	• Changes in prison disciplinary environment • Changes in prison climate
	• Surveys of faculty	N = 20	• Changes in corrections officers' views of and experiences with prison • Changes in attitudes of women not in the college program about college • Changes in faculty's views of college program
What are the post-release effects of college on the women and on their reincarceration rates?	• In-depth interviews with former inmates	N = 20	• Lower reincarceration rates • Economic well-being • Improved health
	• Student narratives	N = 18	• Civic participation • Persistence in pursuing higher education
	• Statistical analysis of former inmates who students attended college while in prison	N = 454 total (N = 274 released)	• Improved relations with family and friends

*Some women participated in more than one data source.

with no college are 18 times more likely to violate parole than women with some amount of college. In other words, college in prison reduces the amount of post-release crime and even more significantly heightens responsible compliance with parole expectations.

To What Extent Does Engagement in College and Completion of a Degree Affect Women's Psychological Sense of Themselves, Past, Present, and Future?

We review, now, how we analyzed the qualitative individual and focus group interviews for evidence of transformation. We were struck, in examining all of the data, with the extent to which women spoke of college as a source of personal change, transformation, and new selves. Theorizing

TABLE 5.2. Key Methodological Decisions

1. Create a research committee consisting of outside researchers and inmates with administrative advisors.

2. Teach inmates how to be researchers in a semester-long research methods college course.

3. Ensure a racial/ethnic mix in research committee leadership and focus group facilitators and co-facilitators.

4. Conduct focus group within prison with teen group children of inmates, rather than conduct interviews in teen homes.

5. Inmate researchers choose between anonymity and authorship.

6. Participants choose a name by which they are known in the report.

7. Sample: Include inmates who left college in sample and those in pre-college program.

8. Conduct focus groups, facilitated by inside and outside researchers, with sub-samples in order to:
   a) Pursue themes that emerged from individual interviews
   b) Maximize opportunities for dissenting opinions

9. Conduct individual interviews rather than focus groups for correction officers.

10. Interpretation session: Data analysis performed by inside and outside researchers.

11. Write final report in a single voice.

transformation, however, proved to be a multilayered task. The process of analysis moved us through four readings of transformation.

Initially we read all the transcripts and heard a discourse of split selves: As the research team first read through the transcripts, we noted recurring talk of old and new selves; the "before-college me" and "after-college me." Women in prison and those recently released repeatedly credited college with facilitating a personal change from their old ways to their new (read better) ways of life. With an intentional and sharp separation of old and new, the women drew clear distinctions between the "me before" and the "me now":

> **Ellie:** I'm not the same person that went to prison. If you knew me before, you would never know it's the same person. [I made] a complete turnaround. And I'm proud of that, 'cause I like me now . . . college made me face me and like me now.

> * * *

> **Denise:** When I first came to Bedford Hills, I was a chronic disciplinary problem, getting tickets [issued for disciplinary infractions] back to back. I had a very poor attitude as well, I was rude and obnoxious for no reason, I did not care about anything or anyone. . . . Then I became motivated to participate in a number of programs, one of which was college. I started to care about getting in trouble and became conscious of the attitude I had that influenced my negative behaviors. . . . College is a form of rehabilitation, one of the best.

Within this discourse of split selves, there was a particularly relentless attempt by the women to derogate their past selves. This, then, produced the occasion for our second reading through the transcripts. We wanted to avoid the tendency to rush too quickly through material that seemed obvious or superficial, even idiomatic. The research team reread and discussed the transcript sections on transformation, generating and pressing for deeper interpretations with each pass.

As the previous excerpts illustrate, we were interested to hear how harshly many of the women described their "former selves": angry, antisocial, drug abusers, disrespectful both to themselves and others, and having little to offer the world. These characterizations were typically followed by descriptions of complete and total personal changes: productive, working, motivated, knowledgeable, and worthy of pride. This trashing of women's past lives was read initially by graduate center researchers as a language of internalized self-blame and self-hatred:

> **Erica:** [Describing herself and her sister early in their incarceration.] 'Cause we were some wild kids when we were younger. We were angry. We didn't understand the system. This was our first time ever being in trouble. So all we wanted to do was fight. We didn't interact with anybody, we weren't social. So now [we're] like totally different. We look forward to coming to college. . . . And it's like I changed, just totally changed. And my sister came [to college] a couple of months afterwards and changed, but we did it together.

The inmate researchers, on the other hand, heard in the same transcripts a familiar language of redemption that echoed the kind of talk heard in counseling, twelve-step programs, support groups, church, and even in discussions about upcoming parole board meetings. An old, bad, unworthy, negative self is vilified and then redeemed as a new positive, productive, good self:

> **Roz:** [W]hen I first came here I had a chip on my shoulder that I wanted somebody to knock off . . . I stayed in trouble. I was disrespectful. I had no self-respect, no respect for others. And it took a while for me to change gradually through the years, and . . . when I started going to college that was like the key point for me of rehabilitation, of changing myself. And nobody did it for me, I did it for myself. . . . And I went and I did it and I accomplished things that I didn't think I could accomplish.

Together as researchers, we worried that this language, used by the women about themselves, sounded so much like the language used by those attacking women in poverty, women of color, and indeed women in prison. Thus, across the transcripts we analyzed for overlapping discourses of redemption as well as social ideologies that place blame for social problems squarely and exclusively within individuals (usually racialized), with no history and no context.

As we theorized the relationship between the discourses of redemption and derogation of poor women, inmate researchers reminded the research team of a simple fact, that though obvious, graduate center researchers had looked beyond: Crimes had been committed by most of the women with whom we spoke. The discourse of redemption, it was suggested, serves as a powerful coping strategy for women desperate to understand themselves as separate from the often destructive behavior that led them to prison. By staying within a story of two separate selves, women can assert judgment over their past actions without having to face the pain of integrating complicated histories—past selves now despised, past behavior now regretted—into their present selves. The task of analysis then became to look back across the data for "connective tissue" between past and present selves for instances where women reflect critically on their lives:

> **Rhonda:** [On documenting her past for her clemency petition.] [B]ut then just to sit down and read it all and discover that you don't even like half of this stuff here about you. But this is you. You know, you from you. And it was like, oooh! . . . so I [re-]wrote it and I read it and I re-read it and I re-wrote it and I sort of like condensed it [from 20 pages] into like about six pages . . . it was like really deep because it was no escaping then.

Through reconceptualizing past, present, and future selves as connected, we began to understand that personal change, or transformation, was not a simple declaration of starting anew with a clean slate. The women were trying to describe personal change or transformation as a process in which a woman recognizes her past, present, and future selves in relation to one another and within social context, both in and outside the prison. And most were articulating the role that college played in helping them draw these lines of connection.

Using this line of analysis, we resisted thinking of lives and selves as existing outside of social context, without community, without history. Further, we began to understand that women bring pieces of "old" selves into "new" selves, and that these pieces of the past selves inform and cocreate, within a social historical context, a present ever-changing self. And that college is one of those sites where women can, in a community, acquire a language and the skills of reflection through which these lines of connection can be drawn. Thus we undertook our third reading of the transcripts, seeking this connective tissue. For Sondra, a student, this means recognizing her multiplicity and negotiating which pieces of herself are useful in moving her life in the direction she chooses:

> **Sondra:** [Addressing past behavior that led to disciplinary problems.] It's still in my character, but I don't let it come out. It doesn't prove anything. Before, I didn't care. Now I see I can achieve, do anything I put my mind to. I have matured. . . . I can set examples now.

> * * *

> **Crystal:** I know the decision to continue my education will help me in the long run, yet my aspiration is to somehow help the young women who are coming into

prison in record-breaking numbers. My past allows me to speak from experience, and the academic knowledge I have obtained allows me to move forward productively, hopefully enabling me to help these younger women recognize and reach their potentials.

In Crystal's comment, we can see that recognizing these connections in oneself can lead to an understanding of self in community and responsibility across generations. Crystal sees her past in the younger women's presents, and her present in their futures. This recognition led our research team to a fourth stage of analysis, in which we sought evidence of transformation talk located within a discourse of community and social responsibility.

Finally, after many readings and much discussion, we came to see that a discourse of responsibility was operating to link old and new selves, and that the women viewed college as the intellectual and personal site where they could develop such a discourse in community while in prison. As fundamental, the women recognized that in the absence of programs like college, they would not have been able to move into re-viewing their pasts, re-seeing their crimes, and narrating a sense of responsibility for past and future:

> **Tanisha:** I can think and talk about my victim now. It's not just "the bitch cut me and I cut her back." Even that idea comes out differently now, "the girl cut me and I chose to strike back." Those words weren't in me before, but now, just having the words to articulate things, puts them into perspective differently.

> ⁕ ⁕ ⁕

> **Vanessa:** My involvement with college . . . has opened my eyes to all of the things that were wrong in my life. Now I have a sense of priority, a sense of accountability and I have made a legitimate premise for myself on which to build . . . my needs are still important, but not at someone else's expense.

As the women above testify, our quantitative and qualitative data confirm what other researchers and prisoners have found: Core elements of higher education, such as self-reflection and critical inquiry, spur the production of critical subjectivities, transformed and connected selves, and in turn, transformed communities (Conway, 1998; Germanotta, 1995; Faith, 1993; Rivera, 1995). These interior transformations in self bear significant consequences for the women and for their incarceration rates. Said another way, individuals move from being passive objects to active subjects—critical thinkers who actively participate in their lives and social surroundings, take responsibility for past and future actions, and direct their lives, networks, and social actions in the world. Moving across readings of the transformation narratives, we came to see the social–psychological links among college, transformation, and social responsibility. We turn now, to our transformations, as researchers on a participatory research team.

We Created Among Us: A Team of Women Scholars

A world may come into being in the course of a continuing dialogue. (Greene, 1995, p. 196)

As a team we met often, sometimes once a month, sometimes more, and sometimes less. Encumbered by limitations on privacy, freedom, contact, and time, we were as profoundly moved by our shared capacity and desire to climb over the walls that separate and carve a small delicate space of trust, reciprocity, and the ability to argue respectfully about what is important to study, to speak, and to hold quietly among ourselves.

In this space for critical inquiry, among us, we walked across barbed wires outside the windows and inside the room, through our racialized and classed histories, between biographies filled with too much violence and too little hope and biographies lined with too much privilege and too little critique. We engaged in what Paulo Freire (1982) would call "dialogue," a "relation of 'empathy' between two 'poles' who are engaged in a joint search" (p. 45). Freire deployed dialogue in an effort to provoke critical consciousness, which "always submits . . . causality to analysis; what is true today may not be so tomorrow" (p. 44). Freire sought to create educational spaces, in our case both a community of learners and a community of researchers, in which "facts" were submitted to analysis, "causes" reconsidered, and indeed "responsibility" reconceived in critical biographic, political, and historical context. The task, then, was not merely to educate us all to "what is," but to provoke analysis of "what has been" and release, as Maxine Greene would invite, our imagination for "what could be."

As one of the inmate researchers, Missy, explained:

> I look at this research project as a way of giving back, motivating, and hopefully helping the program and the participants, and even the researchers—I want them to hopefully have a different outlook on what education means in prisons. I'm hoping that we reach a younger generation. To pass on our stories.

And Yet: Between Us Inside and Out

This space of radical openness is a margin—a profound edge. Locating oneself there is difficult yet necessary. It is not a "safe" place. One is always at risk. One needs a community. (hooks, 1984, p. 149)

We are, at once, a team of semifictional coherence, and, on the ground, a group of women living very different lives, defined in part by biographies of class, race, and ethnic differences. Half of us go home at night; half of us live in prison. Many of us bring personal histories of violence against women to our work, while all of us worry about violence against, and sometimes by, women. Some of us have long-standing experiences in social movements for social justice; others barely survived on the outside.

Some of us are White, Jewish, Latina, Caribbean American, African American, and some mixed. Most of us are from the mainland of this country, but a few were born outside the borders of the United States. The most obvious divide among us is freedom vs. imprisonment, but the other tattoos and scars on our souls weave through our work, worries, writings, and our many communities. Usually these differences enrich us. Sometimes they distinguish us. At moments they separate us. We understand ourselves to carry knowledge and consciousness that are, at once, determined by where we come from and shaped by who we choose to be (Harding, 1983; Hartsock, 1983; Jaggar, 1983; Smith, 1987).

Pamela Smart, inmate researcher, writes that

> Most research on prisons is conducted by outside investigators. However, there is an incredible source of skills right inside these walls. Inmate researchers can establish a comfort zone with interviewees that many outside researchers cannot. Because a lot of people in prison are less trusting of outsiders, they may not be entirely forthcoming with their responses. However, inmate researchers, by the nature of their statuses as inmates, are often viewed by participants as more trustworthy. Just because I am in prison does not negate the fact that I am also a competent researcher. Using prisoners as researchers is a valuable experience that is beneficial to both the participants in the study and the readers of the results.

Questions of Design: How Participation Shifted Our Questions, Methods, Analyses, and Writings

We offer next a series of key methodological, ethical, and theoretical decisions we, as a team, made within the prison project and try to articulate what difference the participatory design made with respect to the questions we asked, the methods we deployed, the sample we selected, the procedures we undertook, the analyses we generated, and the writings we produced.

Creating the Conditions for Collaboration: The Undergraduate and Graduate Seminars

With the wisdom of C. Wright Mills (1959) and Franz Fanon (1967), and buoyed by the commitments of participatory researchers before us, we began our work with an understanding that full participation of all researchers requires common and complementary skills, understandings, trust, and respect. Artificial collaboration would have been easy to accomplish. Simply having women in prison around the table would have been an exercise in what Nancy Fraser (1990) recognizes as the bourgeois version of a public sphere: inviting political unequals to the table and calling that democracy. A number of the women from inside the prison were already published (Boudin, 1993; Clark, 1995), but most were not. Thus, from the start, we committed to working through questions of power, trust, and skill by offering a set of courses on research methods within the prison facility, an undergraduate course and a graduate seminar. In the undergraduate course, students were assigned a final project in which they would have to generate a specific question of personal interest under the larger umbrella question: "How does college impact the women in the facility, the prison environment, and the women and their children post-release?" Once questions were formed and re-formed, each inmate interviewed at least five other women about her question and analyzed, interpreted, and wrote up her results.

What was profound about this experience—a simple exercise in building a cadre of "inmate researchers"—was that the women came to see their personal experiences as fundamentally social and political. And they acquired research experience.

In the graduate seminar, the same kinds of social scaffolding occurred. Personal problems of "having a crazy neighbor who screams all night" unraveled crucial analyses of the politics of mental health and prisons. An offhand remark about the proliferation of gangs in women's prisons sparked a rich theoretical discussion of the power of college and other programs to create intellectual and political spaces for personal and community engagement.

Thus, a crucial feature of participatory work is the building of a community of researchers—this means shared skills, respect, trust, and common language. This does not, however, mean consensus.

Creating Space for Dissent and Insider Knowledge

As indigeneous researchers (Smith, 1999) and participatory action researchers have long recognized, insiders carry knowledge, critique, and a line of vision that are not automatically accessible to outsiders (Park, Brydon-Miller, Hall, & Jackson, 1993; QSE, 2000). There were three ways in which insider knowledge profoundly moved this project. First, prison staff and administrators, as well as inmates, simply know things that outsiders do not—for example, formal and informal procedures, lines of authority, practices, and their consequences. Second, insiders understand the profound connections between discrete features of a community that outsiders might erroneously see as separate and divisible. Understanding life at the intersections, as Kimberle Crenshaw (1991) has so beautifully articulated, is critical to the sustenance of an organization and can be perversely misunderstood by researchers who work to extract "variables" from the tightly woven fabrics of organizational life. And third, these insiders understand the power and politics of privilege, privacy, vulnerability, and surveillance.

Privacy, Vulnerability, and Surveillance

Women living in prison have little privacy. Layering a participatory research project atop of this absence of privacy seemed problematic to the graduate center researchers. Even in this facility—one recognized nationally as respectful, participatory, high on commitments to women's growth, and low on troubles—women's diaries and books have been searched during our time in the facility, notes taken away, poetry confiscated. Questions of where to store the data and still provide access to the inmates for analysis and interpretation continue to plague us as outsiders. Indeed at one point, one of the inmate researchers asked the appropriate question about exploitation: "So we just collect the data with you, and then you get to analyze and interpret it?"

Although all the inside interviews were co-conducted by an inmate and a graduate center researcher it was clear that the graduate center researchers would interview the corrections officers. Some inmates we interviewed wanted to change their names for the final report and others demanded that their original names be kept intact, pointing out that in too many instances they have been erased from the outside world. At many moments in our work, we would need a document, a report, or materials from offices around the prison. When an inmate would ask for such information, there might be nervous caution about giving her requested documents, and yet when one of the graduate center researchers would ask, she would more often be told, "take it—return it whenever you finish." These incidents constantly reminded us of the realities of being in a prison and about our denial about prison.

Self-Censorship: An Insider's Dilemma

An inmate doing research is also a person trying to survive and get out of prison. This dual reality is always present in the mind of the inmate researcher. As researchers and writers of the research, we are always looking for truths, or the closest that we perceive to be true. As prisoners we are always saying "Is it safe to say this?" "What kind of harmful consequences might flow from this either for ourselves personally or the program or individuals about whom we are writing?" Self-censoring is as much a part of being an inmate researcher as truth seeking.

We worry that writing something negative about the prison or a program may lead to negative consequences, removing those of us who are inmate researchers from a program, from one living unit to another, far from friends, or increasing pressure around any of the details of living in prison. As inmate researchers, we worry that defining negative truths may create tension between ourselves and the women with whom we live and work. Our relationships with our peers are a basis for survival. We live in a closed community in which everything is tied together. There is no exit.

All researchers have to make decisions about what to put in or take out of the research. These decisions relate to protecting individuals, communities, or groups or programs within a particular community. In this sense, insider researchers in a prison are not alone in making choices—many of these issues have been raised by Linda Tuhiwai Smith (1999) regarding indigeneous researchers and by feminists of color including Aida Hurtado (1996), bell hooks (1984), and Beth Richie (1996), all working on questions of gender and sexuality subordination within racialized communities. However, operating among these choices for inmate researchers is a tendency for self-censorship that is almost survival instinct. Self-censoring comes from the instinct of self-protection in a context that is one of total control over one's day-to-day living conditions, day-to-day work, and personal freedom.

Issues of Power Among the PAR Team

One of the values of qualitative research is its challenge of the traditional power relation between those who do the research and the object of the research, through a participatory process. But the realities and dynamics of prison, as the social context of this project, also affect the quality of work and the participation of the prisoner researchers in stated and unstated ways. As prisoners, we are always bounded by roles and rules of a closed institution. Some argue that we are in prison to be punished; others argue that we are here to be rehabilitated. But in any case, we are essentially objects who must be controlled. On the other hand, we are striving to take responsibility for our lives, to become active, responsible subjects. This conflict of roles and expectations plays itself out in our roles as researchers in this project.

As the research evolved over time, some of us felt more constraints. Inmate researchers each had some area of involvement, but we had less knowledge of the whole. What was our role and how did it differ from that of the "outsiders?" Toch (1967) argues that prisoners can be useful as translators or "bridgers" in the interviewing and analysis of the data. But what is their relationship to the larger project, its conclusions and results?

At points some inmate researchers felt cut off from the project. An inmate researcher explained these feelings as a series of plaguing questions: "Was it just my imagination? Should I raise this in a meeting? Would I be seen as an interloper, a troublemaker? Am I stepping over the bounds? Whose bounds? Who has the power?" Some of these power issues can be addressed by creating a process among all the researchers. But another dimension has to do with the great divide between inside and out, the very physical and practical nature of our being cut off and limited as prisoners. As *inmate* researchers, we cannot meet among ourselves without permission and oversight. We cannot tape-record interviews. At the end of the day, graduate center researchers leave and we stay.

As we moved toward the data analysis stage of the research project and each of us took on some writing, a few of us began to articulate some of these questions and concerns. The research team talked about how to overcome some of the restraints imposed by time and place. Transcripts of focus group interviews were brought in so that the insider researchers could read through them. This provoked a conversation about how to increase researcher access to the data without compromising the confidentiality and privacy of the participants. When two of the outside researchers raised the point that they were presenting some of our work at a conference outside, we discussed how to include the insiders' perspectives and spirits. These discussions went beyond seeking practical solutions, as we became aware of the dimensionality of time and space, shaping the contours of our collective efforts. Over time (time—that trickster enemy/ally of all prisoners!), particularly in the process of analysis and writing, we became a research team in which the distinctions between insiders and outsiders faded as other dimensions of our experiences emerged—women, mothers, graduate students, Spanish-speaking, comfortable with writing, spiritually focused, and so on. Our team had a life and a spirit, which grew inside our walls; now all of us together had to figure out how to transcend the walls to communicate what we had learned together.

As our work moved toward analysis of the data, our roles got fuzzier. Often the inmate researchers were the ones to caution against romanticizing inmates or using a highly politicized phrase like "the prison industrial complex," fearing that we would alienate our audience. We are not just "insiders," a term that denotes place. Most of us feel acutely responsible for the crimes that brought us here, and for the impact of our actions on others. We truly do feel for the public's anger about crime and feel responsibility to address the legitimacy of that anger in our work. But it is hard for us to climb out of our own sense of responsibility, to feel entitled to claim a critical voice. Our work with outside researchers, who brought their sense of freedom to level clear critiques of social policy so long as it was grounded in the data, stretched our capacities to think the unimaginable, to be socially responsible and critical.

Emotions at the Table

The consequences of our work are many. We research and write to document the impact of college on women in prison; to support the continuing of a college program, one that is on what one inmate researcher described as "sandy footing"; to encourage other prisons and universities to consider similar collaborations; and to illustrate the power of education in prison. On a personal level, we write to secure a program of which some of us are students, some are staff, and some are board members. These intimate relationships bring both a passion and fever to the work, as the future of the program moves between solid and unstable ground. The emotions that flow around this tenuous nature of the program impact our research effort as they demand time and space from us, often in our meetings together. In a research meeting it is common for us to flip-flop between hope and despair, possibility and fear as we face the realities of our relationships to the college program, the research, and to each other. These emotions and our commitments to reflexivity in our work at times leave us numb—the result of too many feelings. Sometimes in a research meeting we pause as a research member details the difficulty of registering new students eager to start the program with one or two courses, as she silently fears the program may close before these students graduate. Other times we deliberately stay clear of conversations that are too painful, keeping on task as a way to feel control when there is little available. We wrestle with how to communicate these emotions in our writings, how to honor their influence, without getting derailed. The context and physical environment of our research is harsh, noisy, and without privacy, by design. We sit, after all, in a maximum security prison where half of us are prisoners and all of us are human.

Lost Bodies

One of the challenges of participatory work is the coordination of bodies around the research table. People bring outside commitments, unexpected illness, and even unexplained absences due to hectic lives. At the prison we have the added challenge of working within the rules, regulations, and limitations set by the facility and the state. Inmate members of our research team have been randomly called out of our meetings by officers and at times have not been given notice about changes in meeting times. As inmates, Bedford researchers have little control over being called to the doctor, the visiting room, or even to a cherished trailer visit with family. One inmate researcher was transferred, mid-project, to a facility near the Canadian border, almost 500 miles away, while another inmate researcher has had to focus her energies on issues related to her case.

This movement of bodies in and out of our meetings has meant that, at points, the research has taken longer. At other moments, the process of updating one another has served to keep our articulations of the research clearer and more focused. In addition, the extra time we have been afforded through this process has strengthened our sense of being a true research "team," as our relationships have grown over time. Each struggle we have individually and collectively undergone has helped us to better understand one another's ideas and theoretical perspectives. Overall, when we sit around the research table we pay attention to who is missing and in this sense the bodies are never truly "lost." Rather, what results is a discussion and writing that is infused with the bodies, minds, thoughts, and spirits of the women, coresearchers, who have come and gone. And though our hearts often ache, our collective work, without question, is richer for it.

Audience

Throughout this project, we were constantly reminding one another, whether subtly or overtly, that we must consider our audience. The inmate researchers, in particular, were extremely cognizant of the public sentiment regarding our crimes and prisoners. We anticipated a hostile, angry audience bred in times when popular "tough on crime" attitudes prevailed. Probably because of our awareness regarding the animosity toward prisoners, the inmate researchers became our own worst enemies. We consistently work as self-censors. We play the roles of devil's advocates forecasting the concerns and arguments of those we imagine will challenge our findings.

Anticipating reaction outside of the prison was often overshadowed by the stark reality that both the inside and outside researchers also had to consider the prison administration's reaction. As the data collected were discussed and analyzed, strong opinions formed. Some of us wanted to include those opinions as part of our interpretation of the findings. However, as inmate researchers we often had to remind ourselves, while we might not actually suffer a typical prison "punishment" (e.g., cell confinement or loss of privileges), there was the risk that vocalizing strong opposition to some policies might result in our angering the very people who hold power over us. As a result, some voices have remained silent. The realization of our limitations has made some of us both disappointed and angry. Interestingly enough, though, those moments have seemed to weigh heavily on the outside researchers as well. Perhaps their concern results from the fact that the suppression of any one voice in the symphony of participatory action research alters the final composition of the project.

Questions of Generalizability

There were many moments in this work, particularly in writing the final report (Fine et al., 2001) and even in writing this chapter, when we sought to understand what is particular to the Bedford Hills experience of college in prison, but just as important, which findings and dynamics are generalizable to other contexts. This question is often asked of qualitative material—if the analysis is so rich, context dependent, and particularized, have we learned anything that can be taken to other contexts?

We believe, with respect to both the substance of college in prison and the praxis of participatory work, that there is much to be generalized. In this project, as in all other projects with which we are connected, we begin with a commitment to theorize the relations of the part to the whole. We ask here and in universities, high schools, community-based organizations, and prisons around the nation: How does education in general transform young adult lives, biographies, and sense of possibility?

How does achievement, earning a diploma, and graduation further affect sense of self and responsibility to community? How do mothers returning to college affect children's academic well-being? How does college afford social critique and personal responsibility? Certainly there are specific features of this prison, with this college at this moment in time, that shape the experience and consequences, but there are also significant dynamics that carry across time and space. The specific features of local communities and resources will vary in rural Minnesota, in a men's prison, or a community college on a Native reservation. But some of the deep complex relations of education, voice, and community appear to resonate across very divergent contexts.

Turning to participatory research, we discover that here, too, many of the issues that have plagued—and defined—our work together are knotty for any group of insiders working within an organization. On topics such as domestic violence in Native communities, racism within gay men's organizations, sexism in a Black church, exploitation of domestic labor in suburban White communities, or domestic violence within the lesbian community, we have met insider researchers and practitioners who have self-censored, worried that the material was "too hot" and would be used against the community, and feared that the researcher would be shunned, the research attacked, and the story further silenced. And in each instance, the researchers ultimately figured out ways to talk about the material so that the right questions of theory, politics, and practice could be opened up. And so we place the concerns of women inmate researchers writing from within prison inside a broad, ethical community of scholars working on critical issues within the local webs of organizational and community life.

How Do We Ever Walk Away?

As we enter the final stages of the research, many of us have been filled with the mixed emotions of pride, hope, and sadness. There is a shared sense of pride in the success of our collective efforts and the potential for our work, hope that this potential will be fulfilled, and sadness that to end this project will end our ability to meet regularly and that we will therefore lose our personal relationships and intellectual intimacy. Again the reality of working across razor wire and steel bars reminds us of the limitations of our social positions.

How do we continue what is no longer allowed? An inmate researcher, perhaps in an attempt to move beyond her own feelings of loss, describes the oncoming transition as "arriving at dessert," recognizing that once the project is over we can indulge in all the digressions and tangential conversations that were put aside due to the time constraints of our rigorous research agenda. But, of course, we are not allowed to bring in food.

What Is to Be Gained From PAR?

We spent much time, as a research collective, discussing what is to be gained from PAR. There are, of course, the instrumental gains—insiders know more, know better, and know in more complicated detail how an organization, a community, and indeed a prison operates. Outsiders, in contrast, have the freshness to ask the deliberately naïve questions (Kvale, 1996) and have the relative freedom to speak a kind of truth to power that may provoke new lines of analysis. We dance between detachment and engagement. Yet, on reflection, rarely did we operate as two separate and coherent constituencies. Instead we grew to be, over time, a group of women with very distinct and sometimes overlapping commitments, questions, worries, and theoretical and political concerns. And yet . . .

In prison, as in any institution under external surveillance, insiders know details of daily life, understand the laser-like penetration of external scrutiny, and are more likely to refuse to simply romanticize—or pathologize— what happens within. Indeed, in our collaborations it has been the inmate researchers who recognized that our design needed to include dissenting voices, narratives of critique, and perspectives from dropouts. It is entirely possible that if outsiders alone collected the qualitative material we would have gathered material that would have been essentially a Hallmark card of praise for the program, collecting discourses of redemption, transformation, and positive effect, unchallenged and underscrutinized. "Research performances" of the good student would likely have gone unchallenged. In contrast, inmate researchers are able and willing to say in an interview, "Are you kidding, *you* have changed? You just got a ticket," identify a correction officer known to be ambivalent about or hostile to the college, or arrange an interview with a recently arrived young woman member of a gang not yet ready for college. To the question, "Don't the inmates *bias* the research design in favor of positive results?" we respond that the inmates, far more than the outsider researchers, knew where to gather more problematic material, knew how to press for complex—not just sugar-coated—responses, and consistently refused to romanticize inmates as powerless or victims.

Inmate researchers understand intimately and thereby theorize profoundly the complex interconnections that constitute prison life, both as inmates and as researchers within the facility. Although graduate center researchers assumed college to be a variable connected to, but relatively insulated from, other aspects of prison life, the inmates understood the connections that had to be recognized. Thus, for example, we learn that due to a recent shift in disciplinary policy in the facility, women can no longer bring pens out to the yard. Anyone seeking or offering tutoring or homework assistance on the yard must be denied—or helped with a crayon. With metal detectors and sometimes pat-frisking required for women to enter the yard, the numbers who do go to the yard have diminished. Tutoring, study groups, and homework assistance in the yard have dwindled. A seemingly remote policy has a profound impact on the college community. Outsiders would never have guessed.

PAR may indeed bend toward a kind of "strong objectivity," as Sandra Harding (1983) would say, because we pool our many partial truths toward understanding the power of college in prison. But PAR also provides an interior legacy and power—within the prison—of respect for insider knowledge and recognition of inmate authority. This research project refuses to speak *for*, but stretches to speak *with*. Inmate "subjects" are not exploited or edited by outsiders, as much as a hybrid team of women have worked together with deeply contradictory material to produce an analysis of rigor, policy, and respect.

So, to the question "What is to be gained from PAR?" we answer that all research is collaborative and participatory, even though typically respondents are given code names and rarely acknowledged as coauthors. More researchers must acknowledge the co-construction of knowledge and that material gathered from, with, and on any community—including a prison—constitutes a participatory process.

We believe, in this work, that we have simply—and with enormous effort—recognized the profound influence of collaboration that is constitutive of research. Insiders *and* outsiders know much, and know much deeply. Between us there is a powerful co-construction of critical knowledge about the effects of college on prison life. We consider participatory work simply an acknowledgment of the strength of our intellectual and action-based collaboration.

CHAPTER **6**

Extraordinary Conversations
in Public Schools

Lois Weis and Michelle Fine

Over the past 25 years, scholars have amassed an impressive array of work
aimed at uncovering the ways in which schools reproduce social inequalities. Forming a corpus of structuralist interpretation, such studies wind
through the ways in which curriculum (Apple, 1982; Anyon, 1983; Gaskell,
1992), standardized testing (Haney, 1993), political economy and bureau-
cratic organization (Anyon, 1997), teacher practices (Kelly & Nihlen,
1982), and university preparation (Ginsberg, 1988) serve to sustain
broader social inequalities. Although it is well understood that schooling
plays a crucial role in offering opportunities for individual social mobility,
it does, at the same time, serve to perpetuate and indeed legitimize wide-
spread structural inequalities.

   Much work over the past 20 years focuses on the ways in which social
inequalities along racial, social class, and gendered lines are sustained
through schools. And, indeed, we have contributed writing in this area
(Fine, 1991; Weis, 1990; Weis & Fine, 1993). Recent excellent work has also
been done on the ways in which schools inscribe heterosexuality and able-
bodiedness through curriculum and social practices as well (Barry, 2000;
Fine, 1988; Friend, 1993; Sapon-Shevin, 1993; Whatley, 1991). Additional
work has focused on the ways in which students themselves, through resis-
tant cultures, further inscribe their own subordinate positions (Giroux,
1983; Solomon, 1992; Valli, 1983; Willis, 1981) along social class, race, and
gendered lines. In the case of gender, for example, Angela McRobbie

(1978) has argued persuasively that it is the girls' own culture, even more than what the school expects of girls, that ensures their (our) position in an ongoing set of patriarchal structures.

This vibrant research agenda has taken us a long way toward understanding how it is that schools sustain that which they purport to eliminate. Nevertheless, in examining the reproduction of social inequalities we may camouflage those truly outstanding moments in today's schools: instances of teachers and kids working against the grain to create more critical and egalitarian structures, to imagine more open opportunities for all, and to truly challenge all that is inscribed in the American Mosaic. These spaces (Katz, 1996; Keither & Pile, 1993) reflect and blend many of the commitments of critical race theorists (e.g., Delpit, 1988; Foster, 1997; Ladson-Billings, 2000; Matsuda, 1995), feminist pedagogy (Ellsworth, 1989; Lather, 1991), and resistance theorists (Cochran-Smith & Lytle, 1992; Giroux, 1983), but with a profound sense of place and space borrowed from radical geographers such as Katz (1996) and Keither and Pile (1993). Organized to create and sustain a sense of intellectual and political community among differences, with a critical eye on power asymmetries within and outside the room, these educators have crafted rich and fragile spaces within public schools—currently sites of enormous surveillance and pressure toward reproduction. Here we wish to honor two such instances of forceful pedagogy that deliberately and directly challenge inequity and that are sustained over time by critical educators working toward a larger political and intellectual project. We suggest, then, that these disruptions deserve critical understanding as politically and pedagogically strategic moments, within traditional schools, for identity and movement work.

Social Spaces for Challenge

Data reported here were collected as part of a larger study on urban spaces (Weis & Fine, 2000; Fine, Weis, Centrie, & Roberts, 2000). As we have argued elsewhere, education does not take place just in schools, as anthropologists have long contended. It occurs at dinnertime, in front of the television set, on street corners, in religious institutions, in family planning clinics, and in lesbian and gay community groups. In the deindustrializing Northeast, those cities ravaged by the collapse of the private sector and the often wholesale abandonment of the public sphere wrought by late 20th-century capitalism, poor and working-class youth sometimes are fortunate enough to find the strength and fortitude to continue educating themselves and one another in spaces they craft and tenaciously hold on to, often against great odds. Young men and women are finding unsuspected places within their geographical locations, even their educational institutions and their spiritual lives, to sculpt real and imaginary corners for peace, solace, communion, social critique, and personal and collective work. These are spaces of deep, sustained community-based educative work—in many cases, outside the bounds of formal schooling.

Serious (re)educative work can flourish in these spaces. Not necessarily rigidly bounded by walls or fences, these spaces often are corralled by a series of fictional borders where trite social stereotypes are precariously contested. Young men and women, in constant confrontation with harsh humiliating public representations of their race, ethnicity, gender, class, and sexuality, use these spaces to re-educate, to break down public representations for scrutiny and invent new ones. It is within this broader theoretical context that the two projects discussed here were conceived. Unlike many of the other sites connected to our larger theoretical project, though, these two are set specifically in public schools and focus on youth, as well as the adults who are connected to these youth, and begin with the following questions: How do adults establish and secure an environment within which critical re-educative work with and for youth can flourish across social class, race, and gender lines? And how do students participate in environments that stretch toward this end?

Political scientist Nancy Fraser (1993) argues that it is advantageous for "marginals" to create what she calls "counterpublics," where they may oppose stereotypes and assert novel interpretations of their own shifting identities, interests, and work. She theorizes that these are formed, ironically, out of the very exclusionary practices of the public sphere. We, too, have found that in the midst of disengagement by the public sector and relocation of private sector jobs "down south," or, more likely overseas, it is into these newly constructed "free spaces" as Evans and Boyte (1992) would call them, that poor and working-class men, women, boys, and girls have fled from sites of historical pain and struggle and reconstituted new identities. It is to these free spaces that we have been led. Together and separately, young people are shaping identities that do and do not resist the structures around them; that will and will not transform their material conditions; that at base promise to inspire re-educative possibilities and new ways to produce "common sense" and to re-imagine social possibilities.

We offer here a theoretical extension of our previous work in this regard. In two public schools we observe and participate with committed adults who push the boundaries of what "would be." These are educators who intentionally and self-consciously challenge the reproductive instincts of public education and create spaces where youth can challenge "common sense" about themselves as well as others and engage intellectual and political projects that are, indeed, counter-hegemonic. Further, these are not simply liberatory spaces for historically oppressed or marginalized youth, but perhaps more pedagogically treacherous, they are integrated sites where youth with biographies of privilege sit side by side with youth from circumstances of poverty, working for a public common understanding across lines of race, ethnicity, and geography. And finally, these educators are not simply engaged in practices of resistance, but they have designed and crafted spaces of public responsibility and intellect, carved by a racially and ethnically diverse group of educators for youths in ways that can easily (and accurately) anticipate opposition from community members, administrators, colleagues, some parents, and many youth.

In so doing, we argue that counterpublics, such as those described by Fraser and others, can and do exist in public arenas such as schools. As the public sphere packs up and walks away from poor and working-class youth, it is absolutely essential for the community to reclaim these spaces. Those of us who work with public schools cannot sit by and accept that schools do no more than reproduce social inequalities, though this may certainly be the case much of the time. We must engage in the creation and protection of counterpublics—spaces where adults and youth can challenge the very exclusionary practices currently existing in public institutions—practices that inscribe inequalities by social class, race, gender, and sexuality.

We have no illusions about the ease, political or pedagogical, of creating or sustaining these spaces—indeed, we are sure (and have lots of evidence) of the likely resistance. We write, instead, with respect for the efforts that are going on and hope to join a public conversation of support for such educational practices within (not despite) the public sphere of public education. As we suggest here, it is not enough to let this form of challenge go on in alternative sites, as important as these alternative sites might be (Bertram et al., 2000; Fine, Weis, Centrie, & Roberts, 2000; Weis & Fine, 2000; Morton-Christmas, 1999; Reichert, 2000). Here we focus on two projects that push against the grain: the first, a voluntary girls group that meets in an urban magnet school in Buffalo, New York; and the second, a detracked 9th grade social studies class in Montclair, New Jersey.

Pushing the Borders of Gender and Race

Data for the first project considered here were gathered during spring semester 1997 at Arts Academy, a 5–12 magnet school geared toward the arts in Buffalo, New York. Students must be accepted into the school on the basis of an audition in dance, theater, music, visual arts, or radio and TV.

The school draws broadly from the city of Buffalo, although many of the students reside in poor and/or working-class neighborhoods within a 10-minute ride of the school. The school is located just south of downtown Buffalo and, like all magnet schools in the city, as part of the desegregation plan, ostensibly acts as a magnet for White students to attend school in neighborhoods populated by people of color. The school is highly mixed racially and ethnically, having 44% White, 45% African American, 8% Latino/Latina, 1% Native American, and 1% Asian students. The ethnic/racial montage is everywhere visible, as students from varying backgrounds participate in academic and arts endeavors, spanning jazz combo to ballet.

Data were drawn from a within-school program entitled My Bottom Line, a program whose officially stated goal is "to prevent or delay the onset of sexual activity, build self-esteem and increase self-sufficiency in young women through an abstinence-based, gender-specific prevention education program." Students voluntarily attend the program during study halls, participating one or two times a week, depending on the schedule. The guidance counselor actively recruited Womanfocus, a non-profit agency designed to deliver the program to local area schools. It has the strong backing of the guidance counseling staff, and group meetings were held in the large, centrally located conference room of the guidance office.

As Shirley, the guidance counselor, states:

> I really want these girls to take good risks with their lives and escape negative situations. I want them to be empowered to make good choices, to be able to leave town for college, to take internships, to take advantage of opportunities, to be able to leave their neighborhoods. Too many are trapped. I want them to delay sexual activity without being a prude so that they will be able to live fuller lives. Too many of these girls don't realistically see what a baby does to one's life. They have babies to make up for their own lost childhood and want to give to the baby what they themselves did not have. But they do not have the resources or maturity to give to their baby what they didn't have.

Shirley invited Womanfocus into the school and used all school resources possible to support the program. She talked with teachers on a regular basis, urging them to send students during their study halls, and worked with teachers to facilitate this.

My Bottom Line is run by Doris Carbonell-Medina, Esq., a Latina Womanfocus staff member.[2] Lois participated in all meetings for a full semester and acted, at times, as co-facilitator of the group. The program runs for 15 weeks. Although the program targets young women in 7th, 8th, and 9th grades, young women from grades 7–12 participated, at the explicit request of Doris. Seventh and 8th graders meet together, and high school students meet in a different session.

The expressed intention of the program is one of encouraging abstinence among girls who are not yet sexually active—generally those in the 7th, 8th, and 9th grades—and this is, in fact, where the funding is (Mecklenburg & Thompson, 1983; Wilcox, 1998).[1] However, Doris insists on working with the older girls as well, specifically tying her decision to the rhetoric of abstinence:

> Many people interpret abstinence-based programs as, you know, very conservative, sort of right wing, concepts. Like that abstinence means they have to be "clamped shut," and you're saying, "that's it." And that's why we target those 7th, 8th, and 9th grade girls, because those are the years that they're going to be facing those crucial decisions in their life, as to whether or not they want to be having sex. And those are the years that girls choose this for their lives. But, on the other hand, those high school girls that have already made that choice [to have sex], or some that haven't, they also need some sort of intervention, and that knowledge that simply because you've been sexually active in one relationship doesn't mean that you have to be sexually active in another relationship. And, you know, young girls need to be given that information, or at least to be given the confidence to say, "Hey, you don't have to sleep around with every single guy." There are some standards that you should have. There are some criteria that you should have in establishing your relationships. And I think those lines get blurred once you become sexually involved, and once you get into that whole world of adolescence and sex.

This space was, then, in addition to dealing with issues of sexual abstinence, intentionally established in order to empower young women, particularly in their relationships with young men. For Doris and Shirley, women's bodies must be under the control of women themselves and should not be a site for male control, abuse, or exploitation. Both state strongly that women need to evidence choices over their bodies and minds and that the lack of such choices means that these young teen women will never venture outside their neighborhoods or their lived economic marginality. Empowering them to stay away from situations of abuse lies at the center of the unofficial programming. This is not, then, simply a program about abstinence, although the abstinence strain is there. Here, mainstream sexuality education curricula are used as the basis for important discussions about gender, sexuality, and, indirectly, race.

In this space, which adults establish and facilitate, teens actively interact. Although the official intent of My Bottom Line is sexual abstinence, there is much other work going on in this site, both by adults and youth, which offers it as a powerful space for re-visioning gendered and race subjectivities as students gain a set of lenses and allies for doing social critique. As we have argued elsewhere, most youth have the potential for social critique, but this critique fizzles as they grow older (Fine, 1991; Fine & Weis, 1998; Weis & Fine, 1996). Here we focus on the preliminary consolidation of critique and enter the site, as Lois lived in it and worked with it for 6 months. It is the gender and race work we visit here, work done under the explicit tutelage of Doris Carbonell-Medina, Esq.

Baring Secrets

A cornerstone of the group is confidentiality, which enables the girls to bare secrets without fear of recrimination or gossip. As Doris states:

> I tell them at the very beginning that this issue I take very seriously. And when we say that in order to build trusting relationships, in order to build relationships [in the group] where we can open up and tell our stories, that we have to be mature. And mature means that you don't go around and you gossip and stuff. Then I say that I get so crazy about this stuff that if it comes back to me that you've opened your mouth and blabbed—and that's how it's seen—you know, we'd ask you to leave. And that would be the way that we separate you from us, because we don't want you to be in our group if you can't keep our secrets. They're very careful about it I tell you. And they don't reveal anything [in group] that they don't want people to know. And then, if they've really got to get it out—and many of them have done this to me—they have said, "Can I talk to you after the group?"

Embedded in the weaving of a new collective of young women across race lines is the baring of secrets. The group is a space where young women tell a great deal about their personal lives—the illnesses within their homes, the violence in their relationships, their fears spoken aloud when their "stepfather's moving back in with mom." Girls share secrets as they share strength and hope, jumping in to help one another with problems, sometimes life threatening, and other times mundane. As they share secrets, they examine themselves and weave new identities, individual and collective. What is particularly striking in these data is the extent to which young White women reveal pieces of their lives normally not told. Although they are relatively quiet in group, as compared with African American girls, for example, those who do open up contest the suffocating silence that envelops them. White women, whether adolescents or adults, are the most silent/silenced group with which we have worked (Weis & Marusza, 1998), speaking softly about the horrors in their lives only in one-to-one interviews, never in a group context. But not so here. White girls are cracking that silence so typical of the group, sharing secrets in protected environments, working beyond the one-to-one encounters. They are hearing one another out as they unburden their problems. Girls from a variety of backgrounds unravel their stories within the group context. Listen to Tiffany, who speaks with Lois and Tia in group:

Tiffany: I love my mother dearly. But, OK, she's manic depressive, but I love her dearly.

Lois: Is she really manic depressive?

Tiffany: Yeah, like she's got medication and everything. She's a manic depressive and my dad is schizophrenic—which is great for me [sarcastically]. . . . She doesn't make friends easily. I have to watch what I say, because I don't want to get her in a bad mood. She's on medication now. She's very caring, but she's smothering. Like, it's my birthday Monday, right. I'm like, since I was like nine, I have like, each birthday, I have a half an hour later that I can stay up. I mean, right now it's 9:30, and all my friends are sitting there going to bed at 11:00. And on Monday, I get to go to bed at 10:00 and that makes me so happy because I can go to bed at 10:00 [laughs].

Tiffany speaks candidly about her clinically ill parents, weaving through her discussions throughout the term her own feelings as she attempts to live in her mother's house. She is not the only one who speaks so openly about home-based problems, and the uniqueness of this, particularly among White girls, should not be underestimated. My Bottom Line offers a space where such secrets can be shared. Tiffany, of course, does not receive professional help in a group of this sort. What she does receive is support and understanding from her peers, monitored by an adult who is sensitive to these issues. In addition, and perhaps most important, Tiffany feels less alone with her problems since she has shared them and learned, oftentimes, that she is not the only one who has them. While teenagers, to be sure, often complain about their parents, this should not be seen simply as a "gripe session." Tiffany's parents are ill, and the sharing of this information, like the sharing of incidents of domestic violence or of violence in a personal relationship, represents one step toward acknowledging the problem and obtaining long-term help. Doris meets regularly with the girls outside the group and urges them, in a more confidential context, to seek additional help.

Distancing

Able to bare secrets, young women use the space of the program to fashion and refashion individual and collective identities. Under Doris's expert guidance, it is a space where selves are tried on, experimented with, accepted, and rejected. A key piece of this identity work among participants involves distancing themselves from those perceived as "not like us." In this space, in this time, they pull away from others. Unlike previous work, however, that suggests that this form of identity work in urban schools takes place largely along we/they racial lines (Bertram et al., 2000; Fine & Weis, 1998; Fine,

Weis, & Powell, 1997; Weis, 1990), particularly among working-class Whites, and most particularly boys and men, the particular form this distancing work takes here is that of distancing from other neighborhood youth, and, more broadly, from other girls or women thought to be heading down the wrong path. Virtually all of the girls, irrespective of race and ethnicity, who attend group use the space to distance themselves explicitly from those they perceive to be "other" than themselves: those who will not make it, those who will end up pregnant at an early age, those who will be beaten at the hands of men. This is not an idyllic presentation of cross-race interactions and friend-ships, but rather reflects the observation that when "difference" is con-structed in group, it is not constructed along racial lines. Girls from all communities articulate carefully that they wish to be different from those in their neighborhoods, those whom they leave behind in their pursuit of schooling and success. Although this may not translate into intimate friend-ships across racial/ethnic lines, it does mean that the racial "other" is not constructed as the "fall guy" for any of the groups under consideration, con-trasting sharply with Julia Hall's data on girls in a White lower-class commu-nity center (2001). For none of the groups under consideration are the racial borders specifically erected against which one's own identity is then elabo-rated. Rather, identity is elaborated across racial and ethnic groups as girls distance themselves from the "other," whether male or female, who will not make it. Certainly there is much racial identity work going on in other sites that reaffirms Whiteness, for example, in opposition to Blackness, much as previous work suggests (Bertram et al., 2000; Weis, Proweller, & Centrie, 1997). However, in this site alternative positionalities are developed.

Witness Connie and Ayisha below. Connie is a White girl of modest means who lives in one of the racial borderlands of Buffalo, a place that is formerly Italian but now largely Puerto Rican and African American. Although Connie draws an "other," this other is racially like self:

> We live in a really small house. I don't have the things my friends have, like all of them at this school are having big graduation parties; I asked my mom to get some small invitations from Party City so that we could at least have the family over; she hasn't even done that. I guess I won't have any celebration. All my friends are having these really big parties. They all have much more money than we do. We live in a really small house; I have a really small bedroom. My one sister lives with us with [her] two kids; another sister lives in a house owned by my father on 14th Street. All my sisters are on welfare. We have been on welfare when my father wasn't driving truck. When he lost his job, we didn't even have food in the house. I would go over to my boyfriend's house to eat. His parents are real nice to me. I have no friends in the neighborhood. All I know is that I don't want to be like my sisters and my mother. Their lives have gone nowhere. I don't want to be like them. I want to have lots of money—and food. I want to go to college [she is currently attending the community

college].... My dad is an alcoholic. He drinks all the time. One time he grabbed my mom's face and held it really hard. He really gets out of control when he drinks. I don't let him put me down though—I just tell him off.

Connie spends much time in the group discussing her own emotional and physical distancing from her alcoholic father, her immediate family, and her neighborhood. The group offers a safe space in which she can air these problems and receive support for remaining emotionally separate from her family, for not being dragged down. At the moment, her boyfriend also offers this safe space. He is 23; they are engaged, having met 3 years ago. The group supports this couple, although concerned that Connie might fall into a pattern of drinking like her father. Doris and the other group members check to make certain that Arturo (her boyfriend) is not abusing her physically. Unlike other White girls and women whom we have interviewed extensively, Connie and other group members talk relatively freely about family histories of alcoholism and physical and sexual abuse, thus engaging in a language through which their and others' circumstances can be understood. In putting this language on the table, they bury such histories far less often than previous research suggests (Weis, Fine, Bertram, Proweller, & Marusza, 1998). Additionally, in breaking the silence about alcoholism, welfare, and violence in the White family, they shatter the myth that the White family has no problems, thereby encouraging young women across race/ethnicity to understand that such problems are indeed shared, as well as helping young women to face their own situations.

Ayisha, a 16-year-old African American woman who has a 1-year-old daughter, also sees her task as one of distancing herself from the neighborhood in which she grew up. This distancing is nuanced, however, since she is entirely dependent on her family, boyfriend, and her boyfriend's family in order to raise her daughter. She walks a fine line—needing to distance herself from those who will hold her back, but simultaneously needing to recognize and respect those who help her move forward. All live in the same neighborhood, which Ayisha discusses here:

Actually there is a small percent who are going to do something with their lives. I hate to see 'em like that, but it's like they're all going to go off, smoke weed and drink, go to parties, and hang around the fellows. You know, my mother always told me, "it's not ladylike to sit there and drink on the corner." It's just . . . I mean, they just don't care about their body. It's terrible to see. And I'll be trying to say, you know, I have some friends and they go do that. And I'll be like "You all shouldn't do that." "Well, just because you don't do it . . . " "OK. Whatever. Whatever you decide to do, I'm behind you. If that's what you're doing, OK, that's what you're going to do." But they're always calling me a preacher or something, you know, every time I try to talk to them.

Many of these young women, particularly the African Americans, are very much connected to their families and neighborhoods, passionately caring about what happens in their communities, while drawing discursive boundaries around themselves that enable them to go to school and stay on the right track. They engage the "other" constantly, telling them that they are going down the wrong path, while setting them up as radically different from themselves.

This work of "othering" is done similarly across race and ethnic lines in the group, thus rewriting dominant race scripts of difference in poor areas (Fine & Weis, 1998) at the same time that they sculpt alternative forms of femininity and womanhood. All are concerned with elaborating a positive present and future for themselves and see themselves in relation to community "others": those who do drugs, drink to excess, wear tight clothes, sleep with a lot of guys, walk the streets, do not take school seriously, or see older men. The group provides an arena for dialogue, a space within which these constructions get worked through, between, and among participants. Witness, for example, the 8th grade group below:

Lois: OK, talk to me about the women in your community.

Krista: About 10:20 they come out. [laughter]

Danielle: Just about every girl, like, on my street, had babies when they were about 14, 15. . . .

Krista: And I know this one girl, she doesn't live on my street anymore, but she had a baby when she was like 14 or 15, and she went back to the same guy and got pregnant again, so now she's got two kids. And I don't know a lot like that. But I know her, because she used to baby-sit me when I was little, but I don't know if he's there and will come back to her, you know, better and everything. But she got pregnant again.

Lois: What about some of the other women?

Shantelle: Well, some of them is fast. They talk to the boys on the corner. All boys on the corner is not bad. They wear a lot of showy clothes.

Tonika: I was watching Jenny Jones, this 12-year-old girl, she wore so much make-up, she acts like she's about 23. And the make-up and stuff. All these girls had these shirts like this [indicates very short], their chest sticking out. I mean, all these short shorts, look like underwear.

Tish: My underwear is not going to be that short.

Tonika: I mean, they're wondering why they'd be getting raped and stuff, even though it's [rape] wrong, but if you walk out of there with your chest sticking out in some short shorts, which is what they do, it's kind of like, what kind of attention you're going to get? You think you're going to get positive attention, you know?

Shantelle: OK. A lot of girls like have babies around my neighborhood. They don't have an education, so like they are kind of, they're low educated, ain't got no money, broken down house and everything, and they're talking to the people in the weed house and everything.

Gloria: The girls around my neighborhood, they all "Hos." And they wear nasty outfits, and they go out with older guys.

Delores: They [older guys] just be using, they use you, and they have like three other girlfriends, and they try to play it off. When they get caught, they'd be trying to like, well, you shouldn't have been doing all this, and all that stuff. And they [the girls] can't do nothing about it.

The 8th grade group, most of whom are African American in this particular session, use the space to talk about "other" girls and women in the neighborhood, carefully distancing themselves from them and asserting that they are different. By publicly solidifying the boundaries of good behavior, they hope to hang together and remain without problems.

This actual (and potential) discursive work takes place across racial and ethnic groups. The fall guy is not a constructed racial other, as is so common in urban (and suburban; Kress, 1997) schools, but rather those neighborhood youth who are perceived to be headed down the wrong path. In the case of young women, it is those other girls and women, those who are fast, wild, and wear tight clothes, who enact femininity and sexuality differently from what they feel is appropriate and safe, and who provide the primary "other" against which their own individual and emerging collective self is created. While this may seem to mirror the good girl/bad girl distinction that is so deeply etched in male culture, and indeed it does in some ways, the fact is that these young women are working cross-racially to live productive lives, lives that enable choices to be made and that are free from abuse. The young 8th graders know that the "older guys just be using them [these other girls]"; they have "three other girlfriends, and they try to play it off." When the guys are caught, they blame the young women for doing something wrong— "You shouldn't have been doing this and that." These 13-year-old girls understand this well and use the group to talk about it. It is exactly this situation that they are trying to avoid, and they know that things only get worse as women grow older. They want to stay in school in order to assert some control over their lives and enable themselves to make choices regarding sexuality, men, marriage, and a future devoid of physical and sexual abuse and harassment. While the officially stated goal of My Bottom Line is to encourage abstinence, much more is happening in this context; it can be argued that young women are weaving a form of collective strength that goes beyond individual abstinence—they are gaining a set of lenses through which to perform social critique and are opening up the possibility of cross-race political work in the future.

It is most interesting in this regard that while "race work" is not in the official curriculum of this project, it is done all the time. The distancing discussed above, which is a by-product of baring secrets, encourages a form of gender collectivity that works across traditionally antagonistic race lines. Abstinence work, on the other hand, which is the official curriculum, is done some of the time, raising interesting questions as to what constitutes the lived curriculum as opposed to the intended curriculum of this or any other project. Curriculum theorists (Apple, 1982; Cornbleth, 1990; McNeil, 1986) have, of course, alerted us to the fact that what is distributed as curriculum in actual classrooms bears, at times, little resemblance to what is seen as the legitimate curriculum (that which is written). The same dynamic is at play here. Doris intentionally stretches what is presented to these teen women as she moves well beyond notions of abstinence in her own understanding of what these young ladies need. The girls, too, stretch the project in that they interact with what is presented and create something new, in this case, a girls' collectivity that works across race lines. By baring their secrets, they create a community, at least in this space at this time, which transcends individual racial and even social class identities. It is the dialectic of lived curriculum creation that is so noteworthy in this particular context—the context of teaching about abstinence. We will see this even more clearly in the next section.

In a contradictory way, of course, these young women, while struggling for their own future health and safety, are positioning themselves as different from "like others" in their communities of origin, thus cutting themselves off potentially from what Robinson and Ward (1991) refer to as group-based "resistance for liberation." At the moment, though, any potential future psychic pain involved in this move and possible inability to do future political work around categories of community of origin cannot be acknowledged. Indeed, it can be argued that these young women must engage in such a move, even if only temporary, in order to save themselves from what they fear is their fate. The moment of disruption chronicled here is not, though, without its own contradictions.

Contesting Social Stereotypes

Spaces such as this can offer places where trite social stereotypes are contested, where individuals and collectivities challenge definitions and constructions perpetuated through media, popular culture, and so forth. This is highly evident in this group in that the girls use the space, under the guidance of Doris, to challenge hegemonic constructions of femininity and race. Doris's role here is important. She urges these young women not to accept prevailing constructions of femininity and masculinity and to challenge race and gender scripts directly.

February 10, 1997 (Field Notes)

Doris and I [Lois] were waiting for the girls to come in for group. Just then Tia walked in for the fifth-period meeting. Tia talked about her former boyfriend who got a 13-year-old girl pregnant and "now it is too late to do anything about it since it is her fourth month." The girl lives two doors down from her. Her mother's best friend is the mother of the young man involved, and that is how she found out. They had broken up already because she [Tia] had no time to see him, with school and working at Wegmans, but she still cares for him. The boy, as it turns out, is 19. Tia can't even look at the girl. She considers her a "slut." She forgives the boy, because "she made him do it," but not the girl.

Doris: What do you mean you forgive the boy but not the girl?

Tia: But she made him do it!

Doris: She made him put his penis into her vagina? He had nothing to do with it at all?

Tia admitted that he had something to do with it, finally, but she still hates the girl since she is a "slut." Since the baby will live only two doors from her, she will see the baby a lot, and she is angry about it. "How is she going to take care of a baby at only 13? She is a slut."

Working off of prevailing understandings that boys are not responsible for their sexual activities because they are hormonally programmed to want sex, unlike girls, whose job it is, therefore, to make sure that boys do not get aroused, Tia's response mirrors notions of sexuality and gender circulating in the broader society and available, as Fine (1988) and Whatley (1991) note, in sexuality curriculum. These understandings have it that if girls get in trouble, it is their fault since they are responsible for ensuring that boys are not enticed by sex. This positions women as sexual victims of hormonally programmed males. Under this formulation, the only subject position for females is keeping men from being aroused. Doris intentionally interrupts this set of understandings by posing the question, "She made him put his penis into her vagina? He had nothing to do with it at all?" While it is not clear that Tia accepts the validity of Doris's disruptive practice, in this instance, her continual challenges are not without consequence.

Below, Doris guides the girls into specifically gendered understandings, offering them space to challenge deeply rooted notions:

April 22, 1997 (8th Grade Group)

Doris: Is it good to be friends before having a boyfriend/girlfriend relationship?

Delores: I think you should be friends first, then if it don't work out, you can still be friends.

Ayisha: That don't work.

Patrice: I hate it when you make friends with a boy and then he doesn't want to take you out because he think you like a little sister.

Tonika: I hate it, most of the guys are taken, conceited, or gay [all laugh].

Doris: How old are you? [she already knows how old they are]

Responses: 13, 13, etc.

Doris: Don't you have a long way to go?

Tonika: No.

Ayisha: This one guy likes me. Everywhere I go he right there. When I go to my friend Phalla's, he right there.

Doris: Why is that a problem?

Ayisha: Cuz I don't like him. I don't want him to be around me.

Doris: Is this a form of sexual harassment? We walk down the street and someone calls after us. Don't we want real romance? You meet and fall in love?

Tish: But then you find out he's married.

Patrice: He's married and he's got a girlfriend.

Delores: He's married, got a girlfriend and got kids by both of them.

Doris: What do we do when someone is in an unhealthy relationship?

Tish: Try to help them out.

Patrice: Get a restraining order.

Tonika: Talk about violence! When my mom was pregnant, her boyfriend hit her.

Patrice: My mom got beat up, then she left.

Doris: Well, we all know that relationships are bad if there is physical abuse.

Doris offers, in the above, the language of sexual harassment and makes certain that the girls understand that violence in relationships should not be tolerated. While these are obviously complicated issues and suggest no easy solutions, it is key that these discussions are taking place in a public school, under the guidance of a trained adult who is suggesting that women need to develop their own power in relationships and not passively accept notions that whatever happens to them is their fault. She is, through the group, encouraging the girls to reconstruct what it means to be a woman/girl, working against the grain, offering an alternative voice to the deafening victim mentality. Helping the girls establish their bottom line—a bottom line that recognizes that women ought not be victims, comes through loud and clear in the group interactions.

Situated in the middle of a public school, young women traverse a variety of subjects regarding race, gender, sexuality, and men. Moving through these issues, under the watchful and caring eye of Doris Carbonell-Medina, young women begin to form a new collective—a collective that surges, at least for the moment, across race and is based on a woman or girl who is different from those left behind emotionally in the neighborhood. We now move to our second instance of "disruptive practice"—this one in a 9th grade detracked social studies class in Montclair, New Jersey.

Creating an Intellectual and Ethical Community Across Borders

With texts, students, anxieties, memories, colleagues, budget crises, faculty cuts, and wild anticipation, the year opens. It is September in a public school, 9th grade. We bend the spines of new books, launch new lives, try novel identities, and sneak toward new relationships among these 14- and 15-year-old bodies filled with delight, dread, hormones, excitement, and premature boredom. For some, the room is filled with friends. For all, the room is also filled with strangers. The room does not look like my other classes. Not everybody looks like me. Everyone is in the room and the teacher thinks that is a good thing. What am I in for? These data are drawn from a 2-year ethnography of a world literature class, detracked and racially integrated, studied by Michelle Fine (see Fine, Weis, & Powell, 1997). The class is in a racially integrated high school of approximately 1,500 youth, just over 50% African American and more than 40% White, ranging from well under the poverty line to extremely wealthy.

The teachers open the year with Name Pieces, invitations to revisit the origins, histories, and "herstories" of student names. And so we hear from a young man I [Michelle] had written off as disengaged:

> My real name is Carlos, but my mother calls me John. She says John means "son of kings." But I know it means a man who hangs out with prostitutes or a toilet. And even though God loves men who pay for prostitutes, and prostitutes, I wish she would call me Carlos.

Next we discuss *Of Mice and Men*, in particular George and Lennie's relationship at the end of the book. Carlton Jordan, the teacher, asks his students to form what he calls a value line: "Stand on my right if you think it was right for George to kill Lennie. Stand on my left if you don't. Stand in the middle if you are of both minds."

Much to my surprise (and dismay?), the room tips to the right. The crowd moves in those loud, clumsy teenage feet over toward the "it's okay to kill" side. I look for patterns of gender and race. Nothing. To the left wander three boys, a bit surprised and embarrassed, two White and one Black, feeling like they are going to lose. "But it's never okay to kill a friend," insists Joshua.

Carlton, momentarily stunned but never stumped by his "pedagogical failure" to get equally distributed groups, undermining his "plan" to set up pairs to discuss their positions, invites them to sit in common position groups and discuss whether George should appeal.

The "it's okay to kill a friend" group gets loud, committed, animated, vile: "Lennie's stupid. He's the biggest retard in the world. He likes to pet dead rabbits. He don't need to live," shouts Kizzy—Muslim, brass, wonderful, noisy, always the voice that provokes Darren, an African American boy, to respond with emotion. Sofia continues, "He should have killed Lennie long ago; he's a burden." Kizzy adds, "He's stupid. He murdered cold blooded. We got to make him bad if we're gonna get George off." Eli joins, "By killing him, it was like saving a life."

Carlton and I exchange glances. I am thrown by the raw but vicious analyses of these young adolescents and their endless creativity. The screams of "stupid, useless, dumb" are rusting my soul.

Carlton is as visibly shaken as I am. A strong, bold African American educator, he begins to teach, preach, and speak with his heart, his eyes, his arms, and his mouth. "Let me say something about Lennie, because, as I walk around, I am disturbed. What are the characteristics of Lennie?"

The class volunteers: "Stupid, slow, dumb!"

Carlton continues. "Dumb. Retarded. When you use language like that, I have to speak. You may say it was right for George to kill Lennie because Lennie killed someone else or Lennie would have been killed. There are many reasons. But because [he] is stupid, slow, no. Some of you have learning disabilities. Some of you have persons with autism or retardation in your family. And none of us know what's coming next. It is important to see Lennie as a man, as a human being, not as something that should be destroyed."

Kizzy says, "But he stupid. You are coming down on our group."

My mind wanders. Remembering the calls (from some White parents) to the superintendent about "them," remembering talk at the school board about how "those students" will hold back "the motivated ones," I am brought back to the room by Carlton's voice. "Some of you have been called stupid by others. You have to think about what it's like to be in a world where everyone seems to be getting it right, and you don't even know that you don't know. Some of you sit in lunchroom and won't eat tuna sandwiches because you're going to save the baby whale, but you'd laugh at Lennie in our school. Some of you will send money to Rwanda and Bosnia to save children over there. But you would make fun of Lennie, throw stones or shun Lennie over here." The students have reproduced the discourse being narrated about them. "George should not be burdened by Lennie." That is just what some at the school board meeting were implying.

Carlton says, "Let me say, I take this personally. If you can't walk with Lennie, if you can't see Lennie as a human, as a brother, what future is there for our community? What possibilities are there for us as a whole?"

Class is over. I'm feeling exhausted and depleted, and amazed at the strength of a teacher willing to speak, interrupt, listen, and educate. After a weekend of worries and exchanged phone messages with Carlton, I returned to class on Monday to refind "community," orchestrated by Carlton, already at play.

The lecture opens with a discussion of first- and third-person narratives. Carlton asks students to "turn to a page of *Of Mice and Men* where George and Lennie are interacting. I want you to rewrite the passage as Lennie. In first-person narrative. To see how Lennie's wheels turn."

"What wheels?" snipes Paul.

The students clip through the text, muttering, but writing eagerly. Carlton waits patiently for volunteers. Hands shoot up. "I am just a happy man, likin' my rabbits." "Why George callin' me a stupid so and so?" Hands of all hues fill the air. The room is alive with Lennies.

"How do you feel?" asks Carlton. "Stupid?" The point was made. Carlton was crafting a community not yet owned by students, but the students were growing extensions with which to connect in the room and beyond.

A parallel exchange occurs in Dana's classroom, early in October. Note how powerfully the character of George is relentlessly protected by the students, while Lennie is ruthlessly discarded as if disposable:

Charles: George is trying and Lennie is holding him back.

Erika: Lennie died happily. George did what he had to do. He gave a final request about rabbits. It's not right to kill, though.

Angela: Whether it was right or wrong, George was the one who had to sacrifice. It was a judgment call. He'd be lonely without Lennie.

Dana [Teacher]: Anyone want to respond?

Dennis: It was a sacrifice. He was sad. Steinbeck tried to make it like he was sad.

Mikel: Maybe he had a bit of remorse because he hesitated, remember? But he thought it was the only decision he could make. They did try to escape.

[Dana comments on their desire to protect George, render him a victim. Lennie is somehow deservedly dispensed with: George is seen as the victim.]

Ben: It's not George's fault.

Dana: Why not?

Ben: If he had known what Lennie was thinking, maybe. But George is off the hook.

Dana: Who is solely responsible for ending the life of Lennie?

Angela: I still feel exactly the way I did before what you said. Lennie couldn't live.

Shana: It was a hidden message. When George shot Lennie, it was his way of setting him free.

Dana: Was it fair for Lennie?

Shana: George wanted Lennie to die. It's not fair for Lennie. Maybe George, in the back of his mind, Lennie was such a burden. Proof he was a burden because George said, "I could do all this stuff, without Lennie."

Mikel: I'm not sure, Curley was going to do something. George protected himself.

Liza: Lennie is a nothing. He's a *sausage!*

Dana: Is it hard to hang out from Lennie's point of view?

Student: Lennie isn't given a point of view in the book.

[Dana and Carlton insist, but don't yet prevail. The students in September and October refuse to view social relations from the bottom.]

Across the five classes echoes a ringing, shared, often painfully victim-blaming consensus, in September and October, in which most *who speak* agree that Lennie is a "loser," a "leech," a "sausage," and that social relations are inherently and fundamentally hierarchical, competitive, and back biting. These are the Reagan, Bush, and now Clinton babies of the 1990s. These are the children who have been raised on policies that are anti-immigrant, anti-welfare, anti-public sector, pro-death penalty, and anti–Affirmative Action as the "national/maternal" ideological milk. And they swallowed. If I [Michelle] were to report only on what I heard from September through November, the Right could relax. These adolescent youths have been well trained by a nation armed with victim-blaming rhetoric. In the beginning of the year, while there are pockets of silence and some raised eyebrows, moments of, "Wait a minute . . ." we hear mostly that "murder and crime can keep the population down," that George was "entitled" and Lennie "dispensable." And so, too, we witness fatigued teachers, still standing in the front of the room, trying to create a space in which a view from the bottom, a moment of empathy, a peek from another angle, or a re-analysis of youth's assumptions could enter.

Having finished *Of Mice and Men*, Dana's class has moved on to *Two Old Women* by Velma Wallis, a Native American woman from Alaska who retells a story told to her by her mother. The story tells the tale of two old women left to die, abandoned by their community:

> **Dana:** In the book *Two Old Women*, where two Alaskan women are left to die by their tribes, should the two old women have forgiven the tribe?
>
> **Ben:** Maybe they should. It was their time to go. It was their survival.
>
> **Dana:** I heard that for George [protection of the powerful].
>
> **Michael:** I don't think they should forgive because they weren't helpless or lame. Just old. It wasn't right. They shouldn't forgive.
>
> **Angela:** I was raised to believe old are wiser and keep heritage alive. From old you get new experiences, but young have little to offer. Even though they were old they were strongest in the book. Like Lennie.
>
> **Ben:** If they didn't forgive, they couldn't last long. If we saved all old, we'd be overpopulated. Murder and crime may keep this earth's population in balance.
>
> **Dana:** Do we bear *no responsibility* in the taking care of?

In the beginning of the school year, there are typically few who will publicly annotate a perspective from the bottom. And yet, by November students like Michael (a Black boy) and Angela (a White girl) are beginning to chance another point of view, beginning to notice that something is different. Their teacher is not simply a carrier of dominant views, reinforcing only the view from above. Dana and Carlton are offering many lines of vision and insisting that, when challenging whispers are voiced, usually late in a class, quietly, in an embarrassed "Please don't read this out loud" paper in an after-school private meeting, they get a hearing.

It is toward the end of this season of victim-blaming chill that parental calls to the superintendent start to come in, demanding to know why Candace didn't get an A on the first draft, why Dana is "bending over backward for *some* students," why Carlton is having "political" and not "literary" discussions. These are the days when "everyone has a choice" is declared as truth by some students, when victims are blamed, and those who challenge social arrangements grow suspect—students and teachers alike. But work is yet to be done. And at this point in the class, all students suspect that something is up. The dominant conversation prevails, but on its last legs for the year. A new moon is rising.

December Through February: The Melting, and Then Partial Restoration, of Privilege

Creating a safe space for all means breaking down the invisible walls that segregate those historically privileged from those historically silenced, that separate traditionally smart from traditionally slow, and that challenge the categories and "right" answers that fit so well in the past. Forcing students to "come out" from behind their performances of nerd, athlete, scholar, clown, or dummy, these educators invite them to reveal their deeper, more complex selves. They venture well beyond the borders of intellectual and political work, modeling, chancing, and pushing the very categories usually taken for granted, categories that have elevated some (smart?) while stunting others ("at risk").

By December, it is clear that the teachers invest in what might be called standpoint theory, an understanding that people think, feel, see, express, resist, comply, and are silent in accordance with their social power and that a view from the bottom may diverge dramatically, critically, and brilliantly from a view from the top. But a view from the bottom may be just as smart. Below students discuss answers to the question, "What are the experiences that told or taught you 'your place'?":

> **Cris [Black boy]:** Mr. G. [former principal] told me I am a shitball and would never develop into nothing.
>
> **Del [Black girl]:** I got kicked out of graduation dinner dance. I was mad and depressed. I just got out of the hospital.
>
> **Cary [White boy]:** Me and my friends couldn't see an R movie. We were kicked out cause of age.
>
> **Eli [White boy]:** I can't think of one.
>
> **Nashama [Black girl]:** You don't expect racist comments, like from White friends, so you don't know what to say.

Even if a view from the top has been the standard, accepted as best, and assured an A+ to date, this standard, oddly, is no longer operating. Equally rigorous, new standards are emerging. We turn now to a discussion of the book *Nectar in a Sieve* (Markandaya, 1998), an analysis of dharma, fate, and hope, to notice the early awkward stages of trying to get *all* voices heard:

> **Seri [Mixed-race boy]:** People *live* based on hope.
>
> **Alison [White girl]:** I think that's *sad*. If it's just based on hope, you need to study.
>
> **Pam [White girl]:** You need not just *hope* but *goals*.
>
> **Cecil [Black boy]:** My *hopes* are to do the best that I can, be a musician and NBA player.
>
> **Danielle [Black girl]:** I think it's true. Everybody has *one dream* and they have to accomplish the dream.
>
> **Carlton:** What keeps you in school?

Chris [White boy]: I think about school, it's the future. College and further, career, family, and support.

James [White boy]: *Work hard.*

Sara [White girl]: My *goals* are based on education, not McDonald's.

Cecil: I would rather have McDonald's.

Sara: I don't want to *depend* on a husband or taxpayers or my parents.

Alison: Most people only have *hope.* That's sad.

Kareem [Black boy]: Animals don't have hope, only people. Animals have instinct.

MF: [Field notes: It's polarizing: Blacks defend hope and Whites defend ambition/goals, as if hope were silly, as if this dichotomy made sense!]

Carlton: Are people different from animals?

Uri [Mixed race boy]: Some animal types that have leaders hope to be the leader in the pack.

Hannah [White girl]: Lennie doesn't know what hope means but he hopes to be as smart as George.

Qwuinette [Black girl]: He does have hope.

Alison: Maybe ignorant people have more hope and smarter people are more cynical.

Cecil: You've got to be kidding!

Cecil carries the momentum here. The room spirals, the conversation stops and then begins again, changed. These critical turns, upon which our pedagogy relies, are as necessary as they are unpredictable. We yearn to understand how we can nurture, cultivate, and fertilize our rooms so that critical turns get a voice and eventually get a hearing.

At this point, "smarts" are popping out of unsuspected mouths, bodies buried into oversized jackets. At the same time, perhaps in response, there is parallel move, a polarizing performance. So, for instance, Blacks defend hope and Whites defend ambitions and goals as though these were separable. As previously unheard voices sing, there is a subtle polarizing, a freezing of positions. Now that the voices are up, there is nothing automatic about creating a community of differences in this space.

It is becoming clear that student identities ranging from smart to disengaged to at risk are unraveling—not so predictably. In integrated schools, as DuBois worried, sorting (Bowles & Gintis, 1976; Ryan, 1981) takes a particularly perverse form. Some students, usually White and/or middle-class students in an integrated school, rise like cream to the top. They blossom as institutional signifiers of merit, smarts, and advanced achievement. It is their loss most profoundly dreaded by public education. Today urban and suburban school boards live in terror of losing Whites and middle-class students across races and do all they can to keep them, even if that means holding other students hostage (Sapon-Shevin, 1993). And yet this categorical elevation is, as Eve Sedgwick would argue, not absolute. It is fundamentally relativistic, parasitic. It *requires* that others (Blacks, working-class/poor, disabled students) are seen as "not" or "lacking." Funneled through a lens of hierarchy and limited goods, standards, achievements, and excellence demand exclusivity. But, in this class, the metric for status enables excellence from otherwise marked bodies.

As new voices emerge, mostly heretofore unheard Black voices, a kind of polarizing occurs. Again a small group of White students may decide to sit together, to reinforce one another's points and synchronize eye rolls when a student of color speaks. In ironic similarity to the oft-repeated, "Why do all the Black students sit together?" at this point in the semester, there is a consolidation of a White-resistant position—not all, just a few—but enough to chill the room. The days of listening to "them" are over. It is important to note that most White and most Black students do not polarize. But most are at a loss for how to engage this conversation outside the polarities. In February, Chante and Erica (two Black girls) discuss this issue:

> **Chante:** Our teacher don't care 'bout the groups, just look at the class. They're all sittin', I'm not gonna say, but just look. At least, when Ms. Little made the groups mixed, we talked to each other, one Black boy, one White boy, one Black girl, one White girl, and we say how we feel. Now, they all sittin' together and scared to talk to us, scared we're gonna yell at them, so they just talk to themselves.

> **Erica:** When Devon [Black boy] was talkin' and Eli [White boy] jumped on him, we all talked but the bell rang and then the conversation went back to the book. But we can't talk about the books until we finish that conversation.

I have a frightening thought: Is it possible that Whites work "optimally," that is, uninterrupted, when we *don't* have to discuss race and ethnicity and that students of color can be engaged and most unburdened only when race and ethnicity are squarely on the table?

Returning to the dynamics of Linda Powell's *Achievement Knot* (1997), it seems likely that students of color are "stuck" until race is discussed, while White students are "stuck" once race is discussed. Then the teacher (or Black students) gets blamed for dwelling on race—again! And a few outspoken White parents "save" the White students (through phone calls) from the conversation. This is not simply about race, it is about what constitutes good and responsible education in a pluralistic society.

By January, midterm grades are in and the old stratification system is not layered like it used to be, no longer a two-tiered White and Black cake.

Carlton and Dana have been reading aloud to the class some of the writings of students who sound like poets, journalists, and creative writers. Sometimes a White kid raises an embarrassed hand when Carlton asks "Whose paper is this?" As often an African American boy from the back of the room will lift a reluctant finger, or an African American girl will hide her giggle as she sashays up to the front of the room to reclaim her text. This moment is one of both racialized melting and desperate consolidation of racial privilege—a tight moment of entrenched contrast sails through a room. The stakes are growing clear and the educators are riding broncos of resistance. This is a crucial moment in an integrated space. One in which many give up. But not these educators.

At this point, a small set of relatively well-off White students (not all, but a few in particular and in full voice) search to reclaim status by displaying their family treasures, what Pierre Bourdieu (1998) would call cultural capital, "My mother is a literary agent and she said *Two Old Women* never would have been published if the author wasn't a Native woman." "Have you read any of Sigmund Freud? My father is a psychoanalyst, and he would contest your interpretation." "My mother is the chair of the board of ____ and she said that Newark is lucky that outsiders have invested money because there was *nothing* there before." Some, at this point, less decorated with biographic merit badges, simply assert that "Today, in this country, we *all* have choices." Oppression and history are deemed largely irrelevant. A few gracefully sneer or turn away when students of color talk about race (not again!). I [Michelle] time the conversations that address race: The average conversation lasts 30 seconds. The record conversation lasted 45 seconds before someone shifted to, "But I don't think it's race, it's class." "It's age." "What about Whites in basketball?" "What about sexism?" "How about when you say faggot?" "But the Holocaust was . . ." And we're off . . .

Old lines are being redrawn, gentrification in academic blood. A sharpened White line of demarcation is being drawn. Interestingly, most White students refuse to employ these displays or barricade themselves but do not know what else to do. They cannot yet invent another discourse of Whiteness. And so they retreat to a kind of silence, sometimes wonder, sometimes embarrassment. A few seem delighted that those who have always "won"—from prekindergarten to 8th grade—are not the automatic victors in this class. Like a fight in a hockey game, it is part of the work—not an interruption and not a failure. Re-vision. There is more to learn on the other end of this struggle.

March Through April: Playing With Power, Shifting, and Reversals
It has been a long stretch but some of those students who never expected to be seen as smart, never expected to get a hearing from teachers or peers, are

now opening their mouths, challenging myths, stereotypes, and lines of vision from the top represented as if natural, or even worse, inherently correct. And they are getting a hearing. There is a long conversation about *The Legend of La Llorana* by Rudolfo Anaya (1991), a literary giant of a text in which the story of Cortes and Malintzin and the conquest of Mexico unfolds with the final scene, one in which Cortes is invited to return to his homeland in Spain. Cortes insists on taking his sons to Spain, lest they become "savages" and "uncivilized." Malintzin, their mother, a native unwilling (and uninvited) to go to Spain, kills the boys in a belief that they will liberate the people of Mexico. Dana has invited the students to prepare a mock trial of Malintzin.

"Is she guilty for having killed her children?" The pros and cons polarize almost immediately. White students form a chorus, "You should never kill your children. She must have been crazy." Most African American students circle around another question, "What do you do to survive oppression?" Four Black boys refuse to take sides, "You never kill *and* it was a time of incredible oppression." And then Aziz, an African American boy, breaks the stalemate, reversing the power and insisting that the trial of Malintzin is itself contained within colonialism. He queries, "Why is Malintzin on trial? Why isn't the Captain (Cortes) on trial?" At once the air thins, the fog lifts, and the fists of power are sitting in the center of the room. The debate is not about Malintzin's innocence or guilt; the debate surrounds the question of who decides what the crime is: colonialism of a race or murder of two?

Now, three quarters of the way through the term, questions of power are engaged (and enraged), often by African American males like Aziz, even more often by African American females who press, sometimes so hard that the White students back off *and* the African American boys move to censor her. Back to another class on *Two Old Women:*

Dana: What's wrong with giving up pride?

Pat [White girl]: It makes me feel lower. Not better.

Mandy [White girl]: It's shocking to realize maybe they're better than me.

Dana: It's really based on hierarchy? Do we define ourselves hierarchically in relation to others? What if it's [social relations] not a triangle [draws on the board] but a flat line [draws]?

Mandy: Then it still goes zero to ten.

Dana: [Looking horrified] What if it's a circle [draws circle]?

Colette [White girl]: I'm on top of the circle.

Lamar [Black boy]: In the center!

Serge [Black boy]: It's like heliocentric versus geocentric. Older ways saw the sun rotating around the earth, but really we're not the center. You're not the center.

Nia [Black girl]: If you're not the center, you're right next to it.

Dana: It has to do with who we value and why. What if I said there is no such thing as better, less than, or equal? We made that up. We made up that conversation. It's a lie.

Joanna [White girl]: We were taught all our life to be the best.

Nefretiti [Black girl]: Not everyone.

MF: Here's the challenge.

Joanna: Everyone wants an A in school.

Serge: It's how a lot of people see things. Superiority complex.

Sharon [Black girl]: I have to disagree with Joanna. Not everyone is taught to be all you can be. Some are raised to grow up and try as hard as you can. Most parents don't talk to kids about getting an A. Half the time parents don't care.

Nina [White girl]: Everyone is taught being the best even though no one taught us. It's there. Everybody gets it. And then there are those who acknowledge they are not going to be the best, but they know everybody thinks they should be.

Dana: Is a triangle really the structure of the school? How is it arranged?

Carl [White boy]: In groups, in classes, outside of school, popular and not so popular and those who couldn't care.

Ravona [Black girl]: I'm not better than anyone else. No one is better than me. Zero to 10, triangle doesn't make sense. The only one who is superior is God. Not everyone is taught to be better. Some parents put their children down. Not everyone is raised in that way it's good for parents to say to try. Not "you better be on the honor roll or I'm going to beat your behind."

Jess [Black boy]: For all the people. You get good grades. My mother expects me to do what I have to do. She wants me, my life, to be better than her life. She doesn't expect me to be better than anyone else. She knows everyone's a pawn in life.

Patrice [White girl]: My dad says if I get a C, don't come home. Society and parents say do good and be better than others.

Joanna: My parents never pressure me, but I am expected to because my sister did. As a society everyone wants to be rich, famous, and we believe we have to be better than everyone else.

Mandy [White girl]: What Joanna said is true. There is an expectation, you are going to college. You have to be better than everyone else. It's a drill. My parents don't want me on unemployment lines. You have to be better.

Sharon: I have a question for you [two White girls]. How can you be better than someone else?

Pat [White girl]: They might have tried harder.

Sharon: There's racism out there. Most people have to work hard all the time.

Pat: Like levels of self-esteem. Ones who can go farther than those who say I can't.

Mary [White girl]: And that's who people want to hear. That makes you better. Everyone is equal but not quite.

Dana: Nobody buys that we are equal? [Fainting] Here are my questions: Tonight's homework, what does it mean to be successful? What does it mean to be better than? What does it mean to be a good student? What if these distinctions didn't matter? What if there was no such things as better, less than, or equal?

The theater is alive. Girls, for the most part, are carrying on the debate about social injustice. Some Black girls assert their position in a discourse of power and inequality. In response, some White girls displace a discourse of power with a discourse of psychology, motivation, and equal opportunity. These White girls, trying to be sympathetic and inclusive, offer up universals ("everyone"), while Black girls, equally insistent, draw attention to power, difference, and inequality. Typically an African American girl is pressing a question of race, class, and gender at once, with the White boys flushed, the White girls scared, and the Black boys actively engaged in muzzling her! And yet she stands sturdy, bold, and alone, courageous often without a support in the room. The room coalesces around its desire for her to just stop.

The end of the year is riddled with a series of power eruptions. Sharon has cracked the dominance in the room and Ravona takes up her analysis. The dominant hold is cracking and freeing everyone. Splinters fly.

April Through June: Coalitions, Standpoints, Speaking Truth to Power... Preparing for the "Real World"

This course is messy. Little can be said that is linear, developmental, moving forward in a predictable line. And yet, on our well-toiled intellectual and emotional grounds, with the reading of great literature these educators invite young minds to travel. With a pedagogy that encourages multiple readings, they are asked to tackle the perspective of others, to re-view their perspectives of self. In this context, there are sometimes fleeting and sometimes sustained moments of coming together.

Students agree to stretch, as a collective, to cross borders of race, class, gender, and "difference" and meet one another in a June Jordan poem, mourning for Rukmani, angry at Cortes, reciting what Lennie in *Of Mice*

and Men might have really been thinking. These moments of coming together are, for us, the hope, the point, the real metaphor for America as it
could be. For in these moments of coming together, students and faculty
embody their differences in a chorus of voices, in a tapestry of cloth. Very
smart and bold, not compromising and not "whiting out," or ignoring differences, these students stand together, even if for a moment, challenging
the separations that we adults—the "other" America—try to impose on
them. They are coming together to build knowledge, community, and
serious intellectual work through and across race, ethnicity, class, and
gender.

From April through the end of the term, students have learned to
engage in this space, for 45 minutes a day, with power, difference, and a
capacity to re-vision. Some with delight and some still disturbed, but
they know that everyone will get a chance to speak and be heard. They
will be surprised, still, to learn that *"She* said something so smart" or *"He*
plays golf?" By now (finally), it is no longer rare to hear White students
refer to, grow a conversation off, interrupt with praise, or even disagree
with students of color. Nor is it unusual when African American students
challenge, extend a comment by, or ask a question of a White student.
These may sound like minor accomplishments, but in a sea of parallel
lives stratified by geography, class, color, friends, language, dress, music,
and structures of tracking around them, the moments of working together, not always friendly or easy but engaged across, are worth comment. For these are moments that, once strung together, weave a frayed
tapestry of cross-racial and cross-class practice inside and outside of
schooling. Students may risk a statement that will get little support from
peers; they may dare not to support a lifelong ally, neighbor, or friend;
they may wander into a more treacherous alliance with someone very
different; they may challenge a comment that sounds, on the face, racist
or homophobic even if a Black person, or a White person, uttered it; they
may opt for a co-authored poem or a joint extension project.

It is at this moment when, after a protracted conversation about race
and power, John, a young man I had "coded" as middle-class and Black, offered, "These conversations are very hard for me. I understand both points
of view. You all think I'm Black, but actually my mom is White and I could
take either position in the room. But I don't talk much because I don't
think anyone will catch my back." His eyes fill with tears as do those of
many others in the room. There is a stunning silence. "I just felt, confused."
At which point from across the room, on the diagonal, we hear the sounds
of applause, strong, hard, deliberate. Eddie has begun the pulse of clapping
that waves across the 24 young men and women. This course is transfor-
mative, and yet it is a moment. Given the ruthless commitment to tracking

students, they are, largely, resegregated in 10th through 12th grades—but there was that moment.

Conclusion

We offer these two scenes, not to argue *against* reproduction theory, for we are deeply implicated and persuaded by such analyses. But we seek to agitate, at the same time, *for* analyses that reveal where, under what conditions, and with what effects schools are promoting extraordinary conversations for and by youth. Although critical scholars have spent the past 30 years engaging in important analyses of reproduction (and later resistance in schools), we now extend the room under the umbrella of critical scholarship for a feminist and antiracist responsibility to produce extraordinary educational projects (see Cochran-Smith & Lytle, 1992).

Social reproduction theorists, and we include ourselves here, have been perhaps too glib in overlooking moments of interruption, material and discursive, within deeply reproductive educational settings. In this essay we have taken seriously these buried moments, what Mouffe (1998) might describe as ripples in an otherwise toxic sea, to try to theorize what it is that youth gain, learn, and teach in these spaces. We offer scholarly respect for educators who dare to carve out such spaces.

These educators, across sites, work with feminist and critical race texts and strategies to accomplish a set of common aims. We elaborate these aims, and their associated pedagogies, in an effort to make explicit the micro-politics of these deeply "disruptive" and responsible pedagogical sites. When we say disruptive, of course, we mean disruptive to reproduction, not necessarily to schools or students, although it needs to be said that any act designed to disrupt the asymmetric relations embedded in a capitalistic economy and racism will, indeed, provoke ripples of resistance inside schools, communities, faculties, and indeed the student body. No one should be surprised at such fallout. We challenge institutions and communities to generate more such dissonance within educational sites for youth.

First, across these two sites, these educators work to create spaces of difference, not merely to engage in practices of resistance. They struggle to create what Mary Louise Pratt calls "contact zones . . . social spaces where cultures meet, clash and grapple with each other, often in the context of highly asymmetric relations of power" (1991, p. 491). They dare to search for the common among differences.

Second, these educators situate, at the center of their intellectual work, crucial questions of power, privilege, standpoint, knowledge, and difference. At once they decenter privilege in the room and in the canon and seek to hear voices of youth whose biographies range broadly (see Hall, 1991).

Third, these educators reframe "private problems" as public issues. In the spirit of C. W. Mills (1959), they make explicit the issues that many youth are grappling with, as though they were normative—for example, domestic violence, racism, pleasure, and surveillance. These issues are posed as intellectual and social concerns, and as potentially shared, not as sources of individual humiliation. By so doing, youth see themselves in a social world and can review themselves as agents with choices rather than as victims swept into a corner of shame with no recourse.

Fourth, these educators work through intersections normally not acknowledged, such as those of race, class, disability (in the New Jersey case), and gender. Thus, all students potentially come to recognize that while they bring situated knowledge from one set of race, class, and gender intersections, other knowledges flood the room. "Organic intellectuals," as Gramsci has argued, emerge, but so do critical allies from unsuspecting corners.

Fifth, these educators have a complex relation to youth voice. While, indeed, they embody Freirian commitments to voice, critique, and liberatory knowledge, these educators also embody a firm standpoint toward community and social justice that requires listening and reflecting. Indeed, like historian Joan Scott, they understand that experience marks the beginning of a conversation, not the end, that "evidence of experience . . . reproduces rather than contests given ideological systems. . . . Experience is, at once, always already an interpretation and in need of interpretation" (1992, p. 37). All youth deserve spaces in which they can engage with critical and supportive analysis, involving prodding and facilitating by other youth and adults.

Sixth, these educators work, at one and the same time, on individual development and community building. That is, they presume and educate toward individual growth but also toward a sense of community, interdependence, and collective responsibility. They refuse to engage what Pierre Bourdieu would call "the return of individualism, a kind of self-fulfilling prophecy which tends to destroy the . . . notion of collective responsibility" (1998, p. 7).

These two instances raise questions about the power of disruption. While most educational settings still fail to educate most poor and working-class youth, and while most schools reinforce structurally and discursively class, race, ethnic, gender, and sexuality stratification, we are taken by the power of spaces designed explicitly to interrupt such dynamics. We are impressed, further, by the consequences of such spaces with respect to young people's abilities to re-view critically social arrangements, challenge stereotypes foisted upon them and others, and realign socially and politically with differently situated young adults. We are not so naïve as to imagine that a pregnancy prevention program, of whatever length, is sufficient to disrupt the weight of structural stratification. Nor do we believe that the introduction of a single detracked course, even if mandatory, can derail the sleek and efficient machine of tracking. But we do ask readers to indulge in the possibilities of interruption. We invite theorizing and strategizing about the potential of stringing together sets of disruptive practices and sites, rather than posing simply unilateral assault on what we still know to be deeply reproductive settings.

That is, we maintain our challenge to educational settings as reproductive sites. Further, we recognize the power of some faculty, community members, and young people to resist. We add now that we encourage spaces that radically alter the power relations around and within school. These spaces enhance the progressive political agenda by generating multiple disruptive sites in which social critique, new alliances, and alternative readings of common sense are available, nurtured, and supported by and among youth, particularly poor, working-class youth of varying racial and ethnic backgrounds.

As strategies for change move away from democratic public education and on to neoliberal private support for vouchers and tax benefits for the wealthy, we find it imperative to return our gaze to spaces inside public schools, such as those focused on here, and to demand more. Thus, we offer these scenes as we promote a collective analysis of the ways in which schools must dare to interrupt reproduction, must engage young people in conversations of intellect and courage, and must dare to educate for critical inquiry and civic participation across lines of "difference."

Epilogue
Lois Weis and Michelle Fine

When we plunged into this line of research more than 20 years ago, we had no way of knowing that years hence it would, unfortunately, continue to be so relevant. We have been privileged to work with gifted and committed teachers, parents, colleagues, students, and community activists. What stands out are both the oppressive conditions under which so many are forced to live, love, and labor, and at the same time, that so many of these same individuals engage life with great dignity and perseverance. It is these twinned conditions that we constantly seek to capture, theorize, and reflect upon in our work—work that spans, over the years, research on and with adults and young people across race, sexuality, religion, ethnicity, class, and gender in a wide variety of contexts, including schools, community colleges, universities, community centers, prisons, churches, organizations devoted to the visual and performing arts, literacy centers, spaces for gay and lesbian youth, desegregated spaces in otherwise segregated schools, as well as separate spaces for identifiable groups within ostensibly desegregated schools.

As we reflect upon the work we have done, we recognize the ways in which we carve out a specific form of ethnographic investigation—one that clearly builds upon the work of numerous others yet simultaneously strikes out in distinct ways. It is this striking out in the context of a deeply embedded desire for social justice that leads us to articulate carefully and fully what we call here "compositional studies." We do this for ourselves obviously, as we codify and name what we have worked to develop all these years, but mainly we do it for those still to come—those committed teachers, scholars, community workers, and students who have years ahead of them in which to continue this work. So we end here not with the last word on this subject, but what we think of as a beginning—a deep theory of method, one that we hope sets the stage for fruitful discussion and intense research both with and about those privileged and not so privileged within a deeply stratified social order.

Although we set this volume inside the context of the United States because that is where our empirical and theoretical work is lodged, we do not see this theory of method as situated and drawing upon U.S. realities alone. The deep fractures evident across social class and race/ethnicity lines explored in this volume are, to be sure, particular to the United States, as structural inequalities and linkages to schools play themselves out in locally specific ways. At the same time, however, such inequalities are evident globally, in part because the United States helps to export and produce inequities. Indeed, all nations and peoples are currently subject to a broader shift in the global economy, a global economy that involves massive realignment of collectivities both within and outside of any given nation state. No one is immune. By way of example, as the old corporate core is being replaced by "global webs which earn their largest profits from clever problem-solving,-identifying, and brokering" and, as the "costs of transporting things and of communicating information about them continue to drop" (Reich, 1991, p. 209), modern factories can now be installed almost anywhere on the globe. This obviously leaves millions of routine production workers in currently industrialized countries such as Australia, the United Kingdom, and Germany, as well as the United States, without a stable foothold in the new economy at the same time that the economies and social relations within numerous nations across the world are being and will continue to be realigned.

Our method of compositional studies, therefore, has far-reaching implications for a continued mapping of new economic, social, and cultural forms, including those associated with existing and emerging social class, race/ethnicity, and gender formations across the globe. The power of our theory of method, then, lies in its malleability and transportability inside a world context that is changing on a daily basis. As the global economy is realigned and social relations are simultaneously reconfigured, our twin passions—mapping and thereby challenging existing oppression and chronicling and moving with the ways in which ordinary people work to contest such oppression—become paramount. It is our belief that though injustice abounds, regular people, such as ourselves and our readers, can do our part to chip away at the edifices of power.

Endnotes

Notes to the Introduction

1. Our continued thanks to Craig Centrie, who offered great insight into our artistic metaphor. Craig, a visual artist in his own right, prompted us to think through the relationship between the visual arts and what we do as ethnographers.

2. We are indebted to Norman Denzin for stretching our thinking on this point. See Maulana Karenga (1982), a theorist of the Black arts movement, as a reaction to "high" European art.

3. Our thanks to Greg Dimitriadis for pushing this point with respect to our work.

Notes to Chapter 1

The authors thank William Cross, Jr. for his enormously helpful feedback.

1. Despite struggles for finance equity (Kozol, 1991), teacher quality in poor urban districts (Darling-Hammond, 2000; Education Trust, 1998; IESP, 2001), school integration (Cross, 1991; Fullilove, 2000), Affirmative Action (Bok & Bowen, 1998), small schools (Wasley et al., 1999), special education and bilingual reform (Nieto, 1996; Rousso & Wehmeyer, 2001; Stanton-Salazar, 1997), and parent organizing (Fruchter, Galletta, & White, 1992) as well as struggles against high stakes standardized testing (Haney, Russell, & Jackson, 1997) and tracking (Dauber & Alexander, 1996; Hurtado, Haney, & Garcia, 1998; New York ACORN, 2000; Noguera, 2003; Oakes et al., 1997; Useem, 1990; Wheelock, 1992), race-, ethnic-, and class-based inequities in educational opportunities and outcomes persist.

2. The youth researchers attend East Side Community High School, a small, detracked urban school on the Lower East Side of New York City, where most of the students come from poor and working-class families, many are recent immigrants from Central and South America, resources are low, and academic expectations high. They are, indeed, neighborhood kids who were lucky enough to find an "alternative" school committed to rigorous education for all.

3. Deborah Meier, Robert Moses, Luis Garden Acosta and Frances Lucerna, Ann Cook, Olivia Lynch, Eric Nadelstern, Peter Steinberg, and hundreds of other dedicated educators.

Notes to Chapter 2

Data in this article are drawn from a larger study that I conducted in collaboration with Michelle Fine, funded by the Spencer Foundation. My thanks to the foundation for its continued support. Thanks also to Amira Proweller and Tracey Shepherd, who conducted some of the interviews reported here.

1. See also Brickman et al., 1982.
2. This is a national construction of the Black male as responsible for all the problems in America and for a local artifact—police harassment. Several African American interviewees point to Rodney King as the logical extension of this discursive construction of the Black man and subsequent police behavior. While many note that the drug economy does not originate at the street level, but rather involves people much higher up including the police, businessmen, and the government, the "war on drugs" targets the poor. "Street sweeps" land African American men in jail. To the people higher up, those working at the street level are expendable; there will always be more of them available. Phillipe Bourgois (1995) explores this point also.
3. See, for example, Amadiume, 1987; Gilmore, 1996; Golden & Shreve, 1995; Hine, 1990; McIntyre, 1997; Spelman, 1988; and Ware, 1992.
4. My thanks to Julia Hall for raising these points.
5. The points regarding political implications benefit from intense discussion with Michelle Fine.

Notes to Chapter 3

This paper has been funded, in part, by the Leslie Glass Institute, the Rockefeller Foundation, and the Spencer Foundation. We offer much appreciation to Morton Deutsch, Susan Opotow, Linda Powell, and Janice Steil for very helpful feedback.

Notes to Chapter 4

A version of this paper was originally delivered as a keynote address at the meetings of the Australian Educational Research Association, December 2002, Brisbane. Thanks to the Spencer Foundation and the Baldy Center for Law and Social Policy, University at Buffalo for supporting this research.

1. The idea of the armed forces as a space that enables/encourages a new masculine form is embedded within a number of the Freeway male narratives. I will take up this point at great length in *Class Reunion* (2004b).

Notes to Chapter 5

1. The authors would like to thank the Leslie Glass Foundation, the Open Society Institute, and the Spencer Foundation for funding the research; Superintendent Elaine Lord, Paul Korotkin, and E. Michele Staley for their feedback; and Shura Saul for her design inspiration.
2. Iris Bowen was transferred to another correctional facility midway through the research. Though her relocation, far from family, friends, and support networks, has put incredible strains on her, she remains a vital member of the research committee.
3. Aisha Elliot, a starting member of the research committee, is no longer active in the research.
4. Migdalia Martinez was granted clemency in December 2000 and released on January 31, 2001, after serving 11 years and 3 months.
5. Staley relied on the following methodology: "[NYSDOCS] matched the file [of college students from the Mercy College registrar's office] with our department's release file that included releases between 1985 and 1999, using DIN (Departmental Identification Numbers assigned to each inmate)... [I]ncluded in the analysis were only the inmates that were released from the custody of NYSDOCS subsequent to their participation in the college program. Of the 454 cases provided, 274 college participants have been released from NYSDOCS since their college participation. This is the sample that was used in the follow-up analysis to determine how many of these participants returned to the custody of NYSDOCS.

With respect to the return-to-custody analysis, I used the same survival analysis methodology that is used to prepare our department's standard return-to-custody report, *1995 Releases: Three Year Post Release Follow Up* (personal correspondence, Staley, August 22, 2000).

Notes to Chapter 6

The authors thank Carlton Jordan for the title of this article. They also thank the Spencer Foundation and the Carnegie Foundation for their support of these projects.

1. My Bottom Line, like most sex education programs currently in schools, is an abstinence-based program. Unlike abstinence-only programs, which are receiving massively increased federal funding under the Family Adolescent Life Act (FALA, Title XX of the Republic Health Act) and the Personal Responsibility and Work Reconciliation Act of 1996 (otherwise known as "welfare reform"), abstinence-based programs offer information about safer sex techniques and contraception in the event that adolescents do not "choose" abstinence.

2. Doris Carbonell-Medina, Esq. has her J.D. from the SUNY Buffalo Faculty of Law and Jurisprudence and is licensed to practice law in New York State. She runs most of the workshops for Womanfocus and now practices law on a referred basis only.

References

Adelman, C. (1997). Action research and the problem of participation. In R. McTaggart (Ed.), *Participatory action research: International contexts and consequences* (pp. 79–106). Albany: State University of New York Press.

Alcoff, L. M. (1995). The problem of speaking for others. In J. Roof & R. Wiegman (Eds.), *Who can speak?: Authority and critical identity* (pp. 97–119). Urbana: University of Illinois Press.

Alford, R. (1998). *The craft of inquiry: Theories, methods, evidence.* London: Oxford University Press.

Amadiume, I. (1987). *Male daughters, female husbands: Gender and sex in an African society.* London: Zed.

Anand, B., Fine, M., Perkins, T., & Surrey, D. (2002). *Keeping the struggle alive: Studying desegregation in our town.* New York: Teachers College Press.

Anand, B., Fine, M., Perkins, T., Surrey, D., & the Graduating Class of 2000 Renaissance School. (2001). *The struggle never ends: An oral history of desegregation in a northern community.* New York: Teachers College Press.

Anand, B. (2003). Personal communication about Sisters and Brothers United.

Anaya, R. (1991). *The legend of La Llorona: A short novel.* Berkeley, CA: TQS Publications.

Ancess, J. (2000, November 3). The reciprocal influence of teacher learning, teaching practice, school restructuring, and student learning outcomes. *Teachers College Record, 102*(3), 590–619.

Ancess, J., & Ort, S. (2001, January 13). *Making school completion integral to school purpose & design.* Paper presented at the conference, Dropouts in America: How Severe Is the Problem? Sponsored by Achieve, Inc. and the Civil Rights Project, Cambridge, MA.

Anyon, J. (1983). Workers, labor and economic history, and textbook content. In M. Apple & L. Weis (Eds.), *Ideology and practice in schools* (pp. 37–60). Philadelphia: Temple Press.

Anyon, J. (1997). *Ghetto schooling: A political economy of urban educational reform.* New York: Teachers College Press.

Anzaldua, G. (1999). *Borderlands/La Frontera.* San Francisco: Aunt Lute Publishers.

Apple, M. (1982). *Education and power.* Boston: Routledge.

Apple, M. (2001). *Educating the "right" way: Markets, standards, God and inequality.* New York: Routledge.

Arnot, M. (2004). Male working class identities and social justice: A reconsideration of Paul Willis' "Learning to Labor" in light of contemporary research. In N. Dolby & G. Dimitriadis (Eds.), *Learning to labor in new times.* New York: Routledge.

Aronowitz, S. (1992). *The politics of identity: Class, culture and social movements.* New York: Routledge.

Aronowitz, S., & Giroux, H. A. (1993). *Education still under siege* (2nd ed.). Westport, CT: Bergin & Garvey.

Ayers, R., Ayers, W., Dohrn, B., & Jackson, T. (2001). *Zero tolerance.* New York: The New Press.

Barry, R. (2000). Sheltered children: Gay, lesbian, and bisexual youth. In L. Weis & M. Fine (Eds.), *Construction sites.* New York: Teachers College Press.

Basch, C. (1987). Focus group interview: An underutilized research technique for improving theory and practice in health education. *Health Education Quarterly, 14*, 411–448.

Baum, A., Singer, J., & Baum, C. (1981). Stress and the environment. *Journal of Social Issues, 37*(1), 4–32.

Bensman, D. (1995). *Lives of the graduates of Central Park East Elementary School: Where have they gone? What did they really learn?* New York: NCREST, Teachers College, Columbia University.

Bertram, C., Fine, M., Weis, L., & Marusza, J. (2000). Where the girls (and women) are. *Journal of Community Psychology, 28*(5), 731–755.

Bettencourt, B. A., Dillman, G., & Wollman, N. (1996). The intragroup dynamics of maintaining a successful grassroots organization: A case study. *Journal of Social Issues, 52*, 207–220.

Bettie, J. (2003). *Women without class.* Berkeley: University of California Press.

Bhabha, H. (Ed.) (1990). *Nation and narration.* New York: Routledge.

Bhavnani, K. K. (1999). Tracing the contours: Feminist research and objectivity. In H. Afshar & M. Maynard (Eds.), *The dynamics of "race" and gender: Some feminist interventions.* London: Taylor & Francis.

Boudin, K. (1993). Participatory literacy education behind bars: AIDS opens the door. *Harvard Educational Review, 63*, 207–232.

Bourdieu, P. (1998). *Acts of resistance.* New York: New Press.

Bourgois, P. (1995). *In search of respect: Selling crack in el barrio.* Cambridge: Cambridge University Press.

Bowen, W. G., & Bok, D. (1998). *The shape of the river: Long-term consequences of considering race in college and university admissions.* Princeton: Princeton University Press.

Bowers, J., & Charles, W. (1989). Effects of physical and school environment in students and faculty. *The Educational Facility Planner, 26*(1), 28–29.

Bowles, S., & Gintis, H. (1976). *Schooling in capitalist America.* New York: Basic Books.

Boyd-Franklin, N., & Franklin, A. J. (2000). *Boys into men: Raising our African American sons.* New York: Dutton.

Braddock, J. H., II, Dawkins, M. P., Wilson, G. (1995). Intercultural contact and race relations among African youth. In W. Hawley & A. Jackson (Eds.), *Toward a common destiny: Improving race relations in American society* (pp. 237–256). San Francisco: Jossey-Bass.

Brickman, P., Carulli Rabinowitz, V., Karuza, J., Jr., Coates, D., Cohn, E., & Kidder, L. (1982). Models of helping and coping. *American Psychologist, 37*(4), 368–384.

Bronfenbrenner, U. (1979). *The ecology of human development.* Cambridge: Harvard University Press.

Brunner, E., & Rueben, K. (2001). *Financing new school construction and modernization: Evidence from California.* Occasional Paper, Public Policy Institute of California.

Brydon-Miller, M. (2001). Participatory action research: Psychology and social change. In D. L. Tolman & M. Brydon-Miller (Eds.), *From subjects to subjectivities: A handbook of interpretive and participatory methods.* New York: New York University Press.

Bryk, A., & Driscoll, M. (1988). *The high school as community.* Madison, WI: National Center on Effective Secondary Schools.

Burhans, K., & Dweck, C. (1995). Helplessness in early childhood: The role of contingent worth. *Child Development, 66*, 1719–1738.

Burns, A. (2004). The racing of capability and culpability. In M. Fine, L. Weis, L. Pruitt, & A. Burns (Eds.), *Off White: Readings in race, power, and privilege*: New York:. Routledge.

Burr, E., Hayward, G., Fuller, B., & Kirst, M. (2000). *Crucial issues in California Education 2000: Are the reform pieces fitting together?* Occasional paper from the Policy Analysis for California Education (PACE).

Butler, J. (1999). *Gender trouble: Tenth anniversary.* New York: Routledge.

Campaign for Fiscal Equity v. State of New York. (2001). www. cfequity.org//littimeline.htm.

Catterall, J. S. (1987, October/November). Social costs of dropping out of school. *The High School Journal, 71*, 19–30.

Chataway, C. J. (1997). An examination of the constraints on mutual inquiry in a participatory action research project. *Journal of Social Issues, 53*, 747–765.

Chataway, C. J. (2001). Negotiating the observer–observed relationship: Participatory action research. In D. L. Tolman & M. Brydon-Miller (Eds.), *From subjects to subjectivities: A handbook of interpretive and participatory methods* (pp. 239–255). New York: New York University Press.

Cherry, F., & Borshuk, C. (1998). Social action research and the commission on community interrelations. *Journal of Social Issues, 54*, 142–199.

Christian, B. (1985). *Black feminist criticism.* New York: Pergamon.

Clark, J. (1995). The impact of the prison environment on mothers. *The Prison Journal, 75*(3), 306–329.

Cochran-Smith, M. (1991). Learning to teach against the grain. *Harvard Educational Review, 61*, 279–310.

Cochran-Smith, M., & Lytle, S. L. (1992). *Inside/outside: Teacher research and knowledge.* New York: Teachers College Press.

Cohen, P., & Ainley, P. (2000). In the country of the blind? Youth studies and cultural studies in Britain. *Journal of Youth Studies, 3*(1), 79–93.

Coleman, J. (1990). *Equality and achievement in education.* Boulder, CO: Westview Press.

Collins, P. H. (1991). *Black feminist thought: Knowledge, consciousness, and the politics of empowerment.* New York: Routledge.

Colven, R. (1990). *The quality of the physical environment of the school.* Paris: Organization for Economic Cooperation and Development.

Connell, J., & Wellborn, J. (1991). Competence, autonomy and relatedness: Motivational analysis of self system processes. In M. Gunnar & L. A. Sroufe (Eds.), *Minnesota Symposium on Child Psychology, 23* (pp. 43–77). Hillsdale, NJ: Erlbaum Publishers.

Connell, R. W. (1989). Cool guys, swots and wimps: The interplay of masculinity and education. *Oxford Journal of Education, 15*(3), 291–303.

Connell, R. W. (1993). Disruptions: Improper masculinities and schooling. In L. Weis & M. Fine (Eds.), *Beyond silenced voices* (pp. 191–208). Albany: State University of New York Press.

Connell, R. W. (1995). *Masculinities.* Cambridge, U. K.: Polity Press.

Connell, R. W. (2000). Arms and the man: Using the new research on masculinity to understand violence and promote peace in the contemporary world. In I. Breines, R. Connell, & I. Eide (Eds.), *Male roles, masculinities and violence: A culture of peace perspective.* Paris: UNESCO.

Conway, K. (1998). *The impact of attending college while incarcerated on women's self-esteem.* Unpublished manuscript.

Cook, A., Cunningham, C., & Tashlik, P. (2000). Unmasking the low standards of high stakes testing. *Education Week, 3/8.*

Cookson, P., & Persell, C. (1985). *Preparing for power: America's elite boarding schools.* New York: Basic Books.

Cooley, C. H. (1998). *On self and social organization.* Chicago: University of Chicago Press.

Cornbleth, C. (1990). *Curriculum in context.* New York: Falmer Press.

Crain, R., & Wells, A. S. (1997). *Stepping over the color line.* New Haven: Yale University Press.

Crenshaw, K. (1991). Mapping the margins: Intersectionality, identity politics, and violence against women of color. *Stanford Law Review, 43*(6), 1241–1299.

Crosby, F. (1976). A model of egotistical relative deprivation. *Psychological Review, 83*(2), 85–113.

Crosby, F., Muehrer, P., & Loewenstein, G. (1986). Relative deprivation and explanation: Models and concepts. In J. Olson, M. Zanna, & P. Hernan (Eds.), *Relative deprivation and assertive action. The Ontario Symposium, 4* (pp. 214–237). Hillsdale, NJ: Erlbaum Publishers.

Cross, W. E., Jr. (1991). *Shades of black: Development in African American identity.* Philadelphia: Temple University Press.

Cummins, J. (1986). Empowering minority students. *Harvard Educational Review, 56*(1), 18–36.

Daiute, C. & Fine, M. (2003). Youth perspectives on violence and injustice. *Journal of Social Issues, 59*(1). 1–14.

Darley, J., & Gilbert, D. (1985). Social psychological aspects of environmental psychology. In G. Lindzey & E. Aronson (Eds.), *Handbook of social psychology: Volume II.* New York: Random House.

Darling-Hammond, L. (2000). Teaching quality and student achievement. *Education Policy Analysis Archives, 8*(1), 27–54.

Darling-Hammond, L. (2002). Apartheid in American education: How opportunity is rationed to children of color in the United States. *Racial Profiling and Punishment in U. S. Public Schools*, 39–44. Oakland Applied Research Center.

Dauber, S., & Alexander, K. (1996). Tracking and transitions through the middle grades: Channeling educational trajectories. *Sociology of Education, 69*(3), 290–307.

Davidson, A., & Phelan, P. (1999). Students' multiple worlds. In D. A. Kleiber & M. Maehr (Eds.), *Advances in Motivation and Achievement, 11* (pp. 233–273). Greenwich, CT: JAI Press.

Deleuze, G. (1992). Postscript on societies of control. *OCTOBER, 59*, Winter, 3–7.

Delpit, L. (1988). The silenced dialogue. *Harvard Educational Review, 58*(3), 280–298.

Delpit, L. (1995). *Other people's children: Cultural conflict in the classroom*. New York: New Press.

DeLuca, S., & Rosenbaum, J. (2001). *Are dropout decisions related to safety concerns, social isolation and teacher disparagement?* Paper presented at the Harvard University Civil Rights Project, Conference on Drop Outs, Cambridge, MA.

Denizin, N., & Lincoln, Y. (1998). *Handbook of qualitative research*. Beverly Hills: Sage Publications.

Desvousges, W., & Smith, V. (1988). Focus groups and risk communication: The "science" of listening to data. *Risk Analysis, 8*, 479–484.

Deutsch, M. (1974). Awakening the sense of injustice. In M. Lerner & M. Ross (Eds.), *The question for justice: Myth, reality, ideal*. Toronto: Holt, Rinehart and Winston.

Devine, J. (1996). *Maximum security: The culture of violence in inner city schools*. Chicago: University of Chicago Press.

Diener, C., & Dweck, C. (1980). An analysis of learned helplessness: II. *Journal of Personality and Social Psychology, 39*, 940–952.

Dolby, N. & Dimitriadis, G. (Eds.) (2004). *Labor in new times*. New York: Routledge.

DuBois, W. E. B. (1935). Does the Negro need separate schools? *Journal of Negro Education, 4*, 328–335.

DuBois, W. E. B. (1990). *Souls of black folks*. New York: First Vintage Books.

Duneier, M. (1994). *Slim's table: Race, respectability, and masculinity*. Chicago: University of Chicago Press.

Duran, V. (2002). *Building quality and student achievement: An exploratory study of 95 urban elementary schools*. Unpublished masters thesis. Environmental Psychology Program, The Graduate Center, City University of New York.

Earthman, G. (1997). The impact of school buildings on student achievement and behavior: A review of research. *PEB Exchange, 30*, 11–15.

Eccles, J. S., Wigfield, A., Midgley, C., Reuman, D., MacIver, D., & Feldlaufer, H. (1993). Negative effects of traditional middle schools on students' motivation. *The Elementary School Journal, 93*(5), 553–574.

Education Trust. (1998). Good teaching matters: How well qualified teachers can close the gap. *Thinking K-16, 3*(2), 1–14.

Edwards, R. (1979). *Contested terrain*. New York: Basic Books.

Elliott, E., & Dweck, C. (1988). Goals: An approach to motivation and achievement. *Journal of Personality and Social Psychology, 54*, 5–12.

Ellsworth, E. (1989). Why doesn't this feel empowering? Working through the repressive myths of critical pedagogy. *Harvard Educational Review, 59*, 297–324.

Epstein, D., Etwood, J., Hey, V., & Maw, J. (Eds.). (1998). *Failing boys? Issues of gender and achievement*. Buckingham, U.K.: Open University Press.

Evans, G., Kliewan, W., & Martin, J. (1991). The role of the physical environment in the health and well being of children. In H. Schroeder (Ed.), *New Directions in Health Psychology Assessment* (pp. 127–157). New York: Hemisphere.

Evans, S., & Boyte, H. (1992). *Free spaces*. Chicago: University of Chicago Press.

Everhart, R. (1983). *Reading, writing, and resistance*. Boston: Routledge.

Faith, K. (1993). *Unruly women: The politics of confinement and resistance*. Vancouver: Press Gang Publishers.

Fallis, R., & Opotow, S. (2002). Are students failing school or are schools failing students? Class cutting in high school. In C. Daiute & M. Fine (Eds.), Youth perspectives on violence and injustice. *Journal of Social Issues*, special volume.

Fals Borda, O. (1979). Investigating the reality in order to transform it: The Colombian experience. *Dialectical Anthropology, 4*, 33–55.

Fanon, F. (1952, 1967). *Black skin, white masks*. New York: Grove Press.

Farmer, P. (1999). *Infections and inequalities*. Berkeley: University of California Press.

Ferguson, R. (1998). Can schools narrow the Black–White test score gap? The Black–White test score gap. In C. Jencks & M. Phillips (Eds.), *The Black–White test score gap* (pp. 318–374). Washington, D.C.: Brookings Institution.

Fine, M. (1982). When nonvictims derogate: Powerlessness in the helping professions. *Personality and Social Psychology Bulletin, 8*, 637–643.

Fine, M. (1988). Sexuality, schooling and adolescent females: The missing discourse of desire. *Harvard Educational Review, 58*, 29–53.

Fine, M. (1990). The "public" in public schools: The social construction/constriction of moral community. *Journal of Social Issues, 4*(1), 107–119.

Fine, M. (1991). *Framing dropouts: Notes on the politics of an urban public high school*. Albany: State University of New York Press.

Fine, M. (Ed.). (1994). *Chartering urban school reform: Reflections on public high schools in the midst of change*. New York: Teachers College Press.

Fine, M., Anand, B., Jordan, C., & Sherman, D. (2000). Before the bleach gets us all. In L. Weis & M. Fine (Eds.), *Construction sites: Spaces for urban youth to reimagine race, class, gender and sexuality*. New York: Teachers College Press.

Fine, M., & Burns, A. (2003). Class notes. *Journal of Social Issues*, special volume on social class and schooling *59*(4), 841–860.

Fine, M., Freudenberg, N., Payne, Y., Perkins, T., Smith, K., & Wanzer, K. (2003). "Anything can happen with police around": Urban youth evaluate strategies of surveillance in public places. In C. Daiute & M. Fine (Eds.), Youth perspectives on violence and injustice. *Journal of Social Issues*, special volume *59*(1), 141–158.

Fine, M., & Powell, L. (2001, October). Small schools as an anti-racist intervention. *Racial profiling and punishment in U. S. public schools*, 45–50. ARC Research Report.

Fine, M., & Somerville, J. (Eds.). (1998). *Small schools, big imaginations*. Chicago: Cross City Campaign for Urban Education Reform.

Fine, M., Torre, M. E., Boudin, K., Bowen, I., Clark, J., Hylton, D., Martinez, M., Missy, Roberts, R. A., Smart, P., & Upegui, D. (2001). *Changing minds: The impact of college in a maximum security prison*. New York: The Graduate School and University Center, City University of New York.

Fine, M., Torre, M. E., Boudin, K., Bowen, I., Clark, J., Hylton, D., Martinez, M., Missy, Roberts, R. A. Smart, P., & Upegui, D. (2002). Participatory action research: From within and beyond prison bars. In P. Camic, J. E. Rhodes, & L. Yardley (Eds.), *Qualitative research in psychology: Expanding perspectives in methodology and design*. Washington, D.C.: American Psychological Association.

Fine, M., Weis, L., & Addelston, M. J. (1997). White loss. In M. Seller & L. Weis (Eds.), *Beyond black and white: New faces and voices in U.S. schools* (pp. 283–301). Albany: State University of New York Press.

Fine, M., Weis, L., Centrie, C., & Roberts, R. (2000). Educating beyond the borders of schooling. *Anthropology and Education Quarterly, 31*(2), 131–151.

Fine, M., Weis, L., & Powell, L. (1997). Communities of difference. *Harvard Educational Review, 67*(2), 247–284.

Fine, M., Weis, L., Powell, L., & Wong, M. (1997). *Off white: Essays on race, power and society*. New York: Routledge.

Fine, M., & Weis, L. (1998). *The unknown city: The lives of poor and working class young adults*. Boston: Beacon Press.

Fiske, E. (1991). *Smart schools, smart kids*. New York: Simon and Schuster.

Flanagan, C., Bowes, J., Jonsson, B., Csapo, B., & Sheblanova, E. (1998). Ties that bind: Correlates of adolescents' civic commitments in seven countries. *Journal of Social Issues, 54*(3), 457–475.

Foley, D. (1990). *Learning capitalist culture: Deep in the heart of Texas*. Philadelphia: University of Pennsylvania Press.

Fordham, S. (1996). *Black out: Dilemmas of race, identity and success at Capital High School*. Chicago: University of Chicago Press.

Foster, M. (1997). *Black teachers on teaching*. New York: New Press.

Foucault, M. (1977). *Discipline and punish: The birth of the prison*. New York: Pantheon.

Frankenburg, R. (1993). *White women, race matters: The social construction of whiteness*. Minneapolis: University of Minnesota Press.

Fraser, N. (1990). Rethinking the public sphere: A contribution to the critique of actually existing democracy. *Social Text, 25/26*, 56–80.

Fraser, N. (1993). Rethinking the public sphere. In B. Robbins (Ed.), *The phantom public sphere*. Minneapolis: University of Minneapolis Press.

Freire, P. (1982). Creating alternative research methods: Learning to do it by doing it. In B. Hall, A. Gillette, & R. Tandon (Eds.), *Creating knowledge: A monopoly* (pp. 29–37). New Delhi: Society for Participatory Research in Asia.

Friend, R. (1993). Choices are not closets: Heterosexism and homophobia in schools. In L. Weis & M. Fine (Eds.), *Beyond silenced voices* (pp. 209–236). Albany: State University of New York Press.

Fruchter, N., Galletta, A., & White, J. (1992). *New directions in parent involvement*. Washington, D.C.: Academy for Educational Development.

Fullilove, M. (2000). The house of Joshua. In L. Weis & M. Fine (Eds.), *Construction sites*. New York: Teachers College Press.

Gangi, R., Schiraldi, V., & Ziedenberg, J. (1998). *New York state of mind*. Washington, D.C.: Justice Policy Institute.

Gaskell, J. (1992). *Gender matters from school to work*. Philadelphia: Open University Press.

Gaventa, J. (1993). The powerful, the powerless, and the experts: Knowledge struggles in an information age. In P. Park, M. Brydon-Miller, B. Hall, & T. Jackson (Eds.), *Voices of change: Participatory research in the U. S. and Canada* (pp. 21–40). Westport, CT: Bergin and Garvey.

Germanotta, D. (1995). Prison education: A contextual analysis. In H. S. Davidson (Ed.), *Schooling in a "total institution": Critical perspectives on prison education* (pp. 103–121). Westport, CT: Bergin & Garvey.

Gilmore, G. E. (1996). *Gender and Jim Crow: Women and the politics of white supremacy in North Carolina, 1896–1920*. Chapel Hill: University of North Carolina Press.

Ginsberg, M. (1988). *Contradictions in teacher education and society: A critical analysis*. New York: Falmer Press.

Giroux, H. (1983). Theories of reproduction and resistance in the new sociology of education. *Harvard Educational Review, 53*(3), 257–293.

Giroux, H., & McLaren, P. (1986). Teacher education and the politics of engagement: The case for democratic schooling. *Harvard Educational Review, 56*, 213–238.

Gladden, M. (1998). A small schools literature review. In M. Fine & J. Somerville (Eds.), *Small schools, big imaginations*. Chicago: Cross City Campaign for Urban Education Reform.

Goffman, E. (1961). *Asylums: Essays on the social situation of mental patients and other inmates*. New York: Anchor.

Golden, M., & Richards Shreve, S. (Eds.). (1995). *Skin deep: Black and white women write about race*. New York: Nan A. Talese.

Gordon, L. (1993). Women's agency, social control and the construction of "rights" by battered women. In S. Fisher & K. Dacis (Eds.), *Negotiating at the margins: The gendered discourses of power and resistance* (pp. 122–144). New Brunswick, NJ: Rutgers University Press.

Gorlitz, D., Harloff, H., Mey, G., & Valsiner, J. (Eds.). (1998). *Children, cities and psychological theories*. New York: Walter de Gruyter.

Gorz, A. (1982). *Farewell to the working class*. London: Pluto Press.

Gramsci, A. (1971). *The intellectual: Selections from prison notebooks*. New York: International.

Greene, J. P. (2001, November). *High school graduation in the United States*. The Manhattan Institute, Center for Civic Innovation. Retrieved on January 16, 2002 from: http://www.manhattan-institute.org/htrnl/cr_baeo.htm.

Greene, M. (1995). *Releasing the imagination: Essays on education, the arts, and social change*. San Francisco: Jossey-Bass.

Guishard, M., Fine, M., Doyle, C., Jackson, J., Roberts, R. A., Staten, T., Singleton, S., & Webb, A. (2003). *I'll keep fighting 'til I stopped breathing*. FINE Evaluation Digest. Cambridge, MA.

Habermas, J. (1971). *Knowledge and human interests*. Boston: Beacon Press.

Hall, B. (1993). Introduction. In P. Park, M. Brydon-Miller, B. Hall, & T. Jackson (Eds.), *Voices of change: Participatory action research in the United States and Canada* (pp. xiii–xxii). Westport, CT: Bergin & Garvey.

Hall, J. (2001). *Canal town youth*. Albany: State University of New York Press.

Hall, S. (1991). Ethnicity, identity and difference. *Radical America, 3*, 9–22.

Haney, C., & Zimbardo, P. (1973). Social roles, role playing and education. *Behavioral Science Teacher, 1*, 24–45.

Haney, W. (1993). Testing and minorities. In L. Weis & M. Fine (Eds.), *Beyond silenced voices* (pp. 45–74). Albany: State University of New York Press.

Haney, W., Russell, M., & Jackson, L. (1997, September). *Using drawings to study and change education.* Center for the Study of Testing, Evaluation and Educational Policy at Boston College.

Hanson, S. (1994). Lost talent: Unrealized educational aspirations and expectations among U.S. Youths. *Sociology of Education, 67*(3), 159–183.

Haraway, D. (1988). Situated knowledges: The science question in feminism and privilege of partial perspective. *Feminist Studies, 14*(3), 575–599.

Harding, S. (1983). *Discovering reality: Feminist perspectives on epistemology, metaphysics, methodology, and philosophy of science.* Dordrecht, Holland: D. Reidel.

Harding, S. (1987). Introduction: Is there a feminist method? In S. Harding (Ed.), *Feminism and methodology* (pp. 1–14). Bloomington: Indiana University Press.

Hart, D., Atkins, R., & Ford, D. (1998). Urban America as a context for the development of moral identity in adolescence. *Journal of Social Issues, 54*(3), 513–530.

Hartsock, N. C. M. (1983). *Money, sex, and power: Toward a feminist historical materialism.* New York: Longman.

Haycock, K. (2001, March). Closing the achievement gap. *Educational Leadership, 58*(6).

Hayduk, R. (1999). *Regional analyses and structural racism.* Paper commissioned by the Aspen Roundtable on Comprehensive Community Reform.

Hill, P. T., Foster, G. E., & Gendler, T. (1990, August). *High schools of character.* The Rand Publication Series.

Hilliard, A. G. (1990). Rx for racism: Imperatives for America's schools. *Phi Delta Kappan, 71,* 593–600.

Hilliard, A. G. (2002). Introduction. In V. G. Morris & C. Morris (Eds.), *The price they paid.* New York: Teachers College Press.

Hine, D. C. (1990). *Black women in white: Racial conflict and cooperation in the nursing profession, 1890–1950.* Bloomington: Indiana University Press.

Hitchcock, P. (1999). *Oscillate wildly.* Minneapolis: University of Minnesota Press.

Hochschild, J. (1995). *Facing up to the American dream.* Princeton, NJ: Princeton University Press.

Hochschild, J. (2002). Social class meets the American dream in public schools. *Journal of Social Issues,* special volume, *59*(4), 821–840.

Holland, D. C. (1990). *Educated in romance: Women, achievement, and college culture.* Chicago: University of Chicago Press.

hooks, b. (1984). *Feminist theory from margin to center.* Boston: South End Press.

hooks, b. (1989). *Talking back: Thinking feminist, thinking black.* Boston: South End.

hooks, b. (1990). *Yearning: Race, gender and cultural politics.* Boston: South End.

Horn, L., & Kojaku, L. (2001). Persistence and transfer behavior of undergraduates through years after entering four year institutions. Educational Statistics Quarterly, National Center for Educational Statistics, U.S. Department of Education.

Howell, J. (1973). *Hard living on Clay Street: Portraits of blue collar families.* Garden City, NJ: Anchor.

Hunter, A. (1987, September). The role of liberal political culture in the construction of middle America. *University of Miami Law Review, 42*(1).

Hurston, Z. N. (1998). In W. E. Martin, Jr. (Ed.), *Brown v. Board of Education: A brief history with documents.* New York: Bedford/St. Martins.

Hurtado, A. (1996). *The color of privilege: Three blasphemies on race and feminism.* Ann Arbor, MI: University of Michigan Press.

Hurtado, A., Haney, C., & Garcia, E. (1998). Becoming the mainstream: Merit, changing demographics and higher education in California. *La Raza Law Journal, 10*(2), 645–690.

Huse, D. (1995). Restructuring the physical context: Designing learning environments. *Children's Environments, 12*(3), 290–310.

IESP Policy Brief. (2001, Spring). *Distributing teacher quality equitably: The case of New York City.*

Jackson, C. (2002). "Laddishness" as a self-worth protection strategy. *Gender and Education, 14*(1), 37–51.

Jaggar, A. M. (1983). *Feminist politics and human nature.* Totowa, NJ: Rowman & Allenheld.

Janoff-Bulman, R. (1979). Characterological versus behavioral self blame: Inquiries into depression and rape. *Journal of Personality and Social Psychology, 37*(10), 1798–1809.

Janoff-Bulman, R. (1992). *Shattered assumptions: Toward a new psychology of trauma.* New York: Free Press.

Joint Committee for California Education System (2000, August 8). *Master plan for education.* California Frameworks.

Jones, J. (1997a). *Prejudice and racism.* New York: McGraw Hill.

Jones, J. (1997b). Whites are from Mars, O. J. is from Planet Hollywood. In M. Fine, L. Weis, L. Powell, & M. Wong (Eds.), *Off white: Readings on race, power and society* (pp. 251–258). New York: Routledge.

Jost, J. (1995). Negative illusions. *Political Psychology, 16*(2), 397–424.

Kahan, J. (2001). Focus groups as a tool for policy analysis. *ASAP, 1*(1), 129–146.

Karenga, M. (1982). *Introduction to black studies.* Inglewood, CA: Kawaida Publications.

Katz, C. (1996). The expeditions of conjurers. In P. Wolf (Ed.), *Feminist dilemmas in fieldwork* (pp. 170–184). Boulder, CO: Westview Press.

Kaufman, P., Kwon, J., & Klein, S. (2000, November) *Dropout rates in the United States: 1999,* National Center for Education Statistics, Statistical Analysis Report, l.

Keither, M., & Pile, S. (1993). *Place and the politics of identity.* London: Routledge.

Kelley, R. (1994). *Race rebels: Culture, politics, and the Black working class.* New York: Free Press.

Kelly, G., & Nihlen, A. (1982). Schooling as the reproduction of patriarchy—unequal workloads, unequal rewards. In M. Apple (Ed.), *Cultural and economic reproduction in education.* London: Routledge.

Kemmis, S., & McTaggart, R. (2000). Participatory action research. In N. K. Denzin & Y. S. Lincoln (Eds.), *Handbook of qualitative research* (2nd ed.) (pp. 567–605). Thousand Oaks, CA: Sage.

Kennedy, E., & Davis, M. (1993). *Boots of leather, slippers of gold: The history of a lesbian community.* New York: Routledge.

Kenway, J., & Fitzclarence, L. (1997). Masculinity, violence and schooling—challenging "poisonous" pedagogies. *Gender and Education, 9,* 117–133.

Kitzinger, J. (1994). The methodology of focus groups: The importance of interaction between research participants. *Sociology of Health and Illness, 16,* 103–121.

Kluger, R. (1977). *Simple justice.* New York: Vintage Books.

Kohl, H. (1994). *"I won't learn from you!": And other thoughts on creative maladjustment.* New York: New Press.

Kohn, A. (2000). *The case against standardized testing: Raising the scores, ruining the schools.* Portsmouth, NH: Heinemann.

Kozol, J. (1991). *Savage inequalities: Children in America's schools.* New York: Crown Publishing.

Krenichyn, K., Saegert, S., & Evans, G. (2001). Parents as moderators of psychological and physiological correlates of inner city children's exposure to violence. *Applied Developmental Psychology, 22*(6), 581–602.

Kress, H. (1997). *Bracing for diversity: A study of white, professional middle class male and female student identity in a U.S. suburban high school.* Unpublished dissertation. State University of New York, Buffalo.

Kurz, D. (1995). *For richer for poorer: Mothers confront divorce.* New York: Routledge.

Kvale, S. (1996). *InterViews: An introduction to qualitative research interviewing.* Thousand Oaks, CA: Sage.

Ladson-Billings, G. (1994). *The dreamkeepers: Successful teachers of African-American children.* San Francisco: Jossey-Bass.

Ladson-Billings, G. (2000). Racialized discourses and ethnic epistemologies. In N. K. Denzin & Y. S. Lincoln (Eds.), *Handbook of qualitative research* (2nd ed.) (pp. 257–277). Thousand Oaks, CA: Sage.

Lather, P. A. (1991). *Getting smart: Feminist research and pedagogy with/in the postmodern.* New York: Routledge.

Lawrence Lightfoot, S. (1983). *The good high school.* New York: Basic Books.

Leach, C., Snider, N., & Iyer, A. (in press). Poisoning the consciousness of the fortunate. In E. Walker & H. Smith (Eds.), *Relative deprivation* (pp. 136–163). Cambridge: Cambridge University Press.

LeCompte, M., & Dworkin, A. (1991). *Giving up on school: Student dropouts and teacher burnouts.* Newberry Park, CA: Corwin Press.

Lederman, L. (1990). Assessing educational effectiveness: The focus group interview as a technique for data collection. *Communication Education, 38,* 117–127.

Lee, V., & Smith, J. (1995). The effects of high school restructuring and size on gains in achievement and engagement for early secondary school students. *Sociology of Education, 68*(4), 271–290.

Lee, V., Smith, J., Perry, T., & Smylie, M. (1999, October). *Social support, academic press, and student achievement: A view from the middle grades in Chicago*. Consortium on Chicago School Research, University of Chicago.

Lefkowitz, B. (1998). *Our guys: The Glen Ridge rape and the secret life of the perfect suburb*. New York: Vintage Press.

Lepore, S., & Evans, U. (1996). Coping with multiple stressors in the environment. In M. Zeidner & N. Endler (Eds.), *Handbook of coping: Theory, research and applications* (pp. 350–377). New York: Wiley.

Lerner, R. (2002). *Adolescence: Development, diversity, context, and application*. Englewood Cliffs, NJ: Prentice Hall.

Lerner, R., & von Eye, A. (1998). Integrating youth- and context-focused research and outreach. In D. Gorlitz, H. Harloff, G. Mey, & J. Valsiner (Eds.), *Children, cities and psychological theories* (pp. 573–597). New York: Walter de Gruyter.

Lewin, K. (1951). *Field theory in social science: Selected theoretical papers*. New York: Harper.

Lewis, M. (1992). *Shame*. New York: Free Press.

Lifton, R. (1994). *The protean self: Human resilience in an age of fragmentation*. New York: Basic Books.

Lindner, E. (2002). The lessons of humiliation. *New Routes: A Journal of Peace Research and Action, 6*(3), 1–10.

Lykes, M. B. (2001). Activist participatory research and the arts with rural Maya women: Interculturality and situated meaning making. In D. L. Tolman & M. Brydon-Miller (Eds.), *From subjects to subjectivities: A handbook of interpretive and participatory methods* (pp. 183–199). New York: New York University Press.

Mac an Ghaill, M. (1994). *The making of men: Masculinities, sexualities, and schooling*. Buckingham, U.K.: Open University Press.

Mac an Ghaill, M. (Ed.). (1996). *Understanding masculinities*. Buckingham, U.K.: Open University Press.

Maguire, P. (2001). The congruency thing: Transforming psychological research and pedagogy. In D. L. Tolman & M. Brydon-Miller (Eds.), *From subjects to subjectivities: A handbook of interpretive and participatory methods* (pp. 276–289). New York: New York University Press.

Markandaya, K. (1998). *Nectar in a sieve*. New York: Penguin.

Marks, J. (2000). *Educational facilities laboratory: A history*. Washington, D.C.: National Clearinghouse for Educational Facilities.

Martín-Baró, I. (1994). *Writings for a liberation psychology*. Cambridge, MA: Harvard University Press.

Martino, W. (1999). "Cool Guys," "Party Animals," "Squids," and "Poofters": interrogating the dynamics and politics of adolescent masculinities in school. *British Journal of Sociology of Education, 20*(2), 239–263.

Martino, W., & Meyenn, B. (Eds.). (2001). *What about the boys?* Buckingham, U.K.: Open University Press.

Marx, K., & Engels, F. (1846). The German ideology. In R. C. Tucker (Ed.), *The Marx-Engels Reader* (2nd ed.) (pp. 146–200). New York: Norton and Company.

Matsuda, M. (1990). Pragmatism modified and the false consciousness problem. *Southern California Law Review, 63*, 1763–1782.

Matsuda, M. (1995). Looking to the bottom: Critical legal studies and reparations. In K. Crenshaw, N. Gotanda, G. Peller, & K. Thomas (Eds.), *Critical race theory: The key writings that formed the movement* (pp. 63–79). New York: New Press.

Mauer, M. (1995). *Young black Americans in the criminal justice system: Five years later*. Washington, D.C.: The Sentencing Project.

Maxwell, L. (2000, Winter). A safe and welcoming school. *Journal of Architecture and Planning Research, 17*(4), 271–282.

McCord, R. (2002). *Declaration of Dr. Robert S. McCord in San Francisco NAACP et al. vs. San Francisco Unified School District, et al.*

McDermott, R. (1987). Achieving school failure: An anthropological approach to literacy and social stratification. In. G. Spindler (Ed.), *Education and cultural process: Anthropological approaches* (2nd ed.) (pp. 82–118). Prospect Heights, IL: Waveland.

McIntyre, A. (1997). *Making meaning of whiteness: Exploring racial identity with white teachers*. New York: State University of New York Press.

McIntyre, A. (2000). *Inner-city kids: Adolescents confront life and violence in an urban community*. New York: New York University Press.

McLaren, P. (2000). *Che Guevera, Paolo Freire and the pedagogy of revolution.* Lanham, MA: Rowman & Littlefield.

McMullan, B. (1994). Charters and restructuring. In M. Fine (Ed.), *Chartering urban school reform: Reflections on public high schools in the midst of change* (pp. 63–78). New York: Teachers College Press.

McNeil, L. (1986). *Contradictions of control.* Boston: Routledge.

McRobbie, A. (1978). Working class girls and the culture of femininity. In Women's Studies Group (Ed.), *Women take issue.* London: Hutchinson.

Mead, G. W. (1988). *Mind, self and society.* Chicago: University of Chicago Press.

Mecklenburg, M. E., & Thompson, P. G. (1983). *The Adolescent Family Life Program as a prevention measure: Public health reports, 98,* 21–29, as cited in Wilcox (1998).

Meier, D. (1998, January). Can these schools be changed? *Phi Delta Kappan,* 358–361.

Merton, R. (1987). The focused interview and focus groups: Continuities and discontinuities. *Public Opinion Quarterly, 51*(5), 50–566.

Miller, D. (2001). Disrespect and the experience of injustice. *Annual Review of Psychology, 52,* 527–553.

Mills, C. W. (1959). *The sociological imagination.* London: Oxford University Press.

Moore, G., & Lackney, J. (1993). School design: Crisis, educational performance and design applications. *Children's Environments, 10*(2), 99–112.

Morris, V., Hilliard, A., & Morris, C. (2002). *The price they paid.* New York: Teachers College Press.

Morton-Christmas, A. (1999). *An ethnographic study of an African American holiness church in the 1990s: An exploration in alternative education empowerment and free space.* Unpublished dissertation, University at Buffalo.

Mouffe, C. (1998). Hegemony and new political subjects. In C. Nelson & L. Grossberg (Eds.), *Marxism and interpretation of cultures.* Urbana: University of Illinois Press.

Mullings, L. (1997). *On our own terms: Race, class and gender in the lives of African American women.* New York: Routledge.

Newmann, F. (1990, April). *Linking restructuring to authentic student achievement.* Paper presented at the Indiana University Annual Education Conference, Bloomington, Indiana.

New York ACORN. (2000). *The secret apartheid.* New York: Acorn Organizing Project.

Nieto, S. (1996). *Affirming diversity: The sociopolitical context of multicultural education* (2nd ed.). New York: Longman.

Noguera, P. (2003). *City schools and the American dream.* New York: Teachers College Press.

Oakes, J., Wells, A., Yonezawa, S., & Ray, K. (1997). Equity lessons from detracking schools. In A. Hargreaves (Ed.), *Rethinking educational change with heart and mind* (pp. 43–72). Alexandria, VA: ASCD.

Ogbu, J. (1974). *The next generation.* New York: Academic Press.

Ogbu, J. (1990). Overcoming racial barriers to access. In J. Goodlad & P. Keating (Eds.), *Access to knowledge.* New York: College Entrance Exam Board.

Ogbu, J. (2002). Black American students and the achievement gap: What else you need to know. *Journal of Thought, 37*(4), 9–33.

Olesen, V. L. (2000). Feminisms and qualitative research at and into the millennium. In N. K. Denzin & Y. S. Lincoln (Eds.), *Handbook of qualitative research* (2nd ed.) (pp. 215–255). Thousand Oaks, CA: Sage.

Orfield, G., & Easton, S. (1996). *Dismantling desegregation.* New York: New Press.

Orfield, M. (1997). *American metropolitics,* Washington, D.C.: Brookings Institution Press.

Oxley, D. (1990, June). *An analysis of house systems in New York City neighborhood high schools.* Monograph.

Park, P., Brydon-Miller, M., Hall, B., & Jackson, T. (1993). *Voices of change: Participatory research in the United States and Canada.* Westport, CT: Bergin and Garvey.

Parsons, T. (1959). The school classroom as a social system. *Harvard Educational Review, 29,* 297–318.

Phillips, M. (1997, Winter). What makes school effective? A comparison of the relation of communitarian climate and academic climate to math achievement and attendance during middle school. *American Educational Research Journal, 34*(4), 633–662.

Phoenix, A., Frosh, S., & Pattman, R. (2003). Producing contradictory masculine subject positions. *Journal of Social Issues, 59*(1), 179–196.

Piran, N. (2001). Re-inhabiting the body from the inside out. In D. L. Tolman & M. Brydon-Miller (Eds.), *From subjects to subjectivities: A handbook of interpretive and participatory methods* (pp. 218–238). New York: New York University Press.

Pittman, K. (2001). *Youth today: The cost of being certain*. International Youth Foundation Search Site.

Poe-Yamagata, E., & Jones, S. (2000, April). *And justice for some*. Washington, D.C.: Youth Law Center, Building Blocks for Youth Report.

Powell, L. (1997). The achievement (k)not! In M. Fine, L. Weis, L. Powell, & L. Wong (Eds.), *Off white*. New York: Routledge.

Pratt, M. L. (1991). Arts of the contact zone. In *Profession '91* (pp. 33–40). New York: Modern Languages Association.

QSE. (2000). Through our eyes and in our words—The voices of indigenous scholars. In F. V. Rains, J. Archibald, & D. Deyhle (Eds.), *International Journal of Qualitative Studies in Education, 13*(4).

Raywid, M. (1997). *Small schools—Reform that works*. Chicago: Small Schools Coalition.

Reay, D. (2002). "Shaun's Story": Troubling discourses of white working class masculinities. *Gender and Education, 14*(3), 221–234.

Reich, R. (1991). *The work of nations*. London: Simon and Schuster.

Reich, R. (1997, January 1). Parting benediction. *New York Times*.

Reich, R. (2001). *The future of success*. New York: Alfred Knopf.

Reichert, M. (2000). Disturbances of difference. In L. Weis & M. Fine (Eds.), *Construction sites: Excavating race, class and gender among urban youth*. New York: Teachers College Press.

Rholes, W., Blackwell, J., Jordan, C., & Walters, C. (1980). Understanding self and others. In E. Higgins & R. Sorrentino (Eds.), *Handbook of motivation and cognition, 2* (pp. 369–407). New York: Guilford.

Richie, B. (1996). *Compelled to crime: The gender entrapment of battered black women*. New York: Routledge.

Rivera, J. A. (1995). A nontraditional approach to social and criminal justice. In H. S. Davidson (Ed.), *Schooling in a "total institution": Critical perspectives on prison education* (pp. 159–171). Westport, CT: Bergin & Garvey.

Robinson, T., & Ward, J. (1991). A belief in self for greater than anyone's disbelief: Cultivating healthy resistance among African American female adolescents. In C. Gilligan, A. Rogers, & D. Tolman (Eds.), *Women, girls and psychotherapy: Reframing resistance* (pp. 87–103). Binghamton, NY: Harrington Park Press.

Rosaldo, R. (1989). *Culture and truth: The remaking of social analysis*. Boston: Beacon.

Rosenthal, R., & Jacobson, C. (1968). *Pygmalion in the classroom: Teacher expectations and pupils' intellectual development*. New York: Rinehart and Winston.

Rousso, H., & Wehmeyer, M. (2001). *Double jeopardy: Addressing gender equity in special education*. Albany: State University of New York Press.

Rubin, L. (1976). *Worlds of pain: Life in the working class family*. New York: Basic.

Rumberger, R. W., & Thomas, S. L. (2000, January). The distribution of dropout among urban and suburban schools. *Sociology of Education, 73*(1), 39–67.

Russell, G. M., & Bohan, J. S. (1999). Hearing voices: The uses of research and the politics of change. *Psychology of Women Quarterly, 23*, 403–418.

Ryan, R. M., & Deci, E. L. (2000). Intrinsic and extrinsic motivations: Class definitions and new directions. *Contemporary Educational Psychology, 25*, 54–67.

Ryan, W. (1981). *Equality*. New York: Pantheon.

Saegert, S. & Evans, G. (2003). Poverty, housing niches and health in the U.S. *Journal of Social Issues, 59*(3), 569–589.

Sapon-Shevin, M. (1993). Gifted education and the protection of privileges. In L. Weis & M. Fine (Eds.), *Beyond silenced voices* (pp. 25–44). Albany: State University of New York Press.

Sarason, S. B. (1974). *The psychological sense of community: Prospects for a community psychology*. San Francisco: Jossey-Bass.

Sartre, J. P. (1968). *Search for method*. New York: Vintage.

Scheper-Hughes, N., & Sargent, N. (1998). *Small wars: The cultural politics of childhood*. Berkeley: University of California Press.

Scott, J. (1990). *Domination and the art of resistance: Hidden transcripts*. New Haven: Yale University Press.

Scott, J. (1992). Experience. In J. Butler & J. Scott (Eds.), *Feminists theorize the political* (pp. 22–40). New York: Routledge.

Seligman, M. (1991). *Learned optimism*. New York: Knopf.

Sennett, R., & Cobb, J. (1972). *The hidden injuries of class*. New York: Knopf.

Simmons, R., & Blyth, D. (1987). *Moving into adolescence.* Hawthorne, NJ: Aldine Publishers.

Smith, D. (1987). *The everyday world as problematic: A feminist sociology.* Boston: Northeastern University Press.

Smith, L. T. (1999). *Decolonizing methodologies: research and indigenous peoples.* London: Zed.

Solomon, P. (1992). *Black resistance in school.* Albany: State University of New York Press.

Spelman, E. (1988). *Inessential woman: Problems of exclusion in feminist thought.* Boston: Beacon.

Spivak, M. (1973). Archetypal place. *Architectural forum, 7*(3), 44–47.

Stacey, J. (1990). *Brave new families.* New York: Basic.

Stack, C. B. (1997). *All our kin.* New York: Basic Books.

Stanfield, J. H. (1994). Ethnic modeling in qualitative research. In N. K. Denzin & Y. S. Lincoln (Eds.), *Handbook of qualitative research* (pp. 175–188). Thousand Oaks, CA: Sage.

Stanton-Salazar, R. (1997). A social capital framework for understanding the socialization of racial minority children and youths. *Harvard Educational Review, 67,* 1–38.

Steady, F. (1981). *The black woman cross-culturally.* Cambridge, MA: Schenkman.

Steele, C. (1997). A threat in the air: How stereotypes shape the intellectual identity and performance of women and African Americans. *American Psychologist, 52,* 613–629.

Stepick, A., Stepick, C., Eugene, E., & Teed, D. (2001). "Shifting identities." In A. Portes and R. Rumbaut (Eds.), *Ethnicities: Coming of age in immigrant America.* Co-published by University Press and Russell Sage Foundation, New York.

Stipek, D., & Tannatt, L. (1984). Children's judgments of their own and their peers' academic competence. *Journal of Educational Psychology, 76,* 75–84.

Suryaraman, M. (2002, May 31). *Private funding divides schools.* www.BayArea.com.

Templeton, R. (1998, November 16). Lockdown walkout. *The Nation, 267*(16), 74–75.

Thorne, B. (1993). *Gender play: Girls and boys in school.* New Brunswick, NJ: Rutgers University Press.

Toch, H. (1967). The convict as researcher. *Style and substance in sociology,* 497–500.

Trusty, J., & Colvin, M. (1999, July). Lost talent: Predictors of the stability of educational expectations across adolescence. *Journal of Adolescent Research, 14*(3), 359–383.

Twine, F. (2000). Racial ideologies and racial methodologies. In F. Twine & J. Warren (Ed.), *Racing research, researching race: Methodological dilemmas in the critical race studies* (pp. 1–34). New York: New York University Press.

Useem, E. (1990). Tracking students out of advanced mathematics. *American Educator, 14,* 24–46.

Valenzuela, A. (1999). *Subtractive schooling.* Albany: State University of New York Press.

Walker, A. (1979). On refusing to be humbled on second place in a contest you did not design: A tradition by now. In Z. Hurston (Ed.), *I love myself when I am laughing....* New York: The Feminist Press.

Walkerdine, V., Lucey, H., & Melody, J. (2001). *Growing up girl.* New York: New York University Press.

Ward, J. (2000). Raising resisters. In L. Weis & M. Fine (Eds.), *Construction sites: Spaces for urban youth to reimagine race, class and gender.* New York: Teachers College Press.

Ware, V. (1992). *Beyond the pale: White women, racism and history.* New York: Verso.

Wasley, P., Fine, M., King, S., Powell, L., Gladden, M., & Holland, N. (1999). *Small schools, great strides.* Report published by the Bank Street College of Education, New York.

Waters, M. (1999). *Black identities: West Indian immigrant dreams and American realities.* New York: Russell Sage Foundation; Cambridge, MA: Harvard University Press.

Weinstein, C., & David, T. (1987). *Spaces for children.* New York: Plenum.

Weis, L. (1990). *Working class without work: High school students in a de-industrializing economy.* New York: Routledge.

Weis, L. (2004a). Re-examining a moment of critique. In N. Dolby & G. Dimitriadis (Eds.), *Learning to labor in new times.* New York: Routledge.

Weis, L. (2004b). *Class reunion: The remaking of the American white working class.* New York: Routledge.

Weis, L., & Fine, M. (Eds.). (1993). *Beyond silenced voices.* Albany: State University of New York Press.

Weis, L., & Fine, M. (1996). Narrating the 1980s and 1990s: Voices of poor and working class white and African American men. *Anthropology and Education Quarterly, 27*(4).

Weis, L., & Fine, M. (1998). What we as educators need to know about domestic violence. *The High School Journal, 81*(2), 55–68.

Weis, L., & Fine, M. (Eds.). (2000). *Construction sites: Excavating race, class and gender among urban youth.* New York: Teachers College Press.
Weis, L., Fine, M., Bertram, C., Proweller, A., & Maruszas, J. (1998). I've slept in clothes long enough: Excavating the sounds of domestic violence among women in the white working class. *Urban Review, 30*(1), 1–27.
Weis, L., & Hall, J. (2001, March). I had a lot of black friends growing up that my father didn't know about: An exploration of white poor and working class female racism. *Journal of Gender Studies, 10*(1), 43–66.
Weis, L., & Maruszas, J. (1998). Living with violence: White working class girls and honest talk. In S. Books (Ed.), *Invisible children in the society at its schools.* Mahwah, NJ: Lawrence Erlbaum.
Weis, L., Proweller, A., & Centrie, C. (1997). Re-examining a moment in history: Loss of privilege inside white working class masculinity in the 1990s. In M. Fine, L. Weis, L. Powell, & M. Wong (Eds.), *Off white: Reading up on race, power and society* (pp. 210–260). New York: Routledge.
Weisenfeld, E. (1999). *The researcher's place in qualitative inquiries: Un-fulfilled promises?* Caracas, Venezuela: The 27th Interamerican Congress of Psychology.
Wells, A. (1995, Summer). Reexamining social science research on school desegregation: Long versus short-term effects. *Teachers College Record, 96*(4), 691–707.
Werner, C., & Altman, I. (1998). A dialectical/transactional framework of social relations: Children in secondary territories. In D. Gorlitz, H. Harloff, G. Mey, & J. Valsiner (Eds.), *Children, cities and psychological theories* (pp. 123–154). New York: Walter de Gruyter.
Whatley, M. (1991). Raging hormones and powerful cars: The construction of men's sexuality in school sex education and popular adolescent films. In H. Giroux (Ed.), *Postmodernism, feminism, and cultural politics* (pp. 119–143). Albany: State University of New York Press.
Wheelock, A. (1992). *Crossing the tracks.* New York: New Press.
Wheelock, A., Bebell, D., & Haney, W. (2000, November). What can student drawings tell us about high stakes testing in Massachusetts? *Teachers College Record.*
Wilcox, B. (1998). Sexual obsession: Public policy and adolescent girls. In N. Johnson, M. Roberts, & J. Worrell (Eds.), *Beyond appearances: A new look at adolescent girls.* Washington, D.C.: APA.
Williams, P. (1992). *The alchemy of race and rights.* Cambridge, MA: Harvard University Press.
Willis, P. (1977). *Learning to labour: How working class kids get working class jobs.* Westmead, England: Saxon House Press.
Willis, P. (1981). *Learning to labor: How working class kids get working class jobs.* New York: Columbia University Press.
Willis, P. (2000). *The ethnographic imagination.* Cambridge, U.K.: Polity Press.
Winant, H. (1994). *Racial conditions: Politics, theory, comparisons.* Minneapolis: University of Minnesota Press.
Wilson, W. J. (1987). *The truly disadvantaged: The inner city, the underclass and public policy.* Chicago: University of Chicago Press.
Wolfe, M., & Rivlin, L. (1987). Institutions in children's lives. In C. Weinstein & T. David (Ed.), *Spaces for children* (p. 89–112). New York, Plenum.
Woodson, C. G. (2000). *The mis-education of the Negro.* Chicago: African American Images. (Reprint).
Wortley, S., & Tanner, J. (2001). *The good, the bad and the profiled: Race, deviant activity and police stop and search practices.* Paper presented at the 2nd Biannual Conference on Crime and Criminal Justice in the Caribbean, Kingston, Jamaica: February 14–17, 2001.
Yates, M., & Youniss, J. (1998). Community service and political identity development in adolescence. *Journal of Social Issues, 54*(3), 495–512.
Yohalem, N., & Pittman, K. (2001, October). *Powerful pathways: Framing options and opportunities for vulnerable youth.* International Youth Foundation.
Zhao, W., Dweck, C., & Mueller, C. (1998). *Implicit theories and depression-like responses to failure.* Unpublished manuscript, Columbia University.
Zimbardo, P. (1970). The human choice: Individuation, reason and order vs. deindividuation, impulse and chaos. In W. Arnold & D. Levine (Eds.), *1969 Nebraska Symposium on Motivation* (pp. 237–307). Lincoln, NE: University of Nebraska Press.
Zinsser, C. (1991). *Raised in east urban: Child care changes in a working class community.* New York: Teachers College Press.

Index